T3-BNT-460

THE YOUNG CHILD
WITH DOWN SYNDROME

THE YOUNG CHILD WITH DOWN SYNDROME

Siegfried M. Pueschel, M.D., M.P.H.

Director, Child Development Center
Rhode Island Hospital
Providence, Rhode Island

HUMAN SCIENCES PRESS, INC.
72 FIFTH AVENUE
NEW YORK, N.Y. 10011

Printed in the United States of America
23456789 98765432

Library of Congress Cataloging in Publication Data

Pueschel, Siegfried
    The young child with Down syndrome.

    Includes index.
    1. Down syndrome.   I. Title [DNLM: 1. Down
syndrome. WS 107 Y691]
RJ506.   D68P84   1984   618.92 '858842   82-21221
ISBN 0-89885-120-3

dedicated to

the Extraordinary Children who taught us so
much—and to their Devoted Parents whose friendship
we cherish, for without their unassuming partnership
the work detailed in this volume could never have been
accomplished.

Contents

CONTRIBUTORS

Lucy P. Buckley, M.D.
Associate in Cardiology
Children's Hospital Medical Center
Assistant Clinical Professor of Pediatrics
Harvard Medical School
Boston, Massachusetts

Claire D. Canning, B.A.
Parent of a Child with Down Syndrome
Pawtucket, Rhode Island

Linda T. Cohen, M.A.
Speech Pathologist
Preschool Language Program
Cerebral Palsy Center
Syracuse, New York

Allen C. Crocker, M.D.
Director, Developmental Evaluation
Clinic
Children's Hospital Medical Center
Associate Professor of Pediatrics
Harvard Medical School
Boston, Massachusetts

Christine E. Cronk, D.Sc.
Anthropologist
Children's Hospital Medical Center
Boston, Massachusetts

Susan Cullen, R.N.
Senior Staff Nurse
Developmental Evaluation Clinic
Children's Hospital Medical Center
Boston, Massachusetts

Kazuie Iinuma, M.D.
Research Fellow
Seizure Unit
Division of Neurophysiology
Department of Neurology
Children's Hospital Medical Center
Research Fellow in Neurology
Harvard Medical School
Boston, Massachusetts

Joan Katz, B.A.
Medical Student
Boston University School of Medicine
Boston, Massachusetts

Daune MacGregor, M.D., D.C.H.
Pediatric Neurologist
Hospital for Sick Children
Assistant Professor of Pediatrics
(Neurology)
University of Toronto
Toronto, Canada

Yoichi Matsumiya, Ph.D.
Director of Special Procedures
Seizure Unit
Division of Neurophysiology

Department of Neurology
Children's Hospital Medical Center
Principal Associate in Neurology
Harvard Medical School
Boston, Massachusetts

Ann Murphy, M.S.W.
Director of Social Service
Developmental Evaluation Clinic
Children's Hospital Medical Center
Clinical Assistant Professor
of Social Work
Boston University
Boston, Massachusetts

Robert A. Peterson, M.D.
Senior Associate in Ophthalmology
Children's Hospital Medical Center
Assistant Professor of Ophthalmology
Harvard Medical School
Boston, Massachusetts

Siegfried M. Pueschel, M.D., M.P.H.
Director, Child Development Center
Rhode Island Hospital
Associate Professor of Pediatrics
Brown University Program in Medicine
Providence, Rhode Island
Lecturer in Pediatrics
Harvard Medical School
Boston, Massachusetts

Robert B. Reed, Ph.D.
Professor of Biostatistics
Department of Biostatistics
Harvard School of Public Health
Boston, Massachusetts

Richard R. Schnell, Ph.D.
Director of Psychology
Developmental Evaluation Clinic
Children's Hospital Medical Center
Associate in Pediatrics (Psychology)
Harvard Medical School
Adjunct Associate Professor
Department of Counseling Psychology
Boston College
Boston, Massachusetts

Martin C. Schultz, Ph.D.
Director, Hearing and Speech Division
Children's Hospital Medical Center
Lecturer in Pediatrics
Harvard Medical School
Research Affiliate
Communications Biophysics Group
Research Laboratory of Electronics
Massachusetts Institute of Technology
Boston, Massachusetts

Alice M. Shea, P.T., M.A., M.P.H.
Director of Training in Physical Therapy
Developmental Evaluation Clinic
Children's Hospital Medical Center
Adjunct Assistant Professor of Physical
Therapy
Sargent College of Allied Health
Professions
Boston University
Special Instructor in Physical Therapy
Simmons College
Boston, Massachusetts

Ann Z. Strominger, M.A., M.S.
Speech and Language Pathologist
Hearing and Speech Division

Children's Hospital Medical Center
Lecturer, Lesley College Graduate School
Boston, Massachusetts

Mindy Winkler, M.S.
Speech and Language Pathologist
Hearing and Speech Division
Children's Hospital Medical Center
Boston, Massachusetts

Liza Yessayan, M.D.
Pediatric Neurologist
Department of Neurology
Children's Hospital Medical Center
Assistant Clinical Professor of Neurology
Harvard Medical School
Neurology Consultant
Crippled Children Services
Department of Public Health
State of Massachusetts
Medical Director and Neurologist
Massachusetts Cerebral Palsy Center
Lawrence, Massachusetts

Elizabeth Zausmer, P.T., M.Ed.
Senior Advisor in Child Development
Children's Hospital Medical Center
Lecturer in Physical Therapy, Simmons
College
Adjunct Associate Professor
Sargent College of Allied Health
Professions
Boston University
Boston, Massachusetts

[Children's Hospital Medical Center's
name has been recently changed to
"The Children's Hospital"]

PREFACE

Allen C. Croker

The present monograph, and the Program which provided the data for it, impart many valuable lessons. Reported here, as the title implies, is a "study," originally undertaken as a clinical investigation seeking a specific answer about a particular therapeutic contention (regarding the effects of 5-hydroxytryptophan and pyridoxine in young children with Down syndrome). This investigation gradually grew into a much broader inquiry about the total phenomenology of the syndrome, and had personal, scientific, and organizational results much beyond the initial expectations. The people and the field were changed by the work as it proceeded.

The first lesson is that detailed and intensive study in a facility of a relatively large number of children with a specific clinical problem allows the development of a portrait of such children which has precision and great utility. In the setting of the Developmental Evaluation Clinic, a new and accurate description of the features and needs of the infant and toddler with Down syndrome emerged. Virtually no element was omitted in the demanding schedule of observation, measurement, and training pursued by Siegfried Pueschel and his coworkers. In such a circumstance there can be a dispelling of myth and bias, with more appropriate guidance and counseling then possible. One is reminded in this regard of the work with the child with acute leukemia in Sidney Farber's Children's Cancer Research Foundation, and of the child with Tay-Sachs disease in the Kingsbrook Jewish Medical Center. This is the proper function of the referral or tertiary center when a fitting team and the necessary support can be gathered.

Next, it can be mentioned that this work has further affirmed the utility of the interdisciplinary mode. There is an exhilaration when complementing professions find a common mission. By mutual feedback and shared insights, the final product is indeed greater than the sum of the parts. This monograph arrives at mature understanding of the functional status of the involved children by allowing correlation across disciplinary perceptions. The possible role of muscle tone, cardiac anomaly, auditory acuity, and blood chemical factors can be examined, for example, in relation to motor function and psychologic development. Direct intellectual stimulation in team activities requires consistent standards from all members.

Another lesson involves the outreaching effects which an intense and specialized study can have. Attitudes about the child with Down syndrome were modified in many departments of the medical center and in the medical community by the simple existence of an advocating team. A generation of trainees looked more positively at these special children, interacted with the program in their own graduate studies, and will carry the interest into career applications. There was support given to many community-based early intervention and educational projects, with the serving of mutual purposes.

And a final lesson was that the potential for reward from true parent/professional partnership has been further demonstrated. The families and the clinical team developed an interdependence which reinforced the commitment of each. As is described in the monograph, there were tribulations aplenty for parents and siblings; sharing and mutual respect between the team and the families enhanced the adventure of surmounting them. In the time together, both learned a new meaning of specialness.

This monograph can be utilized as a definitive resource and guide for those involved in the support system for the young child with Down syndrome and his/her family. The Program described was a pioneering one, which had the good fortune of coinciding with critical years in the social revolution which did so much to assure the full citizenship of persons with special needs. The past decade has seen the emergence of creative understanding for exceptional humans. The child with Down syndrome can stand proudly now. He deserves an authorative and empathic system of knowledge to form the base for action extending his guidance and support. To this, the present monograph is a signal contribution.

ACKNOWLEDGEMENTS

We are foremost indebted to Dr. Allen Crocker, Director of the Developmental Evaluation Clinic of Children's Hospital Medical Center, Boston, for the guidance and support he unselfishly provided to the Down Syndrome Program. We are also grateful to our colleagues from the Developmental Evaluation Clinic, too many to be named here, who in some way contributed to the project.

Furthermore, we appreciated the assistance and cooperation of the personnel from the Children's Hospital Medical Center's Pharmacy who prepared the "medications" to be administered to the children. The invaluable contribution by Professor Reed from the Harvard School of Public Health who not only coauthored several chapters but also carried out biostatistical analyses of most of the work presented in the monograph deserves special acknowledgement.

During the beginning of the program a few children stayed at Crystal Springs Nursery. We would like to acknowledge the outstanding care and attention that was given to those children. We are most grateful to the former Director of this facility, Eunice Brayton, for her collaboration.

We thank the personnel in Research Administration of the Children's Hospital Medical Center who were always available with advice and counsel. Moreover, officials from the National Institute of Child Health and Human Development who provided valuable suggestions were most cooperative during the entire grant period.

We acknowledge the outstanding administrative services provided by Susan Cullen, Diane Berendse, Linda Duchak, Anita Wilson, and Mark Peterson. In particular, we thank Robin O'Reilly and JoAnn Meehan for their secretarial assistance as well as Cynthia Clay for proofreading and assisting with the artwork of illustrations.

We are also indebted to Dr. Thomas Cone for copy-editing our manuscript.

Our publisher, Human Science Press, was most patient and cooperative throughout the time period of manuscript preparation; in particular, we are grateful to Norma Fox for her ever-ready guidance and support.

Most of all we would like to express our gratitude to the children we were permitted to study and care for, and we thank their parents for their loyalty and trust.

The study was in part supported by the Maternal and Child Health Study Project 928, and by the National Institute of Child Health and Human Development, Grant HDO 5341-03, U.S. Department of Health and Human Services.

INTRODUCTION

During the past century numerous reports concerning the phenotype, epidemiology, etiology, therapy, education, and various other aspects of Down syndrome have appeared in the literature. In spite of the abundance of information that has accumulated over the years, there remain many unanswered questions such as what is the cause of Down syndrome, is there an effective therapy available for children with this chromosomal disorder, what are the psychomotor abilities of the child, and what kind of support and assistance do these families require.

The recognition of this lack of knowledge in certain areas of Down syndrome, the impatience of an active parents' group awaiting answers from the scientific community, the willingness of government agencies to support investigators, and the readiness of scientists to pursue studies in Down syndrome have brought about an upsurge of augmented research efforts in this field.

Our involvement in a comprehensive study that focused on the young child with Down syndrome is a reflection of these renewed scholarly endeavors to be detailed in this book. We were fortunate to work in a newly established University Affiliated Facility with a talented interdisciplinary professional staff in the midst of the stimulating academic milieu of a Harvard teaching hospital. Our staff, including social workers, psychologists, educators, physical therapists, audiologists, nurses, anthropologists, speech therapists, and physicians from various subspecialties, was motivated to engage in a long-term study with the goal to gain new insights into this chromosomal disorder, and to improve the quality of life of the child with Down syndrome and his/her family.

While the primary objective of this study was to examine the effects of 5-hydroxytryptophan and/or pyridoxine administration upon motor, social, intellectual, and language developments in young children with Down syndrome, we also became involved in a number of other activities. We studied audiological, otological, ophthalmological, cardiac, neurophysiological, and cytogenetic aspects of children in our cohort. In addition, we counseled parents, developed a siblings program, and focused attention on nutritional factors and a variety of other related issues. These diverse involvements permitted us to develop a truly comprehensive program for the child with Down syndrome and his/her family.

This monograph is comprised of four major sections: Part I will introduce the reader to the basic design of the Down Syndrome Program and the underlying rationale of the research components. Moreover, it provides demographic data which define certain characteristics of the study population's composition. Part II will highlight the analysis of 5-hydroxytryptophan and/or pyridoxine effects on the children's various functions. In subsequent chapters, the "drug effect" will not be further taken into consideration. Hence, Part III and Part IV will concentrate on other study elements offering additional important information on the children enrolled in the program. As expected of an interdisciplinary study approach there will be some overlap of certain subject matters. Although outright duplications have been avoided, certain circumstances necessitate reiteration of specific study aspects in order to provide a better understanding of the contextural framework and cohesiveness of a given chapter. Finally, in the Epilogue, a parent whose child was an active study participant will express her view of what this program meant to herself, her child and her family.

In describing the multiple facets of this program, this text will provide valuable information to the scholar involved with early childhood education, to the investigator in developmental disabilities, and to other interested professionals from both the biomedical and the behavioral sciences involved in the care and management of the child with Down syndrome.

The reader will readily discern, however, that beyond the scientific components as they relate to the evaluation of the drug administration and to the investigations of the individual disciplines involved, there are basic human concerns that are of equal importance to the authors. Surely, the alliance of these two elements which allowed the successful completion of this project will also set the cornerstone for a better future for persons with Down syndrome.

Part I

Chapter 1

DESCRIPTION OF
THE DOWN SYNDROME PROGRAM

Siegfried M. Pueschel

*

THE BEGINNING

As any scientific endeavor necessitates thoughtful preparations and a well-conceived rationale, this project also started out with such basic efforts.

A thorough literature search preceded detailed planning. While initially a general review of the subject matter was pursued, we studied primarily articles discussing genetic, biochemical, assessment, and treatment aspects relating to Down syndrome. Thus, we learned that the discovery of aneuploidy in Down syndrome by Lejeune and coworkers (1) had challenged biochemical geneticists to investigate the teleological function of the supernumerary 21 chromosome (2). Although numerous metabolic derangements had been reported, of paramount interest to us were abnormalities of tryptophan metabolism (3-8). A most constant finding was the markedly reduced serotonin level in the peripheral blood of children with Down syndrome (9-12). The latter observation which was of central concern to us led to questions such as what is the significance of the reduced serotonin blood level in children with Down syndrome, what are the interfering mechanisms producing the low serotonin level, are there any available means to raise the serotonin levels, and, if the latter were feasible, how would it influence the development of the child with Down syndrome?

At about the same time that our preparations progressed, some investigators reported the apparent beneficial effects of 5-hydroxytryptophan administration to young children with Down syndrome. In particular, Bazelon and colleagues noted that children with Down syndrome receiving 5-hydroxytryptophan displayed improved muscle tone and exhibited increased motor activity (11).

Further impetus to engage in a study of children with Down syndrome came from the Director of the Developmental Evaluation Clinic of Children's Hospital Medical Center. Also, discussions with officials of the National Institute of Child Health and Human Development were encouraging and indicated that a well-designed project might find financial support by this agency.

Subsequently a research protocol was developed and a grant application was submitted to the National Institute of Child Health and Human Development. After a few months, wait, we were notified of the project's approval and that a grant would be awarded to us.

Preliminary work included the setting up of a laboratory that would enable us to carry out the biochemical investigations, the acquisition of a spectrophotofluorometer, and the purchase of other needed miscellaneous supplies. An application for an IND number was forwarded to the Food and Drug Administration asking for permission to use the experimental drug 5-hydroxytryptophan. Moreover, we contacted several drug companies known to manufacture 5-hydroxytryptophan in order to find the most purified and least expensive tryptophan compound available.

Other preliminary work involved the design of the individual discipline protocols and their review by members of the Department of Biostatistics of the Harvard School of Public Health. Plans for randomization of patients, data retrieval, and aspects of computer analysis were also discussed with the consultants from this department.

Guidelines for parents to stimulate their children's sensory, motor, and language development were drawn up. We hoped that by providing parents with such information, the overstimulation likely to be pursued by some parents would be minimized, and neglect of these aspects by other parents would be avoided. We also outlined dietary suggestions, primarily emphasizing proteins with increased tryptophan content.

Furthermore, in discussions with pediatricians, nurses, and social workers of maternity hospitals and obstetric services in general hospitals in the greater Boston area, we explained the essential study objectives. We also contacted hospitals with obstetric services in the eastern part of Massachusetts, southern New Hampshire, and the northern part of Connecticut and Rhode Island in order to introduce them to the project and invite referrals to our program.

STUDY RATIONALE

In this prospective study a multidisciplinary team investigated in a double-blind fashion the application of a "treatment" program for the child with Down syndrome. Although there were other program elements (see below) the primary component of this project encompassed the evaluation of the effect of 5-hydroxytryptophan and/or pyridoxine administration upon the motor, social, language, and intellectual development in the young child with Down syndrome.

The rationale for the study was as follows:

1. There was ample documentation in the literature that the 5-hydroxytryptamine (serotonin) concentration in the blood of children with Down syndrome was significantly lower compared to such levels in the normal child.
2. There was also experimental evidence that the serotonin blood level can be raised by the administration of 5-hydroxytryptophan, a precursor of 5-hydroxytryptamine.

3. In this context, the neurophysiological role of serotonin as a neurotransmitter within the central nervous system appeared to be of particular importance.

4. It had been demonstrated that 5-hydroxytryptophan could improve the reduced muscle tone of young children with Down syndrome and would also enhance their motor activity.

5. It was then postulated that the increased motor activity might lead to augmented exploration of the environment at an earlier age, which in turn might affect positively the sensory input, and hence be beneficial to the overall development of the child.

6. It was further hypothesized that the potential improvement in the "treated" patients' general development—including mental abilities—would lead to appropriate education, a more independent, productive, and purposeful life, avoiding expensive institutionalization or significant economic strain within the family.

An important element of this program was an implicit human concern. Parents experienced genuine support and understanding from professional workers who, apart from their basic investigational efforts, assisted families in crisis.

STUDY DESIGN

According to the admitting criteria only newborn children with Down syndrome who had the chromosomal complement of trisomy 21 were to be enrolled.

Before the individual child entered the program, his/her parents were informed of the study's basic elements, its experimental nature, and the double-blind design. Parents were made aware of the fact that we did not consider 5-hydroxytryptophan and/or pyridoxine to be an established "treatment" for Down syndrome, nor did we promise any improvement which might derive from administration of the "medications." We explained the known risks and possible side effects. An approved consent form had to be signed by the parents prior to enrollment of their child into the study. The children then were randomly assigned to one of four groups: (1) placebo, (2) pyridoxine, (3) 5-hydroxytrypophan, and (4) 5-hydroxytryptophan/pyridoxine.

Throughout the study we made sure that none of the members of the evaluation team nor personnel from administration or laboratory staff ever knew the drug code, which was available only to certain senior staff of the Children's Hospital's pharmacy.

We anticipated that the majority of children would be reared in the home and that perhaps a small number of children might be placed by their parents into a residential facility. Although our general philosophy supported the upbringing of children with Down syndrome within the family, we had made arrangements with a private facility, Crystal Springs Nursery in Assonet, Massachusetts, to have children admitted if there were a need for placement. This well-staffed residential facility provided a homelike environment, excellent care, and appropriate stimulation for the children. (Out of our study population of 114 children only 4 infants were admitted to Crystal Springs Nursery, and for a short time period only). The study period for each child commenced soon after birth and the third birthday was chosen as cutoff point.

Our initial estimate of admitting three children with Down syndrome each month was very close to the actual enrollment throughout the study. In the graphical description below, the total study period is shown in relation to the individual study period and the total patient load at any time during the study.

According to our projections there would be 36 patients after the first year, 72 patients after two years, and a total of 108 children would be enrolled in the program after three years. Since each child's individual study period comprised three years and recruitment was gradual over a three-year period, the study in its entirety lasted for six years.

STUDY PARTICIPANTS

In order to make the program as comprehensive as possible, professionals representing ten disciplines participated in this study: pharmacist, pediatrician, social worker, anthropologist, neurologist, physical therapists, nurse, psychologists, audiologist, and speech therapist.

With assistance of the Children's Hospital Medical Center's pharmacy, 5-hydroxytryptophan and/or pyridoxine as well as the

ESTIMATED NUMBER OF PATIENTS AT STUDY YEAR 1 TO 6

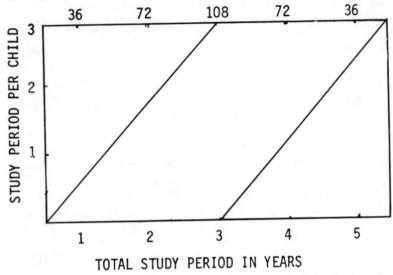

placebo (lactose) were capsuled indistinguishably from each other in appearance and taste. The relative safety of 5-hydroxytryptophan had been studied and its use was approved by the Food and Drug Administration (IND #6400).*

The initial contact with parents of a newborn child with Down syndrome was frequently made by the pediatrician and the social worker. These first encounters were felt to be of paramount importance in the subsequent adjustment of the parents.

The pediatrician usually introduced the family to the Down Syndrome Program. A blood sample of the infant and the parents were obtained and sent for karyotyping. After the results of the chromosome analysis were received, genetic counseling was provided. The pediatrician further elicited information concerning family history as well as preconceptional, antenatal, perinatal, and neonatal histories. He or she examined the children initially and recorded phenotypic characteristics. Reexaminations usually took place at three-month intervals or more frequently if needed. Specific emphasis was placed on the evaluation of muscle tone, general activity level, and signs of "drug toxicity" (hyperactivity, marked tongue protrusion, diarrhea, flushing of face, elevated blood pressure, seizures). During these visits interim histories were recorded, blood was taken for 5-hydroxyindol determination, and the dosage of the "medications" was adjusted according to the weight gain of the child.

Social service involvement included both data gathering and provision of services to the parents. During the initial social service interview, information of family characteristics and social history were obtained. Support was offered at this critical time of parental stress. When significant problems were identified, the social worker aided in planning and implementing appropriate remedial action. During follow-up interviews at one month, six months, one, two, and three years, the state of adjustment, parental attitudes, and quality of the child's home life were assessed. The longitudinal nature of the program allowed documentation of family adaptation to the child with Down syndrome. It also provided an opportunity to elucidate those factors which seem to influence successful integration of the child with Down syndrome into the family.

The anthropologist focused on a variety of physical measurements including recumbent length, weight, circumference of head and chest, as well as head length and breadth. These measurements which were done at three-month intervals had been selected both for the availability of age-appropriate normal standards and for comparison with previously studied populations of children with Down syndrome. Bone age was evaluated radiographically.

Neurological assessment involved 66 variables, concentrating primarily on major neurological functions, with emphasis on motor activity, muscle tone, and reflex activity. These examinations were carried out in the newborn period, at six months, and at the first, second and third birthdays respectively. Electroencephalographic studies were performed annually or more often if indicated.

---

*Details of "drug" administration are provided in Part II of this monograph.

The physical therapist examined the children's muscle strength, muscle tone, range of motion, motor behavior at rest and during activity, reflexive motor function, developmental level of gross and fine motor skills, and responses to selective visual, auditory, tactile, and kinesthetic stimuli. The quality of performance, independence, speed, and endurance was evaluated and scored shortly after birth, at three-month intervals during the first year, and semiannually thereafter. Based on the results of such assessments a motor stimulation program was developed for all children utilizing generally accepted neurophysiological principles. Parents were taught the necessary skills of stimulation through demonstration and written guidelines. Exercises and activities to improve muscle strength and coordination, sensory stimulation to elicit appropriate early motor responses, and other aspects of environmental enrichment were emphasized.

The nurse documented social competence development provided through the use of the Vineland Social Maturity Scale administered at six-month intervals. Further study variables included self-help skills, communication, locomotion, and socialization. Particular attention was paid to feeding, nutrition, and mealtime activities.

Psychological evaluations employing the Bayley Scales of Infant Development were carried out semiannually. The obtained data provided longitudinal as well as cross-sectional comparisons between the different groups. Standard scores were obtained for the mental and motor scales, while the behavior record documented qualitative observations.

Audiological assessments were done both at 15 and 36 months. These examinations involved hearing-testing in pure tone and in sound field, impedance testing, and discrimination studies.

Initially, speech and language examinations were scheduled at three-month intervals during the first year and every six months thereafter. Yet, practical considerations and budgetary limitations permitted such evaluations only at the end of each child's study period using the Receptive-Expressive Emergent Language Scale and measuring vocabulary size as a primary means for communication.

When other disciplines were needed to provide specific services for a child, or when additional medical complications required subspecialty examinations, appropriate consultations were obtained. Children with suspected or diagnosed congenital heart disease were evaluated and followed by pediatric cardiologists at the Children's Hospital Medical Center. Likewise, orthopedic, respiratory, hematological, and other services were occasionally requested when their respective needs were uncovered during routine examinations.

Biochemical investigations dealt with the qualitative and quantitative determinations of tryptophan metabolites. Spectrophotofluorometric, column and paper chromotographic methods were employed to estimate blood and urine concentrations of metabolites in the serotonin pathway.

The primary evaluation goals were to obtain unbiased assessments of various developmental parameters in order to derive interpretable data allowing meaningful statistical analysis.

OTHER PROGRAM ACTIVITIES

Shortly after the initiation of the research program it was felt that there was a need for parents to meet with each other and to have an opportunity to exchange their views and thoughts and to ventilate their feelings and frustrations. Consequently, we held informal discussion meetings on clinic days with the senior social worker and the pediatrician in attendance. These group meetings were of therapeutic value to the parents and provided us with insights into parental coping.

During the six-year project period, parents were also invited to formal seminars where professionals from rehabiliation, special education, orthopedics, ophthalmology, dentistry, and cardiology discussed a variety of aspects relating to Down syndrome in their respective subspecialties.

Brothers and sisters of children with Down syndrome had also been asking for information about Down syndrome. We responded to this need and arranged occasional siblings' meetings on Saturdays. Staff members explained various activities of the Down Syndrome Program. We discussed the chromosomal abnormality in Down syndrome, psychological testing, approaches to sensory-motor stimulation, and other services provided at the clinic. In subsequent discussions, brothers and sisters often talked about their feelings toward the child with Down syndrome.

Since we were frequently asked by parents for literature on Down syndrome, we started a parent library which contained a variety of pamphlets and books on Down syndrome, on general mental retardation issues, and on the education of the handicapped child. Parents who previously had not found any reading materials or had been dissatisfied with outdated books in local libraries were now able to become better informed by making use of our resource library.

Another by-product of the Down Syndrome Program was the development of a resource parent program. Since parents had told us that many physicians had been insensitive to the parents' needs at the time of the birth of their child with Down syndrome, it was felt that new parents would gain from talking to families who had an older child with Down syndrome. Therefore, we set up a statewide network whereby hospital personnel, physicians, nurses, and social workers could contact our resource parents in their communities when a child with Down syndrome was born. The resource parents who had allowed us to give their name, address, and telephone number to their local hospital were provided with guidelines and reading materials.

As our program progressed, we had many professionals in the New England region requesting participation as observers. In response, we initiated a seminar that dealt with concepts of sensory-motor stimulation of the young child with Down syndrome. Later we held a more comprehensive four-day workshop. The focus of discussion was on new developments in assessment and early education of the young child with Down syndrome. During subsequent years small workshops were conducted periodically by the staff of the Developmental Evaluation Clinic of Children's Hospital Medical Center to present various aspects of our work.

Soon after we had begun this program, we received many applications from parents who had children with Down syndrome beyond the neonatal age. Since those children, according to our admission criteria, could not join this Down Syndrome Program, we decided to develop a new program for those children between the ages of one month and three years with emphasis on service aspects. This Down Syndrome Program II has been steadily expanding, and more than 250 children have been served in this program.

In summary, we became engaged in a number of activities which included scientific aspects that involved evaluations of the effect of

5-hydroxytryptophan and/or pyridoxine administration as well as service-related activities geared to help the families.

Chapter 2

THE STUDY POPULATION

Siegfried M. Pueschel

GENERAL DEMOGRAPHIC DATA

Children with Down syndrome admitted to the program were recruited from maternity hospitals and obstetric services of general hospitals from Massachusetts and neighboring states. Of the 114 children with Down syndrome in this study, 89 resided in Massachusetts, 14 in New Hampshire, 6 in Rhode Island, 3 in Connecticut, and 2 in Vermont. Ninety-two percent of the parents whose children participated in the program lived within a 60 mile radius of Boston.

Considering the birth rate in Massachusetts during the time of the study and the incidence rate of Down syndrome, it was estimated that approximately 1/4 to 1/3 of the children with this chromosomal disorder born in this geographic area were admitted to our program. No specific selection process could be identified, and it was assumed that the study population was representative of all children born with Down syndrome in this geographic region.

During the planning period, we had estimated that approximately 36 children would be admitted annually (see above) so that after three years a total of 108 children would have joined the program. We came very close to our initial projections, since at the end of enrollment 114 children with clinically diagnosed Down syndrome had entered the program. In the first study year 43 children came into the program, 39 in the second, and 32 in the third.

Of the 114 children there were 63 boys and 51 girls. With the exception of three, all children were of European ancestry; only two children were black. As expected, the karyotype of the majority of children (110) was trisomy 21, three children had D/G translocation, and one child had mosaic Down syndrome.

CHILDREN NOT INCLUDED IN THE ANALYSIS OF THE DATA

Twenty-five of the 114 children were excluded from the study sample since they did not have adequate follow-up throughout the three-year study period. Table I shows the random assignment of the 25 children to the different study groups.

These children (13 boys, 12 girls) were eliminated from analysis of the results for the following reasons:

TABLE I

CHILDREN WITH DOWN SYNDROME WHO WERE EXCLUDED FROM THE ANALYSIS
OF DATA ACCORDING TO RANDOM ASSIGNMENT INTO STUDY GROUPS

Group	Placebo	Pyridoxine	5-hydroxy-tryptophan	5-hydroxy-tryptophan/pyridoxine	Total
Deceased	3	3	4	3	13
Lost to follow-up	6	0	2	2	10
Excluded	1	1	0	0	2
Total	10	4	6	5	25

1. Thirteen children (seven boys, six girls) died during the course of the study; five children during the first 6 months, five children between 7 and 12 months, two children between 13 and 18 months, and one child at 24 months. All but one of the children had severe congenital heart disease: seven children had endocardial cushion defects, one child suffered from tetralogy of Fallot, one child had transposition of the great vessels, and three children had a combination of cardiac defects. In addition, most of these children had terminally significant respiratory disease and cardiac failure. The child without congenital heart disease died from complications of an operation to correct an intestinal obstruction.

2. Ten children (five boys, five girls) were lost to follow-up: parents of four children had moved out of state, another four children were withdrawn because of increased social and intrafamily problems, one child did not continue the study after foster placement, and another child left the program without ready explanation. Five of these ten children did not have any additional congenital anomalies, four had congenital heart disease, and one had congenital cataracts. One of these children had expired one and a half years after leaving the program. Three of the 10 children were alive and well at the end of the study. The whereabouts and the health status of the remaining six children are not known.

3. Two other children were excluded from the analysis of the study: one child's karyotype revealed mosaic Down syndrome which was considered outside the definition of the reference population; the other child had not completed the full three-year study course after the official closing date.

STUDY SAMPLE

After elimination of the 25 children from the analysis of the data, the final study population consisted of 50 boys and 39 girls. These 89 children were followed regularly throughout the entire study period.

Three children did not receive the randomly assigned "medication" for the full three years. Since they had developed infantile spasm, the "medications" were discontinued* as it was uncertain at that time whether or not 5–hydroxytryptophan was causatively related to the development of seizures in these children. These three children, however, were included in the group of their original assignment since we reasoned that the results obtained from their evaluations would be representative of program effects in typical clinical drug administration.

There were a number of conditions and circumstances which conceivably could have influenced the course of development of the children and thus the outcome of the study. These variables were analyzed to determine the comparability of the four study groups:

1. Since antenatal events such as maternal infections, intoxications, or other medical and environmental conditions during pregnancy may interfere with normal embryonic/fetal development, antenatal and perinatal historical data were carefully evaluated. As noted in Table II, mothers whose children were in the 5–hydroxytryptophan study group had markedly more prenatal difficulties including infections, vaginal bleeding, and other medical problems. Furthermore, a slightly larger number of mothers in the pyridoxine group experienced complications during labor.

    It is of note that infants assigned to the 5–hydroxytryptophan group had a significantly lower birth weight (Table III) when compared with the other groups. This is only partially explained by the slightly shorter mean gestational period of children in the 5–hydroxytryptophan group. If children with a gestational age of less than 37 weeks are excluded from the analysis, the mean birth weight of children in the 5–hydroxytryptophan group is still significantly lower as seen in Table IIIC.

2. As additional congenital anomalies and increased morbidity are frequently observed in children with chromosomal aberrations, we also identified a number of congenital defects and medical problems in our study population. Since such complicating factors may compromise the children's development and

---

*After breaking the code, two children were found to be in the 5–hydroxytryptophan group and one child in the placebo group.

TABLE II

ANTENATAL AND PERINATAL CONDITIONS REPORTED

BY MOTHERS OF CHILDREN WITH DOWN SYNDROME

ACCORDING TO STUDY GROUPS

Condition	Placebo	Pyridoxine	5-hydroxy-tryptophan	5-hydroxy-tryptophan/pyridoxine	Total
Infection	5	4	7	4	20
Vaginal Bleeding	4	5	10	3	22
Other gestational medical problems	2	3	8	6	19
Complications during labor	4	9	2	4	19
Difficulties during delivery	4	3	4	5	16
5 min. Apgar less than 7	1	0	0	2	3
Total	20	24	31	24	99*

*Some mothers reported more than one of the listed antenatal or perinatal conditions.

performance, they will have to be taken into consideration in the analysis of the data.

We diagnosed congenital heart disease in 26 of our 89 children.* The congenital cardiac defects observed in these 26 children are listed in Table IV. Since specific cardiac diagnosis, however, does not describe the child's limitations caused by his/her congenital heart disease, we attempted to classify children with congenital heart disease according to the degree of severity (Table V).

The degree of cardiac involvement was determined as follows: Children with mild congenital heart disease had single

*For detailed description of the cardiac data, see chapter on Cardiac Assessment. Note that only the 89 children of the final study sample are considered here, while the chapter on Cardiac Assessment describes all infants with cardiac defects from the entire study sample of 114 children including those who expired and those who were lost to follow-up.

TABLE III

GESTATIONAL AGE AND BIRTH WEIGHTS OF CHILDREN WITH DOWN SYNDROME ACCORDING TO STUDY GROUP

	Placebo		Pyridoxine		5-hydroxy-tryptophan		5-hydroxy-tryptophan/pyridoxine		Total	
	Mean	SD	Mean	SD	Mean	SD	Mean	SD	Mean	SD
A Gestational age (weeks)	39.1	2.0	39.1	1.8	38.7	2.2	38.0	1.7	38.9	1.7
B Birth weights (kg) of the 89 study Children	3.25	0.46	3.17	0.51	2.83	0.52	3.03	0.48	2.91	0.43
C Birth weights (kg) of children with gestational age < 37 weeks	3.30	0.41	3.24	0.51	2.96	0.38	3.11	0.43		

TABLE IV

SPECIFIC DIAGNOSIS OF 26 CHILDREN WITH

CONGENITAL HEART DISEASE ACCORDING TO STUDY GROUPS

Congenital Heart Defect	Placebo	Pyridoxine	5-hydroxy-tryptophan	5-hydroxy-tryptophan/pyridoxine	Total
Endocardial cushion defect	5	5	1	2	13
Tetralogy of Fallot	0	0	0	1	1
Ventricular septal defect	0	1	2	2	5
Atrial septal defect	0	0	2	1	3
Combined* defects	1	0	0	1	2
Other**	2	0	0	0	2
Total	8	6	5	7	26

*One child had both a ventricular septal defect and a patent ductus arteriosus; the other child had a double outlet right ventricle and an endocardial cushion defect.

**Two children in this category had ventricular septal defects that closed spontaneously during the evaluation period.

cardiac defects such as atrial or ventricular septal defects without pulmonary vascular involvement. These children usually did not require cardiac medications or cardiac surgery. Their growth rate and weight gain was similar to that of children without congenital heart disease. Moderate congenital heart disease refers to more complex cardiac problems such as endocardial cushion defects. These children often required digitalis. Their longitudinal growth and weight gain were sub-optimal. Severe congenital heart disease signifies serious anatomical heart lesions such as complex endocardial cushion defects, tetralogy of Fallot, etc. These children were often in cardiac failure and were in need of digitalis and various

TABLE V

CLASSIFICATION OF DEGREE OF SEVERITY OF
CHILDREN WITH CONGENITAL HEART DISEASE
ACCORDING TO STUDY GROUPS

Congenital heart disease	Placebo	Pyridoxine	5-hydroxy-tryptophan	5-hydroxy-tryptophan/ pyridoxine	Total
None	12	17	17	17	63
Mild	1	1	4	3	9
Moderate	6	4	1	1	12
Severe	1	1	0	3	5
Total	20	23	22	24	89

diuretics. They often had pulmonary complications and their growth rate and weight gain were significantly reduced.

In the analyses of the data, frequently children without and with mildcongenital heart disease were combined since there was no significant difference between the respective combined groups (chi square = 6.51, df = 3, p< 10).

As seen in Table V, the random assignment of children in the various study groups placed more children with severe and moderate degree of congenital heart disease in the placebo group as compared to the other groups, in particular if contrasted with the 5-hydroxytryptophan group. This heavily weighted placebo group with children having significant cardiac involvement was accommodated during later analysis.

There were several children who had other congenital anomalies: two children had hip dislocation; two others had patella subluxation; one child each had congenital leukemia, diabetes mellitus, congenital cataracts, imperforate anus, hiatal hernia, and cleft palate. Table VI lists these children according to assignment into study groups.

TABLE VI

CHILDREN WHO HAD OTHER SIGNIFICANT ILLNESSES

AND/OR CONGENITAL ANOMALIES ACCORDING TO STUDY GROUPS

Condition or malformation	Placebo	Pyridoxine	5-hydroxy-tryptophan	5-hydroxy-tryptophan/pyridoxine	Total
Hip dislocation	0	0	0	2	2
Patella subluxation	0	0	1	1	2
Congenital leukemia	0	0	1	0	1
Diabetes Mellitus	0	1	0	0	1
Congenital cataracts	0	1	0	0	1
Imperforate anus	0	0	0	1	1
Hiatal Hernia	0	0	0	1	1
Cleft Palate	0	0	0	1	1
Total	0	2	2	6	10

3. Another set of variables relates to environmental circumstances. In order to ascertain whether there were differences in the various study groups in terms of social conditions, we obtained information on occupation, education, and religion of both father and mother, family income, and possible existing financial problems. The means of socioeconomic scores which take into consideration most of the above mentioned variables did not uncover any significant differences among the four study groups (Table VII). The average family in the program was made up of parents having completed high school and earning $12,000 to $15,000 per year in a skilled labor or white collar occupation.

Additional social service investigations (for details see below) dealt with the parents' marital relationship, the possibility of new stress factors in the family, and the status of parental adjustment. The analysis of these data again did not reveal any dissimilarity among the four study groups.

TABLE VII

SOCIO-ECONOMIC SCORES OF FAMILIES WHOSE

CHILDREN WITH DOWN SYNDROME WERE INCLUDED

IN THE FINAL STUDY SAMPLE ACCORDING TO STUDY GROUPS

	Placebo	Pyridoxine	5-hydroxy-tryptophan	5-hydroxy-tryptophan/pyridoxine
Mean	39.0	43.0	45.00	38.96
Standard deviation	1.6	1.9	1.5	1.5

TABLE VIII

MEANS AND STANDARD DEVIATIONS OF

PARENTAL AGE AT TIME OF THEIR CHILDS BIRTH

ACCORDING TO STUDY GROUPS

	Placebo		Pyridoxine		5-hydroxy-tryptophan		5-hydroxy-tryptophan/pyridoxine	
	Mean	S.D.	Mean	S.D.	Mean	S.D.	Mean	S.D.
Father	33.4	8.9	31.9	8.7	33.1	7.7	33.8	7.3
Mother	30.9	8.1	29.0	6.5	30.6	6.9	30.6	6.7

We also studied mother's and father's age at the time of the child's birth (Table VIII) as well as birth order of the study child. No significant differences were evident for any of these variables among the study groups.

PHYSICAL CHARACTERISTICS

Children with Down syndrome in our program underwent a thorough physical examination during the initial visit and the presence or absence of 28 common phenotypic characteristics were recorded (Table IX). In addition, some functional variables were assessed (Table X). Other abnormal physical features such as growth characteristics, cardiac involvement, neurologic dysfunctions and ophthalmologic abnormalities were also studied and will be described in the following chapters.

As noted in Table IX, the most frequent finding was a separation (>5mm) of the sagittal suture (98.3%) often with a third (false) fontanel (94.7%) between the anterior and posterior fontanels. The second and third most often noted characteristics were the presence of oblique palpebral fissures (97.7%) and a wide space between the first and second toes (95.5%) respectively.

Further analysis of our data revealed that a high correlation exists between certain phenotypic features observed in children participating in our program. Table XI lists positive correlations of physical features including oblique palpebral fissures, increased neck tissue, abnormally shaped palate, single palmar crease, wide space between first and second toes, hypoplastic nose, hyperflexibility of joints, Brushfield spots, and an open sagittal suture.

Studying the relationship between the frequency of phenotypic features noted shortly after birth and mental age at 36 months, we did not find any correlation ($r = -.149$).

SELECTED ILLNESSES WHICH OCCURRED DURING THE STUDY PERIOD

We recorded the frequency of upper respiratory infections, lower respiratory infections, otitis media, other illnesses and hospitalizations throughout the study period (Table XII). The

TABLE IX

FREQUENCY (%) OF POSITIVE PHENOTYPIC FINDINGS IN CHILDREN

WITH DOWN SYNDROME AT THE TIME OF ENROLLMENT INTO THE PROGRAM

Sagittal suture separated	98.3
Oblique palpebral fissure	97.7
Wide space between 1st and 2nd toes	95.5
False fontanel	94.7
Plantar crease between 1st and 2nd toes	94.1
Increased neck tissue	86.9
Abnormally shaped palate	85.1
Hypoplastic nose	83.1
Brushfield spots	75.0
Mouth kept open	65.4
Protruding tongue	58.4
Epicanthal folds	57.3
Single palmar crease, left hand	54.5
Single palmar crease, right hand	52.2
Brachyclinodactyly, left hand	51.1
Brachyclinodactyly, right hand	50.0
Increased interpupillary distance	46.5
Short stubby hands	37.9
Flattened occiput	35.2
Abnormal size of ears	33.7
Short stubby feet	32.6
Abnormal structure of ears	28.1
Abnormal implantation of ears	15.8
Other hand abnormalities	12.9
Other abnormal eye findings	11.2
Syndactyly	10.7
Other feet abnormalities	8.3
Other oral abnormalities	2.3

analysis of the data revealed that the majority of children with Down syndrome did not have significantly more upper respiratory infections and otitis media than children without chromosome abnormalities. There were seven children who, according to their parents, "always had a cold." They were frequently congested when they came to the clinic, and presented with mucopurulent nasal

TABLE X

FREQUENCY (%) OF POSITIVE FINDINGS RELATING TO

JOINT MOBILITY, MUSCLE STRENGTH, AND

MOTOR ACTIVITY OF CHILDREN WITH DOWN SYNDROME

Hyperflexibility	90.5
Muscle weakness	81.0
Hypotonia	77.4
Hypoactivity	52.1

discharge. Children with significant congenital heart disease suffered more often from lower respiratory infections (bronchitis, bronchopneumonia, pneumonitis) and had frequent hospitalizations. Other illnesses included children with gastroenteritis, meningitis, and fracture of the leg. One child developed diabetes and was in a coma for nearly one week. Six other children had seizure disorders, which will be described in more detail in a subsequent chapter. While we did not observe children with thyroid disease during the study period, we uncovered three children with hypothyroidism after their third birthday.

In summary, the above detailed description of the study population noted that of 114 children admitted to the program, 89 were included in the final study sample. The characteristics of the 25 children who were excluded from later analysis are described. Moreover, we identified a number of conditions in the 89 study children and in their parents which could have interfered with their developmental course as reflected in the performance at the time of

TABLE XI

POSITIVE CORRELATIONS OF PHYSICAL FEATURES
(the numbers indicate the frequency of both characteristics being present).

	%
Oblique palpebral fissures - wide space between 1st and 2nd toes	76
Oblique palpebral fissures - single palmar crease	74
Oblique palpebral fissures - hypoplastic nose	67
Oblique palpebral fissures - abnormally shaped palate	65
Oblique palpebral fissures - hyperflexibility	62
Oblique palpebral fissures - increased neck tissue	62
Oblique palpebral fissures - Brushfield spots	59
Oblique palpebral fissures - open saggital suture line	55
Increased neck tissue - wide space between 1st and 2nd toes	61
Increased neck tissue - single palmar crease	60
Increased neck tissue - hypoplastic nose	59
Increased neck tissue - abnormally shaped palate	56
Increased neck tissue - hyperflexibility in joints	53
Increased neck tissue - Brushfield spots	50
Abnormally shaped palate - wide space between 1st and 2nd toes	67
Abnormally shaped palate - single palmar crease	66
Abnormally shaped palate - hypoplastic nose	62
Abnormally shaped palate - hyperflexibility in joints	57
Abnormally shaped palate - Brushfield spots	51
Single palmar crease - wide space between 1st and 2nd toes	80
Single palmar crease - hypoplastic nose	68
Single palmar crease - hyperflexibility	63
Single palmar crease - Brushfield spots	58
Single palmar crease - open saggital suture line	54
Wide space between 1st and 2nd toes - Brushfield spots	60
Wide space between 1st and 2nd toes - open sagittal suture line	54
Hypoplastic nose - Brushfield spots	53
Hypoplastic nose - open saggital suture line	50
Hyperflexibility in joints - wide space between 1st and 2nd toes	65
Hyperflexibility in joints - hypoplastic nose	59

the evaluation. Some of these factors will need to be considered in further evaluation of the data. We also presented the frequency of phenotypic features of children with Down syndrome in our program.

Moreover, the majority of children with Down syndrome did not have more upper respiratory infections than did normal children. There was a small group of children who had frequent nasal discharge and congestion, and children with congenital heart disease often had pneumonia. A small number of children had a variety of other

TABLE XII

FREQUENCY (%) OF SELECTED ILLNESSES OF CHILDREN WITH DOWN SYNDROME

WHICH OCCURRED DURING THE STUDY YEARS.

		None	x1	x2	x3	x4	x5
Upper respiratory infections	1st year	6.3	15.2	21.5	34.2	13.9	8.9
Upper respiratory infections	2nd year	5.1	11.4	26.6	30.4	13.9	12.7
Upper respiratory infections	3rd year	3.7	7.5	27.5	32.5	25.0	3.7
Lower respiratory infections	1st year	76.4	15.7	5.6	0	2.2	0
Lower respiratory infections	2nd year	75.3	21.3	2.2	0	1.1	0
Lower respiratory infections	3rd year	76.4	20.2	2.2	1.1	0	0
Otitis media	1st year	85.2	10.2	2.3	2.3	0	0
Otitis media	2nd year	77.5	13.5	3.4	3.4	2.2	0
Otitis media	3rd year	65.2	25.8	5.6	2.2	1.1	0
Other significant illnesses	1st year	60.7	30.3	5.6	3.4	0	0
Other significant illnesses	2nd year	62.9	28.1	6.7	1.1	1.1	0
Other significant illnesses	3rd year	66.3	24.7	5.6	3.4	0	0
Hospitalization	1st year	68.5	20.2	11.2	0	0	0
Hospitalization	2nd year	67.4	24.7	5.6	2.2	0	0
Hospitalization	3rd year	76.4	14.6	7.9	0	0	1.1

medical problems which have been described. It is of note, however, that most of the children in our Down Syndrome Program enjoyed good health during the first three years of life.

REFERENCES

1. Lejeune, J., Turpin, R. and Gauthier, M. Le Mongolisme, Premier example d'aberration autosomique humaine. *Annals De Genetique* (Paris) 1:41, 1959.

2. Rosner, F., Ong, B.H., Paine, R.S., and Mahanand, D. Biochemical differentiation of trisomic Down's syndrome (Mongolism) from that due to translocation. *New England Journal of Medicine.* 273:1356, 1965.

3. Penrose, L.S. and Smith, G.F. *Down's Anomaly.* Boston: Little Brown and Co., 1966, p. 86-98.

4. Gershoff, S.N., Hegsted, D. and Trulson, M.E. Metabolic Studies of mongoloids. *American Journal of Clinical Nutrition,* 9:526, 1958.

5. O'Brien, D. and Groshek, A. The abnormality of tryptophan metabolism in children with mongolism. *Archives of Diseases of Childhood,* 37:17, 1962.

6. Jerome, H., Lejeune, J. and Turpin, R. Etude de l'excretion urinaire de certains metabolites du tryptophane chez les enfants mongoliens. *Comptes Rendus de l'Academie des Sciences* (Paris), 251:474, 1960.

7. Pare, C.M.B., Sandler, M. and Stacey, R.S. 5-hydroxy indoles in mental deficiency. *Journal of Neurology, Neurosurgery and Psychiatry* (London), 23:341, 1960.

8. McCoy, E.E. and Chung, S.I. The excretion of tryptophan metabolites following deoxypyridoxine administration in mongoloid and non-mongoloid patients. *Pediatrics,* 64:227, 1964.

9. Rosner, F., Ong, B.H., Paine, R.S., and Mahanand, D. Blood serotonin activity in trisomic and translocation Down's syndrome. *The Lancet,* 1:1191, 1965.

10. Tu, J. and Zellweger, H. Blood serotonin deficiency in Down's syndrome. *The Lancet,* 2:715, 1965.

11. Bazelon, M., Paine, R.S., Cowie, V.A., Hunt, P., Houck, J.C. and Mahanand, D. Reversal of hypotonia in infants with Down's syndrome by administration of 5-hydroxytryptophan. *The Lancet,* 1:1130, 1967.

12. Berman, J.L. The metabolism of 5-hydroxytryptamine (serotonin) in the newborn. *Journal of Pediatrics,* 67:603, 1965.

Part II

Chapter 3

EVALUATION OF THE EFFECT OF 5-HYDROXYTRYPTOPHAN AND/OR PYRIDOXINE ADMINISTRATION IN YOUNG CHILDREN WITH DOWN SYNDROME*

Siegfried M. Pueschel
Robert B. Reed
Christine E. Cronk

INTRODUCTION

During the past decades a multitude of treatment modalities in Down syndrome has been reported (1-10). In the attempt to improve physical features and mental abilities of the child with Down syndrome, a variety of medications including hormones, vitamins, sicca cells, dimethylsulfoxide, and various combinations of these and other compounds have been employed. The ineffectiveness of the majority of those therapeutic approaches has been discussed in recent publications (11-13).

*Part of this paper was published in the American Journal of Diseases of Children, September, 1980, Volume 134, pages 838-844 under the title "5-Hydroxytryptophan and Pyridoxine" (copyright 1980 American Medical Association). Permission to reproduce obtained from publisher.

It was shortly after several investigators had reported decreased 5-hydroxytryptamine (serotonin) levels in peripheral blood in children with Down syndrome (14-19) that 5-hydroxytryptophan was introduced as a form of therapy. Bazelon and coworkers noted improvement in muscle tone, reduced tongue protrusion, and increased motor activity in infants with Down syndrome who had been given 5-hydroxytryptophan (20). In a subsequent study, the same investigator compared a group of children with Down syndrome who received 5-hydroxytryptophan with children in a placebo group; no significant difference of developmental parameters between children in these two groups was found (21). In 1971, Partington and coworkers reported a controlled trial of 5-hydroxytryptophan administration to children with Down syndrome. These investigators did not detect any improvement in motor, behavioral, and neurological functions (22). Weise and coworkers who gave 5-hydroxytryptophan to young children with Down syndrome also observed that this compound was not effective in accelerating the children's rate of development. Moreover, no discernible behavior differences between treated and nontreated children were noted (23).

METHODS

In the foregoing chapter, details of study design, study population and the roles of participating disciplines in the Down Syndrome Program are described. It is mentioned that prior to initiation of the Down Syndrome Program, random assignment to the different study groups (placebo, pyridoxine, 5-hydroxytryptophan, 5-hydroxytryptophan/pyridoxine) was carried out by our biostatistical consultant from the Harvard School of Public Health and transmitted directly to the pharmacist so that the evaluation team was blind to the random assignment.

The four "medications" were provided in capsules indistinguishable from each other and were administered in divided doses of 1 to 2 mg/kg/day 5-hydroxytryptophan and 5 to 10 mg/kg/day of pyridoxine. Because the children required larger dosage of "medications" as they grew and gained weight, three types of capsules were prepared for each of the three active "medications."

For 5-hydroxytryptophan, capsule I contained 5 mg, capsule II 10 mg, and capsule III 20 mg. For pyridoxine, capsule I contained 15 mg, capsule II 30 mg, and capsule III 60 mg. For 5-hydroxytryptophan/pyridoxine respective combined dosages were prepared in capsules I, II, III. Lactose which was placed into the placebo capsules was also used as filler for all the other capsules thus providing a similar taste to all four "medications."

A three-month supply of "medications" was given to the parents during their visits to the Developmental Evaluation Clinic. The parents were asked to keep the "medications" refrigerated. If the "medications" were lost or for some reason unusable, the parents were to call us immediately so that new "medications" could be mailed to them.

Parents were advised to mix the content of the capsules in applesauce or with other fruits and to give it at mealtimes to their child. On occasion urine samples were examined for tryptophan compounds to assure that parents were in compliance with the recommended administration of the "medications."

At each clinic visit, the pediatrician obtained approximately 5 ml of venous blood which was usually drawn from the anticubital vein into a heparinized syringe. The blood was transferred into a polyethylene tube and immediately deep frozen.

One or two days after the blood was obtained it was analyzed in duplicate. The total 5-hydroxyindol was determined by a method described by Rosner and coworkers (14). After thawing, 2.0 ml of blood was transferred with a Mohr pipette to a polyethylene test-tube containing 5.0 ml of triple distilled deionized water. After thorough mixing by inversion, 2.0 ml of cold 10% zinc sulfate was added to precipitate the protein. Following repeated mixing by inversion, 1.0 ml of cold [1N] sodium hydroxide was added and the tube again inverted several times to ensure even mixing. The resulting mixture was centrifuged at 4 °C at 5000 r.p.m. for 10 minutes. 3.0 ml of the clear, colorless supernatant was transferred to another tube, and 0.9 ml of 12N hydrochloric acid was added. Serotonin activity was then measured directly, spectrophotofluorometrically (Aminco-Bowman 4-8202) at 290 mμ activation and 355 mμ fluorescence.

The muscle tone of the children in the study was evaluated independently by three examiners: pediatrician, neurologist, and physical therapist. Each of the examiners followed his/her individual protocol: During the physical examinations, the pediatrician recorded a composite score for muscle tone, ranging from 0 = extremely poor muscle tone to 4 = hypertonic. The neurologist gave separate ratings for muscle tone of upper extremities, lower extremities, neck, and trunk; in addition, posture, arm recoil, leg recoil, ventral suspension, and traction responses were recorded. The individual assessments were averaged to produce a single muscle-tone score for each examination. The physical therapist focused on resistance against passive movements in trunk, hip, knees, and elbows. An average score was obtained from each examination.

The cognitive-adaptive function of children in the study was evaluated utilizing the Bayley Scales of Infant Development (26) and the Vineland Social Maturity Scale (27). Both instruments were given at six-month intervals during the study period. At the third birthday each child's language abilities were examined using the Receptive-Expressive Emergent Language Scale (28).

Support to parents and instructions regarding various aspects of care and stimulation were provided throughout the study. The parents' ability to comply and follow through with furnished guidance was rated as *yes* or *no* by the participating nurse after a lengthy interview with the parents at six-month intervals. The individual ratings were summed in the final analysis of the data.

The rationale for this study (which has been discussed in detail in the previous chapter) was that 5-hydroxytryptamine levels in children with Down syndrome can be raised by administration of either 5-hydroxytryptophan, which is the precursor of 5-hydroxytryptamine, and/or of pyridoxine which is the coenzyme in the decarboxylation reaction. It also had been demonstrated that 5-hydroxytryptophan would improve the usually observed hypotonia and enhance motor activity in the young child with Down syndrome.

RESULTS

After breaking the drug code at the end of the study, it was found that out of 89 subjects in the study there were 20 children in the placebo group, 23 in the pyridoxine group, 22 in the 5-hydroxytryptophan group, and 24 in the 5-hydroxytryptophan/pyridoxine group. As had been mentioned in the previous chapter, the random assignment of children to the study groups placed more children with moderate and severe congenital heart disease in the placebo group than in the 5-hydroxytryptophan group (Table I). Therefore, children with moderate and severe cardiac conditions were excluded during specified analyses.

In the analysis of the total 5-hydroxyindol concentration in the blood of children with Down syndrome it became apparent that 5-hydroxytryptophan, pyridoxine and 5-hydroxytryptophan/pyridoxine all raised the blood levels to an equal degree (Figure 1). The effect of pyridoxine alone was similar to the effect of 5-hydroxytryptophan and the combination of 5-hydroxytryptophan/pyridoxine was not more effective than each of the individual "medications." There was a gradual decline of 5-hydroxyindol blood levels over time in the treatment groups as well as in the placebo group although the latter trend was less marked (Table II and Figure 1).

In each of the three treatment groups the effect on total 5-hydroxyindol blood levels was confined to about 40 percent of the children while the remaining children had mean 5-hydroxyindol blood levels

TABLE I

CONGENITAL HEART DISEASE OF CHILDREN

WITH DOWN SYNDROME IN THE VARIOUS STUDY GROUPS

Study Group	Congenital Heart Disease[*]				
	A None	B Mild	C Moderate	D Severe	Total
Placebo	12	1	6	1	20
Pyridoxine	17	1	4	1	23
5-hydroxytryptophan	17	4	1	0	22
5-hydroxytryptophan/pyridoxine	17	3	1	3	24
Total	63	9	12	5	89

[*]A definition of mild, moderate, and severe congenital heart disease is provided in Part I of this monograph.

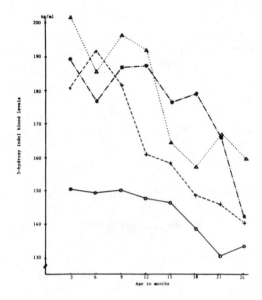

Figure 1:   Mean 5-hydroxyindol blood levels of children with Down syndrome according to study group.

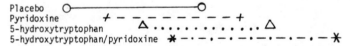

(Since after 24 months less than 50% of blood 5-hydroxyindol levels were available we did not include these incomplete data in this figure).

within the range of the placebo group (Table III). This was not influenced by other conditions such as congenital heart disease or parental compliance.

   Muscle tone examinations done by pediatrician, neurologist and physical therapist revealed a good interexaminer agreement with an average correlation of 0.55. The examiners observed a gradual increase of muscle tone in children from the four groups over the study period (Figure 2).*

---

*Brief discussions on muscle tone are also provided in chapters on Motor Development and Neurological Investigations.

TABLE II

MEANS AND STANDARD ERRORS

OF 5-HYDROXYINDOL BLOOD LEVELS ACCORDING TO AGE

AND STUDY GROUP

ng/ml

				Age in Months				
	3	6	9	12	15	18	21	24
Placebo								
Mean	150.3	149.2	151.0	147.8	146.6	138.9	130.2	133.3
Standard Error	11.3	10.8	11.1	11.4	9.9	6.7	7.4	8.3
Pyridoxine								
Mean	180.3	191.5	181.7	165.3	158.4	145.4	146.8	140.7
Standard Error	15.9	13.2	11.4	9.1	8.6	11.3	7.6	7.8
5-Hydroxytryptophan								
Mean	201.3	185.1	196.6	191.8	164.1	157.4	166.8	159.9
Standard Error	19.3	15.0	12.3	13.7	13.0	11.6	11.1	10.4
5-Hydroxytryptophan/Pyridoxine								
Mean	189.1	176.7	186.9	187.7	176.6	179.5	165.7	142.6
Standard Error	14.1	16.2	14.0	16.2	14.2	10.3	12.6	9.3

Children who had been randomly assigned to the 5-hydroxytryptophan group initially had higher muscle tone ratings than children in the other two treatment groups and in the placebo group, but the difference was not statistically significant. The slightly increased muscle tone in children from the 5-hydroxytryptophan group as compared with the other three groups continued throughout the study. The muscle tone ratings by the pediatrician during the second and third year of study were noted to be significantly higher in children in the 5-hydroxytryptophan group. However, when children with moderate and severe cardiac disease were excluded, no significant difference was observed among the four study groups (Figure 2).

It has been noted previously that the 5-hydroxyindol blood levels had been elevated in approximately 40 percent of the children in the

TABLE III

DISTRIBUTION OF CHILDREN WITH DOWN SYNDROME
ACCORDING TO MEAN 5-HYDROXYINDOL BLOOD LEVEL AND STUDY GROUP

| Study Group | 5-Hydroxyindol levels in ng/ml* | | | |
	< 135	135-175	>175	Total
Placebo	9	8	1	18
Pyridoxine	6	10	7	23
5-Hydroxytryptophan	6	5	11	22
5-Hydroxytryptophan/Pyridoxine	7	6	9	22
Total	28	29	28	85**

*Each child was classified according to blood 5-hydroxyindol levels averaged over a period from 3 to 24 months.

**Four children were not included because of insufficient blood data.

three treatment groups, whereas the remainder of the children in the treatment groups maintained blood levels comparable to the placebo group. Consequently the 27 children with the highest average blood levels were studied to determine whether possible effects of treatment had been confined to these apparent responders.

When the muscle tone analysis was carried out contrasting children with high (>175 ng/ml) and low (≤175 ng/ml) total 5-hydroxyindol blood levels, no significant difference was noted.

In further analyses the treatment effects were studied for selected variables from anthropometric examinations, motor assessments, neurological evaluations, psychological assessments, and the language examination. There were no statistically significant treatment effects for these variables at the .05 level comparing the four study groups. The only findings that were statistically significant occurred on the Vineland Social Maturity Scale at ages 6, 12, 18, and 36 months ($.05 < p > .01$) for the overall F-test (Table IV). At 6, 12, and 18 months the source of significant findings was a negative interaction, i.e. children treated with 5-hydroxytryptophan/pyridoxine performed less well than would have been expected on the

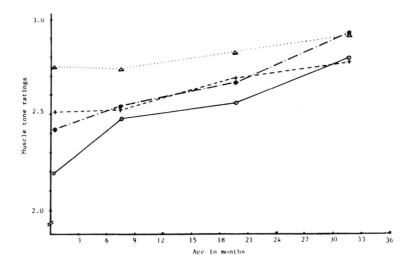

Figure 2: Mean muscle tone ratings of children with Down syndrome by age according to
study groups. Children with moderate and severe congenital heart disease were omitted.

Muscle tone ratings:

    0 - extremely poor muscle tone
    1 - markedly decreased muscle tone
    2 - mildly decreased muscle tone
    3 - normal muscle tone
    4 - increased muscle tone

Study groups:

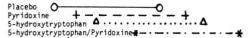

basis of 5-hydroxytryptophan and pyridoxine groups. At 36 months
the negative interaction on the Vineland Social Maturity Scale was
not significant by itself. However, the pattern of effects was the same
as at the earlier ages 6, 12 and 18 months when there was a slight
positive effect of 5-hydroxytryptophan, a slight negative effect of
pyridoxine, and a negative interaction (Table IV).

    Since there is no biochemical basis for expecting or interpreting
the negative interaction effect, it was decided to investigate other

TABLE IV

MEANS, STANDARD DEVIATIONS, AND INTERACTION EFFECTS OF

VINELAND SOCIAL MATURITY SCALE RAW SCORES

OBTAINED AT SIX MONTH INTERVALS

Age in Months*	Study Group**	Mean	Standard Deviation	N***	F	P	Interaction Effect****
6	1	5.7	1.6	12			
	2	6.9	.9	18	3.9	.05	-1.4
	3	6.9	.9	20			
	4	6.8	1.0	18			
12	1	13.2	3.6	10			
	2	13.8	2.1	14	3.9	.05	-3.3
	3	15.1	1.8	20			
	4	12.4	2.6	20			
18	1	18.0	5.0	10			
	2	19.5	2.8	14	2.8	.05	-4.6
	3	20.3	2.8	16			
	4	17.1	2.5	16			
24	1	22.3	5.3	12			
	2	23.4	3.8	15	1.5	NS	-2.6
	3	25.3	3.4	19			
	4	23.8	3.2	15			

cont'd

possible explanations for this peculiar aspect of the data. Subsequently, parental follow-through, a nonrandomized variable, was introduced into further analyses. Table V shows the follow-through data according to study group. While chi-square analysis did not reveal a significant difference among the groups ($p < .05$) there was a disproportionate number of "good" follow-through cases in the 5-hydroxytryptophan group. Forty-two children whose parents had been less able to follow through on furnished guidance were placed in one group and 47 children whose parents carried out recommendations successfully were placed in the other group. There was no evidence of drug effect in the latter group. However, in the former

Table IV continued

Age in Months*	Study Group**	Mean	Standard Deviation	N***	F	P	Interaction Effect****
30	1	28.3	5.6	13			
	2	27.6	3.8	12	1.5	NS	-2.3
	3	30.5	4.5	16			
	4	27.5	3.1	15			
36	1	32.4	6.4	10			
	2	31.5	3.7	15	3.4	.05	-3.6
	3	35.7	3.8	18			
	4	31.2	4.5	17			

*Children were tested close to the specified times at 6, 12, 18, 24, 30, and 36 months $\pm$ 6 days.

**Study Group 1: Placebo
Study Group 2: Pyridoxine
Study Group 3: 5-Hydroxytryptophan
Study Group 4: 5-Hydroxytryptophan/Pyridoxine

***This includes children with mild and without congenital heart disease; the numbers change slightly since not all children always were available for testing.

****Interaction Effect - $Mean_1$ - $Mean_2$ - $Mean_3$ + $Mean_4$
(The interaction effect measures the extent to which the combined treatment groups had a mean score that differed from what would be expected as a simple additive effect of 5-hydroxytryptophan and pyridoxine alone).

group of children whose parents had difficulties with follow-through, the statistically significant negative interaction on the Vineland Social Maturity Scale at 6 and 18 months was noted. The group whose parents were rated as successful on follow-through showed consistently higher levels of accomplishment than children in the group with ''poor'' follow-through, as shown in Table VI. Thus it appeared that if there was any positive drug effect it was overshadowed by the parental follow-through variable. Moreover, analysis of cognitive-adaptive function comparing individuals with relatively high 5-hydroxyindol blood levels with those of lower 5-hydroxyindol blood levels showed no significant treatment effects.

TABLE   V

RATINGS OF PARENTAL ABILITY TO FOLLOW THROUGH

WITH FURNISHED GUIDANCE ACCORDING TO STUDY GROUPS

Study Group	Dichotomous Ratings of Parental Follow-through*		Total
	Yes	No	
Placebo	8	12	20
Pyridoxine	10	13	23
5-hydroxytryptophan	17	5	22
5-hydroxytryptophan/pyridoxine	12	12	24
Total	47	42	89

*chi-square = 7.48; df 3; p < 0.10

In order to separate out further the effects of 5-hydroxytryptophan and the ability of parental follow-through on the various outcome variables, linear contrasts were carried out on the means that examines the difference between the mean of the groups with adequate follow-through and the mean of the total group with 5-hydroxytryptophan. The result is the "effect" in the units of the outcome variable.

Table VII shows that effects for the follow-through variable holding 5-hydroxytryptophan constant is significant at at least the .05 level for all tests except the results from the Bayley Mental Scale at 6 months. The 5-hydroxytryptophan effect was not statistically significant at any point in the assessments.

Table VIII presents the linear contrasts on total 5-hydroxyindol blood levels comparing the 5-hydroxytryptophan and follow-through effects. While a follow-through effect at the .05 level was found at 30 months, a significant 5-hydroxytryptophan effect was noted at 12, 15, 18, 21, 27 and 36 months.

TABLE VI

BAYLEY MOTOR AND MENTAL SCALES
ACCORDING TO THE PARENTAL ABILITY TO
FOLLOW THROUGH WITH FURNISHED GUIDANCE

Age in Months	Bayley Scales of Infant Development	Ratings of parental follow through	Mean	Standard Deviation	F	P
12	Motor	yes	8.0	1.5	16.6	.001
		no	6.5	1.3		
	Mental	yes	7.5	1.7	14.2	.001
		no	6.0	1.3		
24	Motor	yes	14.9	2.8	14.3	.001
		no	12.1	3.0		
	Mental	yes	15.1	2.8	32.2	.001
		no	12.0	2.1		
36	Motor	yes	21.6	4.7	7.9	.02
		no	17.9	4.2		
	Mental	yes	23.0	4.5	19.1	.001
		no	18.2	3.5		

DISCUSSION

As noted in Figure 1, pyridoxine, 5-hydroxytryptophan and the combination of 5-hydroxytryptophan/pyridoxine all raised the total 5-hydroxyindol blood level in 40 percent of the children in the treatment groups. Why did not the remaining 60 percent of the

TABLE VII

LINEAR CONTRASTS ON VARIABLES FROM THE BAYLEY SCALES OF INFANT DEVELOPMENT,
VINELAND SOCIAL MATURITY SCALE, AND RECEPTIVE-EXPRESSIVE EMERGENT LANGUAGE SCALE
(REEL) COMPARING 5-HYDROXYTRYPTOPHAN (5-HTP) AND FOLLOW-THROUGH EFFECTS

Age in months	Examination	N	Study**** Group	Mean	F	Follow-through	5-HTP effect	Interaction
6	Bayley Mental Scale	67	1	3.40	.572	.659	.321	.307
			2	2.92				
			3	3.41				
			4	3.23				
6	Bayley Motor Scale	67	1	4.73	* 3.51	* 1.51	.418	1.122
			2	3.42				
			3	3.96				
			4	3.77				
12	Bayley Mental Scale	70	1	7.63	** 5.47	** 2.95	.559	1.069
			2	5.62				
			3	7.37				
			4	6.43				
12	Bayley Motor Scale	69	1	8.31	*** 6.047	*** 3.07	.517	.725
			2	6.42				
			3	7.74				
			4	6.57				
18	Bayley Mental Scale	64	1	11.93	*** 7.172	*** 4.86	.167	1.142
			2	8.83				
			3	11.35				
			4	9.58				

children have elevated total 5-hydroxyindol blood levels? Since we
made frequent spot checks concerning parental compliance in the
administration of the "medications," we estimated that the vast
majority of parents (at least 95%) gave the "medication" to their
children. Laboratory errors and pharmacy miscalculations as
responsible elements for this finding are highly unlikely. Decreased
absorption from the intestinal tract may in part account for the low

Table VII continued

Age in months	Examination	N	Study**** Group	Mean	F	Follow-through	5-HTP effect	Interaction
18	Bayley Motor Scale	64	1	11.50	* 3.814	** 4.372	.934	.462
			2	9.08				
			3	11.54				
			4	9.58				
24	Bayley Mental Scale	62	1	15.19	*** 11.112	*** 6.308	.934	1.142
			2	11.46				
			3	15.08				
			4	12.50				
24	Bayley Motor Scale	63	1	14.69	** 5.472	*** 5.533	2.013	1.205
			2	11.31				
			3	15.09				
			4	12.92				
30	Bayley Mental Scale	66	1	18.40	*** 6.549	*** 6.06	-.194	1.006
			2	14.87				
			3	17.80				
			4	15.27				
30	Bayley Motor Scale	66	1	17.93	* 3.369	* 5.091	3.043	2.509
			2	14.13				
			3	18.20				
			4	16.91				
36	Bayley Mental Scale	61	1	23.50	*** 6.519	*** 9.719	.355	2.051
			2	17.62				
			3	22.65				
			4	18.82				

total 5-hydroxyindol blood levels in some children who received the "medications" (30). Although some investigators have reported deficiencies in the 5-hydroxyindol pathway (see Figure 3), there is evidence that this pathway is essentially intact in children with Down syndrome (21). It is more likely that failure of 5-hydroxytryptamine

Table VII continued

Age in months	Exami- nation	N	Study**** Group	Mean	F	Follow- through	5-HTP effect	Inter- action
36	Bayley Motor Scale	48	1	22.00	* 3.809	*** 7.148	2.748	3.459
			2	16.39				
			3	21.33				
			4	19.80				
	REEL (Receptive)	56	1	31.35	*** 6.819	*** 9.195	1.059	3.459
			2	24.92				
			3	30.05				
			4	27.18				
	REEL (Expressive)	60	1	34.14	** 5.392	*** 9.013	2.727	1.273
			2	29.00				
			3	34.87				
			4	31.00				
6	Vineland	85	1	6.77	1.116	.0672	.392	.218
			2	6.32				
			3	6.85				
			4	6.63				
12	Vineland	81	1	14.13	* 3.245	** 3.504	.196 -	.446
			2	12.15				
			3	14.00				
			4	12.47				
18	Vineland	67	1	20.44	*** 6.854	*** 6.74	-.42	2.00
			2	16.07				
			3	19.23				
			4	16.86				

uptake, transport, and/or binding in addition to limited availability of adenosine triphosphate may have been responsible for the low total 5-hydroxyindol blood concentration in some children of the treatment groups (31-34). It is also possible that some unidentified metabolic factor made some children respond to the administration of the three compounds in raising 5-hydroxyindol blood levels, while in other

Table VII continued

Age in months	Examination	N	Study Group	Mean	F	Follow-through	5-HTP effect	Inter-action
24	Vineland	77	1	25.00				
			2	20.27	***7.591	***9.031		1.273
			3	25.24				
			4	21.79				
30	Vineland	71	1	30.64				
			2	25.05	***8.105	***9.231	-.055	1.959
			3	29.64				
			4	26.00				
36	Vineland	74	1	34.14				
			2	29.40	***6.111	***9.13	.71	.356
			3	34.32				
			4	29.33				

Legend:

* $p < 0.05$

** $p < 0.01$

*** $p < 0.001$

****Study group 1 – combined groups (placebo and pyridoxine) parents follow-through with furnished guidance.

2 – combined groups (placebo and pyridoxine) parents do not follow-through with furnished guidance.

3 – combined groups (5-HTP and 5-HTP/pyridoxine) parents follow-through with furnished guidance.

4 – combined groups (5-HTP and 5-HTP/pyridoxine) parents follow-through with furnished guidance.

children the total 5-hydroxyindol blood levels were not affected by the administration of 5-hydroxytryptophan, pyridoxine, or 5-hydroxy-tryptophan/pyridoxine.

Compared with Coleman's study (21), the placebo group in this investigation had higher 5-hydroxyindol blood levels, yet the treatment groups as noted above had similar total 5-hydroxyindol blood levels as children in Coleman's study who received 5-hydroxytryptophan (21). Coleman also observed that in some children the 5-hydroxyindol level was significantly raised by 5-hydroxytryptophan administration while in others the 5-hydroxyindol level was only minimally elevated.

It is generally agreed that the conventional assessment of muscle tone is not an accurate science. Therefore, the investigators of this study attempted to objectively quantify the muscle tone of children with Down syndrome by computerized electromyography; however, these efforts failed. Thus the examiners evaluated the muscle tone in the usual fashion. Good correlation was found among the three examiners' individual assessments.

Bazelon and coworkers had initially reported that 5-hydroxytryptophan administration would markedly increase the reduced muscle tone in children with Down syndrome (20). In her second study, only a mild increase in muscle tone was noted in children with Down syndrome who had received 5-hydroxytryptophan during the first few months of life, and after the fourth month of age children in the placebo group tended to have even higher muscle tone ratings than children in the treatment group (21). Similarly, Partington and coworkers as well as Weise and co-investigators who had administered 5-hydroxytryptophan to children with Down syndrome did not find a consistent effect on long term improvement of muscle tone in their patients (22,23).

Of primary interest are the results of the cognitive-adaptive assessments. A selective, simple analysis of the data could have interpreted 5-hydroxytryptophan as having a positive effect on the adaptive functioning of children with Down syndrome since those children receiving 5-hydroxytryptophan had significantly higher scores on the Vineland Social Maturity Scale at 6, 12, 18, and 36 months than those who were not administered this "medication." However, this difference was primarily due to an uninterpretable negative interaction of pyridoxine and 5-hydroxytryptophan. Moreover, when children with moderate and severe congenital heart disease were excluded from the analysis and the follow-up variable was taken into consideration, no significant difference among the children's cognitive-adaptive functioning was apparent. While this study analyzed in much more detail various aspects of the Down

TABLE VIII

LINEAR CONTRASTS ON TOTAL 5-HYDROXYINDOL BLOOD LEVELS
COMPARING 5-HYDROXYTRYPTOPHAN (5-HTP) AND FOLLOW-THROUGH EFFECTS

Age in months	Study*** Group	N	Mean (ng/ml)	F	Follow-through	5-HTP effect	Inter-action
3	1	18	170				
	2	24	164				
	3	28	206	1.903	41.304	43.304	-29.554
	4	15	171				
6	1	18	185				
	2	24	169				
	3	29	184	.537	16.5	14.916	16.215
	4	16	184				
9	1	18	180				
	2	23	163				
	3	29	186	1.689	.984	49.85	35.172
	4	16	204				
12	1	17	164				
	2	24	153			*	
	3	28	185	2.590	-7	70.334	28.834
	4	15	203				
15	1	16	160				
	2	24	151	*		*	*
	3	29	156	2.999	35.323	44.911	54.363
	4	14	200				

syndrome child's abilities, it is in agreement with previously reported negative results of investigations administering 5-hydroxytryptophan to children with Down syndrome (21-23).

In an attempt to explain the negative findings on children who were given tryptophan compounds, the known effects upon the central nervous system need to be briefly discussed. It is conceivable that the same defect observed in transport, uptake, and binding of 5-hydroxytryptamine in platelets also exists in the neurons of children

Table VIIIcontinued

Age in months	Study*** Group	N	Mean (ng/ml)	F	Follow-through	5-HTP effect	Inter-action
	1	17	141				
18	2	24	143	2.894*	26.863	60.015**	22.535
	3	29	160				
	4	15	188				
	1	17	137				
21	2	24	141	2.521	21.364	54.014**	13.652
	3	28	157				
	4	15	175				
	1	17	125				
24	2	22	141	1.853	31.829	31.701	1.209
	3	27	140				
	4	14	157				
	1	7	121				
30	2	9	147	1.858	57.921*	30.937	5.793
	3	14	133				
	4	7	165				
	1	8	107				
27	2	11	127	1.927	37.007	74.923*	3.673
	3	13	146				
	4	8	163				
	1	6	113				
36	2	7	131	3.071*	32.777	69.699**	.271
	3	11	148				
	4	7	166				

with Down syndrome. While several studies suggested normal synthesis of 5-hydroxytryptamine in the central nervous system (35, 36), Fellstrom and coworkers reported low levels of 5-hydroxy-indolacetic acid in cerebral spinal fluid of children with Down syndrome (37). Yet, it is uncertain whether 5-hydroxyindol compounds measured in spinal fluid accurately reflect concentration

Table VIII continued

Legend:

  *<p .05
 **<p .01

*** Study groups 1 - combined groups (placebo and pyridoxine) parents follow-through with
furnished guidance.

2 - combined groups (placebo and pyridoxine) parents do not follow-through
with furnished guidance.

3 - combined groups (5-HTP and 5-HTP/pyridoxine) parents follow-through
with furnished guidance.

4 - combined groups (5-HTP and 5-HTP/pyridoxine) parents follow-through
with furnished guidance.

of 5-hydroxytryptamine at the neuronal level. No controlled studies are available on 5-hydroxytryptophan and 5-hydroxytryptamine transport across blood-brain barrier. If 5-hydroxytryptophan administered to children with Down syndrome were transported adequately into the central nervous system we still would lack information on how increased 5-hydroxyindol compounds in the central nervous system might affect the overall mental functioning.

SUMMARY

During this double-blind study, 89 children with Down syndrome were administered 5-hydroxytryptophan and/or pyridoxine in the first three years of life. The analysis of 5-hydroxyindol blood levels revealed that 5-hydroxytryptophan, pyridoxine and 5-hydroxytryptophan/pyridoxine raised blood levels of 5-hydroxyindols equally well in 40 percent of the children. The assessment of muscle tone ratings showed no significant difference among the study groups once children with moderate and severe congenital heart disease were excluded. Detailed studies of cognitive-adaptive function of children in the various groups found a significant difference on the Vineland Social Maturity Scale at ages 6, 12, 18, and 36 months; yet the source of significance was a negative interaction affecting children whose parents were able to follow through with furnished guidance; these children showed consistently higher levels of accomplishment.

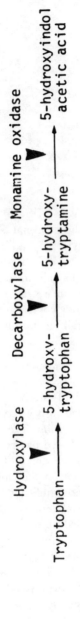

Figure 3: 5-hydroxyindol pathway.

Further analyses of possible treatment effects for selected variables from anthropometric examinations, motor assessments, neurological evaluations, Bayley Scales of Infant Development, and language examination did not reveal any statistically significant differences for these variables at the .05 level.

REFERENCES

1. Benda, C.F. *The Child with Mongolism.* New York: Grune and Stratton, 1960.
2. Koch, R., Share, J., and Graliker, B. The effects of cytomel on young children with Down's syndrome (mongolism): a double blind longitudinal study. *Journal of Pediatrics,* 66:776, 1965.
3. Goldstein, H. L-glutative as a therapeutic aid in mentally retarded children. *Medical Times,* August, 1961.
4. Marsh, R.W. and Cabaret, J.J. Down's syndrome treated with a low phenylalanine diet: case report. *New Zealand Medical Journal,* 75:364, 1971.
5. Blumberg, E. Two years of pituitary treatment in mongoloids: a clinical study. *Journal of Maine Medical Association,* 50:120, 1959.
6. Aspillaga, M.J., Morizon, G. and Avendano, I. Dimethylsulfoxide therapy in severe retardation in mongoloid children. *Annals of the New York Academy of Sciences,* 243:421, 1975.
7. Schmid, F., Haus, E., Moradof, S. and Dyck, H. Beeinflussung der mongoloiden Dyszephalie durch Injektionsimplantationen fetaler, heterologer Gehirngewebe. *Fortschritte der Medizin* 90:1811, 1972.
8. Oestreicher, P. Die Behandlung des Mongolismus. *Monatsschrift der Kinderheilkunde.* 121:316, 1973.
9. Black, D.B., Kato, J.G. and Walker, G.W. Improvement in mentally retarded children accruing from sicca cell therapy. *American Journal of Mental Deficiency.* 70:499, 1966.
10. Turkel, H. Medical amelioration of Down's syndrome incorporating the orthomolecular approach. *Journal of Orthomolecular Psychiatry.* 4:102, 1975.
11. Share, J.B. A review of drug treatment for Down's syndrome persons. *American Journal of Mental Deficiency.* 80:388, 1976.

12. De la Cruz, F. Medical management of mongolism or Down syndrome. In: *Research to Practice in Mental Retardation: Education and Training.* Vol. III, P. Mittler, (Ed.), Baltimore: University Park Press, 1977.

13. Pueschel, S.M. Therapeutic approaches in Down syndrome. In *Trisomy 21 (Down syndrome) Research Perspectives.* de la Cruz, F.F. and Gerald, P.S. (Eds.), Baltimore, University Park Press, 1981.

14. Rosner, F., Ong, B.H., Paine, R.S. and Mahanand, D. Blood-serotonin activity in trisomic and translocation Down syndrome. *The Lancet,* 1:1191, 1965.

15. Tu, J. and Zellweger, H. Blood serotonin deficiency in Down syndrome. *The Lancet,* 2:715, 1965.

16. Berman, J.L. The metabolism of 5-hydroxytryptamine (serotonin) in the newborn. *Journal of Pediatrics,* 67:603, 1965.

17. Saxl, O. Down syndrome: New aspects. *Acta Pediatrica Academia Scientiarum Hungaricae (Budapest)*

18. Bazelon, M. Serotonin metabolism in Down syndrome. *Clinical Proceedings of Children's Hospital,* Washington, D.C. 23:58, 1967.

19. Carpenter, W.T. Serotonin now: Clinical implications of inhibiting its synthesis with p-chlorophenylalanine. *Annals of Internal Medicine,* 73:607, 1970.

20. Bazelon, M., Paine, R.S., Cowie, V.A., Hunt, P., Houck, J.C. and Mahanand, D. Reversal of hypotonia in infants with Down syndrome by administration of 5-hydroxytryptophan. *The Lancet,* 1:1130, 1967.

21. Coleman, M. and Steinberg, L. A double blind trial of 5-hydroxytryptophan in Trisomy 21 patients. In *Serotonin in Down syndrome.* M. Coleman (Ed.), New York: American Elsevier Publishing Company, Inc., 1973, pp. 43-60.

22. Partington, M.W., MacDonald, M.R.A. and Tu, J.B.: 5-hydroxytryptophan (5-HTP) in Down syndrome. *Developmental Medicine and Child Neurology,* 13:362, 1971.

23. Weise, P., Koch, R., Shaw, K.N.F., and Rosenfeld, M.J. The use of 5-HTP in the treatment of Down syndrome. *Pediatrics,* 54:165, 1974.

24. Udenfriend, S., Weissbach, H. and Brodie, B.B. In *Methods of Biochemical Analysis,* Vol. 6. D. Glick (Ed.), New York: Wiley-Interscience, 1958, p. 112.

25. Sjoerdsma, A., Weissbach, H., Terry, L.L. and Udenfriend, S. Further observations on patients with malignant carcinosis. *American Journal of Medicine,* 23:5, 1957.

26. Bayley, N. *Bayley Scales of Infant Development*. New York: Psychological Corporation, 1969.

27. Doll, E.A. *Vineland Social Maturity Scale*. Minnesota: American Guidance Service Inc., 1965.

28. Bzoch, K.R. and League, R. *The Receptive-Expressive Emergent Language Scale for the Measurement of Language Skills in Infancy*. Gainesville, Florida: The Tree of Life Press, 1970.

29. Pueschel, S.M. and Murphy, A. Counseling of parents of infants with Down syndrome. *Postgraduate Medicine,* 58:90, 1975.

30. O'Brien, D. and Groshek, A. The abnormality of tryptophane metabolism in children with mongolism. *Archives of Diseases of Childhood,* 37:17, 1962.

31. Jerome, H. and Kamoun, P. Diminution du taux de la serotonine associee a un defaut de captation dans les plaquettes sanguines des sujets trisomiques 21. *Comptes Rendus de l'Academiedes Sciences* (Paris), 264:2072, 1967.

32. Boullin, D.J. and O'Brien, R.A. Abnormalities of 5-hydroxytryptamine uptake and binding by blood platelets from children with Down syndrome. *Journal of Physiology,* 212:287, 1971.

33. McCoy, E.E. and Bayer, S.M. Decreased serotonin uptake and ATPase activity in platelets from Down syndrome patients. *Clin. Res.,* 21:304, 1973.

34. Lott, I.T., Chase, T.N. and Murphy, D.L. Down syndrome: Transport, storage and metabolism of serotonin in blood platelets. *Pediatric Research,* 6:730, 1972.

35. Dubowitz, V. and Rogers, K.J. 5-hydroxyindoles in the cerebrospinal fluid of infants with Down syndrome and muscle hypotonia. *Developmental Medicine and Child Neurology,* 11:730, 1969.

36. Tu, J. and Partington, M.W. 5-hydroxyindole levels in the blood and CSF in Down syndrome, phenylketonuria and severe mental retardation. *Developmental Medicine and Child Neurology,* 14:457, 1972.

37. Fellstrom, P., Liedholm, M. and Lundborg, P. Evidence of altered cerebral serotonin metabolism in Down syndrome from measurement of cerebro-spinal fluid acids. *Pediatric Research,* 7:53, 1973.

Part III

Chapter 4

SOCIAL SERVICE EVALUATIONS

Ann Murphy

INTRODUCTION

Since Down syndrome can be identified in the newborn period, the diagnosis is made at a time critical for the formation of the parent-child relationship. In the past it was thought that separation of the child with Down syndrome from the family at birth would minimize the stress on family members and promote their return to normal functioning. Thus, previously many infants with Down syndrome were placed in residential facilities shortly after their birth.

For some time specialists in mental retardation have been concerned with the negative impact of institutionalization on the development of retarded children and the effect upon the family. When our Down Syndrome Program was started, Massachusetts' state institutions were no longer accepting young children with Down syndrome for admission. Child welfare agencies were subsidizing some private placements and were just beginning to develop alternative programs such as foster homes. However, this information and this philosophy had not permeated the thinking and attitude either of many professionals or of the general public.

Our program provided an opportunity to meet a large number of families who were confronted with the diagnosis of Down syndrome in their newborn child. We were enabled to learn what coping mechanisms parents utilize and what influenced the decisions they made. It is important to note that at that time no specialized community-based support services were available to parents for child rearing until the child was 3 years of age. Families were dependent upon their own resources, their family physician or pediatrician, and the grassroots supports potentially available to parents of normal children.

METHODS

Several factors seemed relevant to examine:

—What information was available to parents about Down syndrome?

—What pre-existing knowledge did they have?

—What were they told by professional people they encountered?

—What values were communicated about an appropriate direction to take?

Since a diagnosis of mental retardation often represents a loss to the parent, a loss of the "normal child" whom they anticipated (1), relevant questions were:

—What had the pregnancy meant to these parents?

—What previous experiences had they had with stress and loss?

—What supports were available which might help mitigate the impact of the loss?

—Was the marriage stable?

—Was there extended family who were supportive and available?

—What were the implications of the socioeconomic status?

—Were people of advanced education and with available economic resources better able to accept a child with special needs, or did such a diagnosis pose greater threat to their values and social position?

—What alternatives were available to families for providing care of the child?

All families were seen on the first day that their child entered the Down Syndrome Program. A few families with whom contact was initiated in the maternity hospital generally offered a different perspective on the development of coping mechanisms. At this stage the families were in far more acute distress and more disorganized in their thinking and feeling than those parents who were interviewed at a later point in the Developmental Evaluation Clinic.

The plan was to have an open-ended relatively unstructured discussion with the parents, but routinely to solicit data on the issues under study. Several factors affected the quality and quantity of the data. Of necessity the interview had to focus on the immediate needs of the family, who almost without exception were in a state of crisis, needing to talk about their feelings, to raise questions about Down syndrome or the program. Parents had come to us with the expectation that the focus would be on the child in terms of more extensive diagnostic investigations. They often wondered whether they should enroll the child in a research-oriented study. Some parents were very open in providing information about other aspects of their life situation, whereas others were guarded or not particularly oriented to such discussions.

RESULTS AND DISCUSSION

Characteristics Of The Families

The distribution of the parental ages is provided in Table I. The parents range in age from 16 to 55 with a mean age of 33 for fathers and 30 years for mothers.

TABLE I

AGE OF PARENTS AT THE TIME OF THE BIRTH

OF THEIR CHILD WITH DOWN SYNDROME

Age range	Father		Mother	
	#	%	#	%
15 - 19	4	4.5	5	5.6
20 - 24	12	13.5	14	15.7
25 - 29	17	19.0	24	27.1
30 - 34	18	20.2	19	21.3
35 - 39	15	16.9	14	15.7
40 - 44	15	16.9	12	13.5
45 - 49	7	7.9	1	1.1
50 - 54	0	0	0	0
55 - 59	1	1.1	0	0

As Table II indicates, the average length of the marriage was 7.8 years; the range was from less than one year to more than 20 years. In a few instances the marriage had been precipitated by the pregnancy. For 17% this was the first child and for 24% the second. For 55% the pregnancy was planned; 38% of pregnancies were unplanned, but the parents felt this was a wanted child, while 7% were unwanted.

Table III shows the educational level of the parents. Forty-four percent of the fathers and 60% of the mothers had completed high school, and 36% of the fathers and 28% of the mothers had additional education, including technical school, college, or graduate school.

The father's occupation as seen in Table IV clustered in the management, technical and skilled categories. As Table V indicates, 79% lived in the suburbs or outlying areas, with few residing in the inner city.

In Table VI it is noted that 61% of our patients' parents were Catholic and 30 percent were Protestant. Of the total population, 69% had an active identification with a church; yet these parents did

TABLE II

YEARS OF MARRIAGE OF PARENTS WHOSE CHILDREN WERE ENROLLED
IN THE DOWN SYNDROME PROGRAM

Years	Families	
	#	%
<1	7	8.1
1 - 2	4	4.7
2 - 5	21	24.3
6 - 10	26	30.2
11 - 15	12	14.0
16 - 20	12	14.0
>21	4	4.7

not necessarily mention their religion as a help in coping with the birth of the child with Down syndrome.

Table VII provides some data on the social history of the parents. Seventy-four% of the fathers and 71% of the mothers described their life before the child's birth as fairly satisfying, without previous major disappointments, family disruptions, or significant illnesses. Fifteen % of the fathers and 18% of the mothers indicated that their early family life was disrupted by illness, impaired relationships with their parents, or unsuccessful previous marriages. Eleven% of the fathers and 12% of the mothers had significant problems, with their early family life which had been sufficiently disturbed to require placement, or because they were victims of abuse. Ninety-five% of the families had close relatives with whom they had active and positive contact; most of them lived in the New England area.

Eighty-nine percent of the parents described their marriage as happy, while 7% acknowledged stress and 4% serious problems. A

TABLE III

EDUCATION OF PARENTS WHOSE CHILDREN WERE ENROLLED

IN THE DOWN SYNDROME PROGRAM

Highest Educational Level	Father		Mother	
	#	%	#	%
High School not completed	17	19.6	11	12.7
High School completed	38	43.7	52	59.8
College	21	24.1	19	21.8
Graduate School	10	11.5	5	5.7
Other	1	1.1		

common stressor was the husband's combining both school and job with little time left for family responsibilities. Problems classified as serious included couples who were separated or had such serious disagreements that they questioned whether the marriage would continue.

Since the Down Syndrome Program was center-oriented, and since there were no resources to develop an outreach component, people who took advantage of the program probably were more prepared to make some investment in the child. Our contacts with individuals in the maternity hospital indicated that this was an issue for many parents, and we encountered a few families who resolved it by arranging for the child to be placed. However, placement alternatives were actually few in number, and it was apparent that those parents who could not afford a private residential facility found it difficult to consider a foster home as an alternative. The latter seemed far more threatening to their self-esteem as parents. Yet an institution with a more "neutral" image seemed to reinforce the idea that this was a very unique individual who required specialized management.

TABLE IV

OCCUPATION OF PARENTS WHOSE CHILDREN WERE ENROLLED
IN THE DOWN SYNDROME PROGRAM

Occupation	Father		Mother	
	#	%	#	%
Executive, Professional, Manager	20	23.0	4	4.5
Technical, Supervisory, Sales	18	20.7	0	0
Clerical, Skilled worker	22	25.3	4	4.5
Factory, semiskilled worker	14	16.1	3	3.4
Unskilled worker	12	13.8	1	1.1
Student	1	1.1	4	4.5
Unemployed	0	0	0	0
Housewife			67	75.3
Housewife, part-time employed			6	6.7

TABLE V

RESIDENCE OF PARENTS WHOSE CHILDREN WERE ENROLLED

IN THE DOWN SYNDROME PROGRAM

	Families	
Place of Residence	#	%
Inner City	3	3.4
City	15	17.2
Suburb	49	56.4
Rural	20	23.0

Early Adaptation

Many parents had some previous awareness of Down syndrome as a form of retardation. The term "mongoloid" was often more familiar than Down syndrome. Fifteen % of families had previous personal contact with Down syndrome through the child of a friend, neighbor, or casual acquaintance. A small number of parents had relatives with this diagnosis. However, their concept of what the diagnosis involved was often incomplete and inaccurate. The term mongoloid was frequently associated with a distorted body, (large head, small body) and disordered behavior (drooling, "insanity"). Retardation conveyed to the parents the image of total inability.

Most parents had been informed on the second day of their child's life that he/she had Down syndrome. Often the word "mongoloid" was used relative to their child's condition. There was mixed opinion about which words would be more informative. Many parents were alienated by the word "mongoloid," because it conveyed offensive stereotypes. On the other hand Down syndrome was not a term that was meaningful to them.

TABLE VI

RELIGIOUS AFFILIATIONS OF PARENTS WHOSE CHILDREN WERE
ENROLLED IN THE DOWN SYNDROME PROGRAM

Religion	Father		Mother	
	#	%	#	%
Roman Catholic	54	64.3	52	61.2
Protestant	23	27.4	28	32.9
Jewish	2	2.4	1	1.2
None	5	5.9	4	4.7

In 62% of the families a consulting pediatrician not previously known to them had first talked with them about the diagnosis. In only 15% of the cases did this discussion take place with both parents together. Almost all of the parents felt that being together at this time would have allowed them to support one another. With only 25% did the obstetrician assume a role in the informing process. The other families experienced this absence as an abandonment by a person with whom they had had a significant relationship. Fifty-seven % of the parents characterized the informant as providing relevant information in a way which indicated sensitivity to their feelings. Rarely did families receive any guidance as to what they should do. Of these a very small number were advised to place the child immediately in an institution for the ''protection'' of their family life. In contrast, equally few parents were specifically advised that the best plan would be to take the child home.

All parents described intense feelings of shock, disbelief and depression on first learning that they had produced a child with Down syndrome. People described themselves as confused and dazed: ''I cried all the time;'' ''I was revolted;'' ''I could not believe it was

TABLE VII

SOCIAL HISTORY OF PARENTS WHOSE CHILDREN WERE

ENROLLED IN THE DOWN SYNDROME PROGRAM

	Father		Mother	
Social Circumstances	#	%	#	%
Satisfactory	63	74.1	60	70.6
Stress	13	15.3	15	17.6
Significant problems	9	10.6	10	11.8

true." Other refused to acknowledge it was a real event until the chromosome analysis was completed.

Most parents were left to their own devices in initiating contact with the child. They felt as though they were in a vacuum. In most instances professional staff maintained a distance. They seemed inaccessible and uncomfortable when parents raised questions about the child. Most parents interpreted this nonverbal behavior as indicating a negative appraisal of the child or an attitude discouraging contact with the child. Sometimes specific negative thoughts were expressed such as, "These children do not suck well, and cannot be breast fed," a "Do you really want to see him?" But it is difficult to determine to what extent this is the parents' projection of their own feelings and conflicts, and what represents the staff's attitudes toward retarded children.

It certainly seemed that the parents' formation of attachment to the infant was disrupted by the attitude displayed by others as well as by their own disappointment and sorrow. They were hypersensitive to the behavior of professionals to whom they looked to help orient them towards this new entity they were encountering. Many parents described apprehension about seeing their baby, fearing that the appearance might be "abnormal" or grotesque. Yet actual contact with the child seemed to have major therapeutic value, since parents felt that the children were much more normal-appearing than anticipated. It was helpful to identify family characteristics in the child's appearance, and to note qualities of alertness and responsiveness which gave indication of individual personality. This seemed to allow parents to utilize their original feelings and plans for child care with the baby, such as rooming-in, breast-feeding, choice of name, etc. Others tended to make compromises which allowed them to move closer or to distance themselves from the child. For example, one mother decided not to breast-feed, feeling other family members should share in the child's care. Another mother who had not planned to breast-feed decided to do so since this might help the child and aid in forming a relationship. One young mother left the hospital early with the child so that she could have "more time to get to know her."

Many parents acknowledge feelings of anxiety or panic about making a long-term commitment to a child with a handicap. A few expressed the wish that the child had a life-threatening heart condition. Then they could invest as a caring parent, but without having the long-term responsibility.

Prior to discharge from the maternity hospital 84% of the mothers became actively involved in the child's care, whereas only 19% of the fathers had this opportunity. More often than not this reflected the hospital's policy regarding the father's role in child care.

Extended family tended to take a more neutral posture toward the infant, waiting cues from the decision of the parents. Once the parents made a commitment, other family members tended to be very supportive (79%), but sometimes unrealistically so, implying there was nothing wrong with the child. A few grandparents were more negative. In their protectiveness of the parents, they seemed to fear that the parents were assuming a responsibility which could be destructive of their wellbeing. A very few grandparents (6%) viewed this child as a threat to the image of the family, and did not want to see the child. Some grandparents initiated a very active and supportive role. One father had difficulty touching or holding his new son. When the maternal grandfather was able to do this easily and spontaneously the father was able to imitate this behavior.

All but four of the families who were enrolled in our program cared for their child at home. Three of the four families who placed their children in a residential facility eventually took the child home; two when the child was 6 months old, and the other when the child was a year old. Two of the three families seemed motivated by their increasingly positive feelings about the child's development and the expressed wish of their other children that the infant be at home. In the third family the father had always actively desired the infant to be at home, but the mother, who had a medical condition, was anxious and fearful about the responsibility involved in the child's care. In the fourth case, the family was not able to pay the costs of private residential care. The child's presence in the home was a channel for the parents to play out conflicts and feelings about one another. The management of the child's care was so poor that protective action was indicated. This child was withdrawn from the program and was not included in the final study sample.

Most families had established contacts with pediatricians but very few of these offered guidance on the developmental needs of the child. On the contrary they tended to deprecate any enthusiasm the parents might show about the child's progress, interpreting it as a denial of the disability.

Common concerns of the parents were:

—What caused the handicap?
—What could they anticipate in terms of future development?
—What would be the impact on family life, particularly on siblings?
—How should one inform other people of the diagnosis?
—Would they and their child experience rejection or social embarrassment?
—Were community resources available to share in the child-rearing process?

The family utilized a number of mechanisms in coming to terms with the child's disability. A major trend was not to attempt to assimilate on a cognitive and affective basis the total implications of producing and caring for a retarded child. Rather, through ventilation of feelings, gradual incorporation of information, and assuming of responsibility for the tasks of immediate caretaking, the parents' energies and concerns became more focused on present issues and the immediate future.

They also developed other mechanisms to defer a full acceptance of the child's retardation. When the child was somewhat responsive, or had few stigma, some convinced themselves that this would mean minimal lags in development: that the child would be slow, but not really retarded. Some parents latched onto the information that these children had a range of abilities, and the conviction that their child would be the exception. Some hoped that the "medications" used in the double-blind study would have a curative effect, although they had been told otherwise. Others felt that the exercises and the stimulation would overcome the disabilities in the child with Down syndrome. They rationalized that possibly these children's deficits and low functioning was in large part due to lack of opportunity and help.

Therapeutic Supports Offered
By The Program

At the time of the initial appointment, over 80% of the parents were quite depressed, and still grappling with the initial shock of learning that they had a handicapped child; needing to relive the moments when they first learned of the diagnosis (2). Almost all families acknowledged feelings of loneliness and isolation. Our program offered them a wide variety of resources which aided them in coping. It provided a supportive environment, free from criticism, where children with this diagnosis were valued. There was almost unlimited opportunity to ask questions, ventilate feelings and obtain information. Many parents were anxious for knowledge as to the cause, and why this had happened to them. Many of the activities provided information and demonstration on caretaking. Specific activities were prescribed which presumably would have some remedial effect. There was also anticipatory guidance around developmental issues.

All the appointments were scheduled on the same day of the week. It was decided to have an open-ended discussion group for parents who wished to participate (3). Most families used this resource to some extent. For some, the opportunity to share with other families was a high point of the program. It enabled them to see their child as an individual with a group of peers. Friends, older siblings and relatives often participated in these meetings at the invitation of the parents. Out of this evolved occasional informational discussion groups for siblings to which entire families came (4).

Although the primary focus was research, overall the program provided structure, warmth and closeness, information and reinforcement for the parents' desire to invest in the child; acceptance of sadness and discouragement when it occurred, help in making decisions affecting the family, and activities which were presumed to be remedial. With the security of these alliances the families were able to reorganize and to invest in a consistent way in the child's potential for development. It helped them to deal with the overwhelming implications of retardation by eventually breaking it down into specific immediate issues, concrete tasks and potentially attainable goals.

Periodically, many parents' adaptation would be threatened. Sometimes this was precipitated by a social event which prompted a renewed focus on the developmental lags of the child, or a prolonged plateau with little observable progress, or periods when behavior was difficult to manage. A particular trigger of crisis was the knowledge that the program would only continue until the children were three years of age. However, when the services to children who passed this age were extended the parental anxiety diminished.

Follow-up Contacts

Each family was scheduled for follow-up interviews with the same social worker when the child reached 6 months of age, 1 year, 2 years, and 3 years. The purpose was to screen for gross changes in family functioning, as well as to determine what the concerns were at the specific time-intervals relating to the child with Down syndrome. Almost all families felt that the progress of the child with Down syndrome was far superior to what they had originally expected. However, for many there were stresses occasioned by the need for prolonged supervision and extended teaching of behavior that with other children was acquired spontaneously (2). The parents' worries were rather for the future than the present, as to what resources might be available for work and adult living situations. They also feared that the child might experience ridicule. Some parents thought of the child as always living with them, or with someone in the extended family. However, most parents assumed that the child would proceed through a succession of community-based programs similar to that offered to their other children at the same developmental stage. They actively evaluated programs to assess their capability to promote the child's development, and spoke of the child as a future worker, living independently but in a protected environment.

Eighteen families had significant marital problems, some culminating in separation and divorce. None of the families identified the handicapped child as the reason for their problems. Most of them described pre-existing tensions and changes in values with advancing age as the major source.

Almost all families indicated that the experience of having a child with Down syndrome had caused them to alter their values, re-examining themselves as people, and their goals and values in life. Some parents felt that this challenge had resulted in personal growth. And there were others who for the first time realized that there were threats and insecurities in life which one cannot anticipate or control.

There was great individual variation in the quality and style of the family's adaptation. Most parents seemed able to relate to the handicapped child in a warm and caring way, perceiving him/her as an individual, and responding to new accomplishments with joy and spontaneous enthusiasm. They were conscious that developmental progress was not in accord with chronological age, but this did not seem to affect their view of the child as a person or as a full family member. For other parents the investment in the child was shadowed by a more continuous awareness of him/her as a retarded person. They were more vulnerable to social embarrassment, anxiety about prolonged dependency, and conscious of the amount of energy required for supervision or instruction. A few families never really accepted that the child was mentally retarded; of these, two had experienced great difficulty in conceiving and bearing a living child.

Except for situations where there was social pathology, the specific identifying characteristics of the family were not particularly predictive of their later coping patterns. Qualitative factors such as optimism, comfort with risk-taking, patience and perseverance, and ability and desire to commit much energy to child-rearing were more relevant to later shaping behaviors. The child's growth and development were also contributive factors, since the progress of some of the children was such that they proved the source of more rewards and fewer stresses.

SUMMARY

Our experience with the families in the program confirmed that all parents who give birth to a child with Down syndrome go through a period of grief and mourning. The first stage is one of shock and disbelief. There are feelings of anger at why it happened to them, followed by a gradual acceptance of the reality of the situation, and awareness of the need to make decisions (5). For each parent this is a unique experience. The manner in which the individual approaches and deals with this stressful event and its intensity and duration varies greatly. If there is preexisting distress and conflict in a family, a handicapped child can be a grievous liability, appropriated as a channel for discharge of feelings.

As to the social context, these children were born in a period when beliefs and values regarding appropriate management of children with Down syndrome were in the process of change. Formerly the "intelligent" family would immediately accept the severity of the disability, and make plans for the child's care in an institution. That resource was no longer available, and was socially devalued during the time-period of our program.

The overwhelmingly positive responses to our program indicated that most families have a desire to invest in caring for and working with their handicapped infant. However, they needed emotional and technical support from professional people who share this commitment. The community resources ordinarily supportive to parents in child-rearing, including pediatricians, had not as yet assimilated this new philosophy toward handicapped infants to the extent that they could offer the help these parents required (6). Rearing a handicapped child can drain family energies and resources, and in making this commitment parents need to know that they will not be alone. These parents prevailed because they had support and could place reliance on the development of an available network of community resources and alternatives such as special education, workshops, etc. to meet the future needs of their handicapped child.

REFERENCES

1. Solnit, A. J. and Stark, M. H. Mourning and the birth of a defective child. *Psychoanalytic Study of the Child,* 16:523-537, 1961.
2. Olshansky, S. Chronic sorrow: A response to having a mentally defective child. *Social Casework,* 43:191, 1962.
3. Murphy, A. Pueschel, S. M. and Schneider, J. Group work with parents of children with Down's syndrome, *Social Casework,* 54:114-119, 1973.
4. Murphy, A. Pueschel, S. M. Duffy, T. and Brady, E. Meeting with brothers and sisters of children with Down syndrome. *Children Today,* Department of Health, Education and Welfare Publication # (OHD) 76-30014 5(2):20-23, 1976.
5. Rapoport, L: Working with families in crisis: An exploration in preventive intervention. In: *Crisis Intervention: Selected Readings,* Parad, H.J. (Ed.) New York: Family Service Association of America, 1965, pp. 129-139.
6. Wolfensberger, W. and Menolascino, F. J. A theoretical framework for the management of parents of the mentally retarded. In: *Psychiatric Approaches to Mental Retardation,* Menolascino, F. J. (Ed.) New York: Basic Books, 1970, pp. 475-491.

Chapter 5

ANTHROPOMETRIC STUDIES

Christine E. Cronk
Siegfried M. Pueschel

INTRODUCTION

Previous anthropometric investigations in Down syndrome have focused on various aspects of physical growth in children with this chromosomal disorder. Studies of birth weight and length have shown that the average child with Down syndrome is smaller and weighs less at the time of birth than normal children of the same gestational age (between 0.5 and 1.0 standard deviations below the normal mean) (1-5). Polani indicated that growth retardation begins at 38 weeks of postconceptional age (6). Assessment of linear growth in Down syndrome has documented reduced growth velocity during infancy and early childhood; however, investigators differ in regard to the exact timing of this growth reduction. Talbot found the greatest growth deficit after 1 year of age; Gustavson after 2 years; Benda and DeToni during the first 3 years; Brousseau and Brainerd and Roche, between 2 and 5 years, and Thelander and Pryor after 4 years (4,7-12). A longitudinal study of children with Down syndrome from age 7 to 18 years revealed an average reduction in height of two standard deviations (13). The average height of adults with Down syndrome was reported in several studies to be more than two standard deviations below the normal (4,5,8-12,14-18). Also, mean values for sitting height, length of the extremities and short bones of the hands have been noted to be significantly less than those for normal individuals (5,10,12,18-23).

Many of the above-cited studies have also investigated weight gain in children with Down syndrome. In most instances, weight showed age-specific differences ranging from significantly underweight infants (in particular those children with congenital heart disease) to marked overweight during adolescence and adulthood. Obesity, which has been observed in many persons with Down syndrome, has not been carefully studied (24).

While the reduction in head circumference in children with Down syndrome has been well-documented, investigators differ with respect to the time period during which head growth slows. Benda, Engler, and Roche observed normal head circumference in infants with Down syndrome at birth, but noted small head sizes by 6 months (14,25,26). Other investigators have also reported the head circumference of children with this chromosomal disorder to be smaller than normal at the time of birth (5,27). Roche, Seward and Sunderland found normal head size increments until 1 year of age, with progressive fall-off thereafter (between 1 to 5 years) (28). Oster observed head circumference to be proportional to body size in his series of children with Down syndrome (5).

There is considerable disagreement concerning skeletal development in children with Down syndrome. Investigators have demonstrated retarded, normal and advanced bone age during the first years of life (5,8,11,16,25,28-31). On the basis of split-line regression analysis, Rundle suggested that the delay of bone maturation was followed by a "catch-up" growth (32). After 6 years of age, the mean rate of skeletal maturation of children with Down syndrome has been reported to differ little from normal children (16,17,29,32). With one exception, studies on bone maturation did not reveal sex differences (33).

The present investigation was carried out within the framework of the Down Syndrome Program and focused primarily on measurement of recumbent length, body weight, head-circumference, and skeletal maturation of young children with Down syndrome.

METHODS

A description of the study population has been provided in the opening chapter. Measurements of length, weight, and head circumference were carried out every three months throughout the study. Measures were made by two investigators (Mary Ann Whelan and Christine Cronk). Recumbent length was measured to the nearest millimeter using a custom-built anthropometric table with fixed head and moveable foot piece. Weight was obtained from a Health-O-Meter beam-balance scale and recorded to the nearest decigram. Head circumference (greatest antero-posterior diameter) was taken with a fiberglass tape measure. Radiographs of the left hand and wrist were used to estimate bone age according to Greulich-Pyle (34).

Since two investigators were involved in the above mentioned measurements, the following procedures for standardized observations were carried out. Various measurements taken at a given age by each of the investigators were pooled and an age-specific mean was calculated. Differences between these means were taken and averaged across all ages using inverse weighting. The mean difference was then added to observations made by the first investigator (Mary Ann Whelan). Height of subsamples of parents and siblings of the study children were measured with a fixed anthropometer using the method described by Cameron (35). Control data were drawn from the Stuart Study of Child Health and Development (36).

RESULTS

Recumbent Length

Table I and Figure 1 present the means and standard deviations for girls and boys with Down syndrome and the control sample. Differences between the two groups were significant at all ages.

TABLE I

MEAN ($\bar{X}$) AND STANDARD DEVIATIONS (SD) OF RECUMBENT LENGTHS (cm)

FOR GIRLS AND BOYS WITH DOWN SYNDROME FROM BIRTH TO THREE YEARS OF AGE

AND COMPARABLE DATA FROM THE STUART STUDY PROGRAM

GIRLS

	Down Syndrome			Stuart Study				
Age	N	$\bar{X}$	SD	N	$\bar{X}$	SD	t	P<
Birth	39	48.5	3.2	105	49.7	2.2	2.2	.05
3 months	38	56.1	3.3	117	58.7	2.6	4.4	.01
6 months	39	62.5	2.3	114	65.3	2.4	6.5	.01
9 months	37	66.3	2.2	112	69.8	2.5	8.1	.01
12 months	37	69.4	2.2	117	73.9	2.7	10.2	.01
18 months	36	75.0	2.3	111	81.0	3.0	12.6	.01
24 months	37	79.7	2.7	115	86.4	3.4	12.3	.01
30 months	37	84.0	3.0	111	91.4	3.7	12.2	.01
36 months	34	87.1	3.3	114	95.8	3.9	12.1	.01

BOYS

	Down Syndrome			Stuart Study				
Birth	50	49.2	3.2	104	50.3	2.1	2.2	.05
3 months	49	58.3	3.1	112	60.2	2.2	3.9	.01
6 months	50	64.5	2.9	110	66.9	2.1	5.3	.01
9 months	46	68.3	2.8	112	71.5	2.2	6.9	.01
12 months	47	71.6	3.0	113	75.6	2.4	8.1	.01
18 months	47	76.9	3.3	109	82.4	2.5	10.2	.01
24 months	45	80.6	3.6	111	88.0	2.9	12.3	.01
30 months	49	89.7	3.6	112	92.4	3.1	13.0	.01
36 months	48	88.2	3.7	111	96.4	3.2	13.3	.01

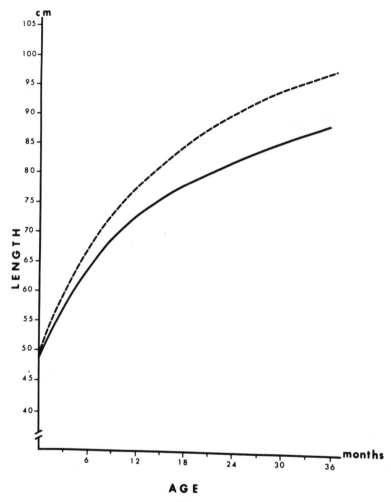

Figure 1:   Means of recumbent length of children with Down syndrome (━━━━)
from birth to three years and comparable data from the Stuart Study
population (━ ━ ━ ━).

Table II offers means and standard deviations for boys and girls with Down syndrome, demonstrating that the differences between the groups become progressively greater with advancing age until 18 months in girls, and up to 24 months in boys. Variability among the

TABLE II

MEANS ($\bar{X}$) AND STANDARD DEVIATIONS (SD) OF RECUMBENT LENGTH (cm)

COMPARING GIRLS (GROUP I) AND BOYS (GROUP II)

WITH DOWN SYNDROME FROM BIRTH TO THREE YEARS OF AGE

Age	Group	N	$\bar{X}$	SD	t	p<
3 months	I	38	56.1	3.3	3.2	.01
	II	49	58.3	3.1		
6 months	I	39	62.5	2.3	3.4	.01
	II	50	64.5	2.9		
9 months	I	37	66.3	2.2	3.7	.01
	II	46	68.3	2.8		
12 months	I	37	69.4	2.2	3.6	.01
	II	47	71.6	3.0		
18 months	I	36	75.0	2.3	2.4	.05
	II	47	76.9	3.3		
24 months	I	337	79.7	2.7	1.3	NS
	II	45	80.6	3.6		
30 months	I	37	84.0	3.0	.93	NS
	II	49	84.7	3.6		
36 months	I	34	87.1	3.3	1.4	NS
	İI	48	88.2	3.7		

boys with Down syndrome was greater than that of controls at all ages, while girls with Down syndrome showed a variance equivalent to, or less than, that of girls in the control group. Within the Down syndrome group, boys were significantly taller than girls until 18 months of age, after which their length were comparable. Length velocity was deficient during each of the six-months intervals, most markedly between 6 and 24 months, when it was 20% less than that for the controls. The growth velocity over the entire three-year period was 14% less than that for the Stuart Study children.

Because of the great variability in individual growth curves, children were classified into three categories according to the timing and magnitude of their respective longitudinal growth. An example of each of the three groups is shown in Figure 2, accompanied by the growth curve of one child from the Stuart Study. Category A represents a pattern exhibited by about 30% of our Down syndrome population. Children in this category showed reduced growth increments at all intervals until three years. All of the children were more than two standard deviations below the Stuart Study mean by age three years. Seventy percent of the children fell into Category B. These children grew deficiently during some of the study intervals, but with interspersed periods of gain within the normal range. Most of these children were growing between one and two standard deviations below the Stuart Study mean by 3 years of age. The growth velocity for children in Category C (10% of the total sample) was within the range of the controls during most intervals. At 3 years of age these children were growing between one standard deviation above and one standard deviation below the Stuart Study mean.

Because a large number of children with Down syndrome were born prior to the estimated date of confinement, means of length and head circumference separating children with gestational age less than 38 weeks (range 32 to 37 weeks, N = 22) from those with gestational age of 38 weeks or more, were contrasted (Table III). The length of children born at normal gestational age were significantly increased between examinations at birth and at 3 months; thereafter, they were similar to the group born prior to 38 weeks of gestation. Birth length of the group with normal gestation were not different from that of the control population.

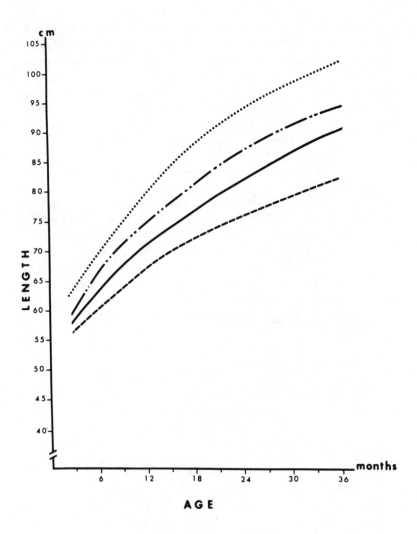

Figure 2:   Three examples of growth pattern variation in children with Down syndrome:

.... nearly normal growth pattern
— ·· — slightly delayed growth pattern
————— mean growth of Down syndrome sample
— — — — markedly deficient growth

TABLE III

MEANS ($\bar{X}$) AND STANDARD DEVIATIONS (SD) OF BIRTH WEIGHT (Kg), RECUMBENT LENGTH (cm)
AND HEAD CIRCUMFERENCE (cm) COMPARING CHILDREN WITH DOWN SYNDROME BORN AT
A GESTATIONAL AGE OF LESS THAN 38 WEEKS (GROUP I) WITH THOSE BORN AT 38 WEEKS OF
GESTATION OR MORE (GROUP II)

	Age	Group	N	$\bar{X}$	SD	t	p
Weight	Birth	I	67	3.95	1.35	4.6	.01
		II	22	3.61	1.40		
Length	Birth	I	59	50.0	2.3	5.1	.01
		II	20	46.8	2.7		
Length	3 months	I	65	57.9	2.5	3.0	.01
		II	22	55.9	3.5		
Length	6 months	I	67	63.8	2.6	1.23	NS
		II	22	62.0	3.3		
Length	12 months	I	62	70.7	2.8	.38	NS
		II	21	70.5	3.1		
Head Circumference	3 months	I	65	38.1	1.4	1.1	NS
		II	22	37.8	1.5		
Head Circumference	6 months	I	64	40.7	1.5	.19	NS
		II	20	40.8	1.2		
Head Circumference	12 months	I	60	43.4	1.5	.27	NS
		II	22	43.5	1.3		

TABLE IV

MEANS ($\bar{X}$) AND STANDARD DEVIATIONS (SD) OF RECUMBANT LENTGH

COMPARING CHILDREN WITH DOWN SYNDROME WHO HAVE NO OR ONLY MILD CONGENITAL HEART DISEASE

(GROUP I) WITH THOSE WHO HAVE MODERATE AND SEVERE CONGENITAL HEART DISEASE (GROUP II)

Age	Group	N	$\bar{X}$	SD	t	p<
Birth	I	64	49.0	2.9	1.15	NS
	II	15	49.9	2.1		
3 months	I	70	57.4	3.0	.04	NS
	II	17	57.4	2.6		
6 months	I	72	63.9	2.8	2.00	.05
	II	17	62.4	2.5		
9 months	I	68	67.6	2.1	1.68	NS
	II	15	66.3	2.4		
12 months	I	69	71.0	2.9	2.27	.05
	II	15	69.2	2.2		
18 months	I	70	76.3	3.0	2.52	.05
	II	13	74.0	2.2		
24 months	I	67	80.7	3.2	2.76	.01
	II	15	78.2	2.7		
30 months	I	71	84.9	3.3	3.16	.01
	II	15	82.0	2.6		
36 months	I	67	88.2	3.6	2.59	.05
	II	16	85.6	2.8		

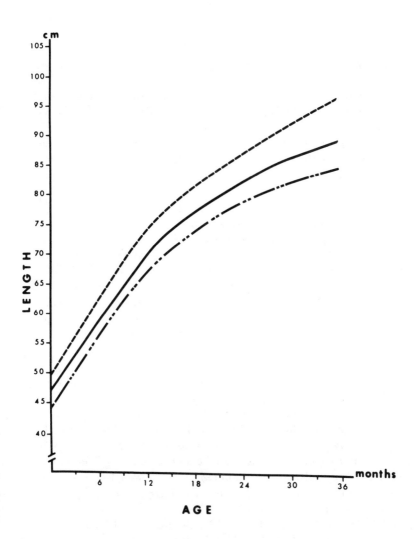

Figure 3: Mean recumbent lengths of young boys with Down syndrome from pooled studies
(————— -- ——) (see text) and from our program (—————————) in comparison
with equivalent data from the Stuart Study (--------).

Table IV presents means for recumbent length of two groups of children with Down syndrome according to cardiac status.* Differences were significant at 6 months and 12 to 36 months of age. Boys and girls showed similar magnitude of additional growth deficiency in the presence of moderate and severe congenital heart disease.

Figure 3 shows the relationship of the means for recumbent length comparing the data from our cohort of children with Down syndrome, the pooled data reported by Roche, Oster and Brousseau and Brainerd (5,10,16) and the Stuart Study (36). In general, the means from the children in this study exceed those from earlier investigations. Roche's means for ages equivalent to those of our study were consistently smaller in males and females, and significantly reduced at 30 to 36 months. On the other hand, the means from Oster's study sometimes exceed the means of recumbent length of children in our study, and vice versa.

Standard scores for height of parents and siblings were calculated using age and sex-specific norms from the Stuart Study (36). Eighteen year-old norms were used for the parents. These data were entered into a Pearson correlation with standard scores for the height at 36 months of the study children. Table V shows that correlations between height of parents and length of the children with Down syndrome were not statistically significant.

Weight

Table VI and Figure 4 provide descriptive statistics for weight of the children with Down syndrome and comparative data from the Stuart Study population. The mean birth weight for the Down syndrome sample was slightly less than the control mean (2). The velocity of weight gain calculated for 6-month intervals was deficient for all intervals between 6 and 18 months when increments were 22% less than those in the control population. Between 18 and 36 months, the weight velocity did not differ significantly from that for controls. At 18 months, the mean weight for the entire study group of children with Down syndrome was reduced by 1.75 standard deviations and at 36 months by 1.5 standard deviations.

*The definition of the various categories of cardiac involvement (mild, moderate, severe) is provided in Part I of this monograph.

TABLE V

CORRELATIONS OF PARENTS' AND SIBLINGS' LENGTHS

WITH LENGTHS OF CHILDREN WITH DOWN SYNDROME AT 36 MONTHS

Children with Down syndrome	Father	Mother	Sibling
Girls	-.091 (13)*	.219 (14)	.411 (21)
Boys	.256 (18)	.073 (21)	.293 (16)
Total			.403 (34)

*Numbers in parentheses give the N of the respective correlations.

Within the Down syndrome group, boys weighed significantly more than girls at all ages, except 30 months. The difference between control and Down syndrome children's mean weight was greater for boys, particularly at later ages. Children with moderate and severe congenital heart disease showed mean weights significantly less than those without or with only mild congenital heart disease, from 3 months until 36 months.

Evaluation of the data for individual children shows that there was an excess number of children who were overweight for length at 12, 24, and 36 months examinations. Two indices were used for classifying children as overweight: ponderal index (weight/height^3) greater than one standard deviation above the mean for the Down syndrome group, and a percentile rank for weight greater than two percentile levels above that for length on the Stuart Study chart. A child was considered overweight when both indices were positive. Approximately ⅓ of the children with Down syndrome were classified as being overweight at some time during the course of the three-year study. Of this group, 22% of children became overweight in the

TABLE VI

MEANS ($\bar{X}$) AND STANDARD DEVIATIONS (SD) OF WEIGHTS (Kg)

FOR GIRLS AND BOYS WITH DOWN SYNDROME FROM BIRTH TO THREE YEARS

AND COMPARABLE DATA FROM THE STUART STUDY POPULATION

Age	N	$\bar{X}$	SD	N	$\bar{X}$	SD	t	p<
				GIRLS				
Birth	36	2.97	.47					
3 months	38	4.48	.69	98	5.39	.69	6.90	.01
6 months	39	5.92	.87	98	7.24	.90	7.94	.01
9 months	37	6.82	.90	98	8.60	1.1	9.62	.01
12 months	37	7.55	.80	98	9.61	1.21	11.42	.01
18 months	38	8.77	.95	98	10.96	1.26	10.96	.01
24 months	38	10.07	1.03	98	12.14	1.39	9.48	.01
30 months	38	11.17	1.11	98	13.29	1.48	9.06	.01
36 months	34	11.97	1.29	98	14.35	1.64	8.61	.01
				BOYS				
Birth	44	3.24	.52					
3 months	49	5.03	.93	101	5.82	.70	5.30	.01
6 months	50	6.55	1.01	101	7.76	.83	7.33	.01
9 months	48	7.58	1.10	101	9.19	1.01	9.79	.01
12 months	48	8.38	1.07	101	10.22	1.11	9.69	.01
18 months	48	9.71	1.20	101	12.75	1.27	14.20	.01
24 months	46	10.60	1.32	101	13.70	1.33	13.17	.01
30 months	50	11.54	1.43	101	14.69	1.48	14.07	.01
36 months	48	12.62	1.53	101	15.72	1.61	11.36	.01

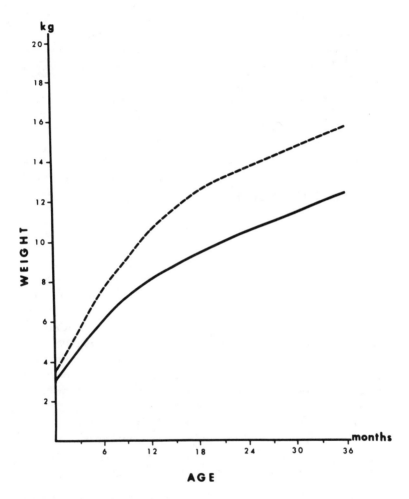

Figure 4: Mean weights of children with Down syndrome (————) and comparative measurements from the Stuart Study population (- - - - -).

first year of life, 55% between 13 and 24 months, and 23% showed increased weight gain beginning in the third year of life.

The relationship of overweight to a number of variables including muscle tone, length, medical history, and parental follow-through was examined. Correlation analyses for the entire group of children with Down syndrome showed a significant inverse relationship between ponderal indices and lengths at 36 months; but no other significant relationships were observed. For girls, relationships between 36 months ponderal indices and muscle tone (.4) were also evident.

The ponderal indices at 12, 24, and 36 months for children whose parents provided firm and consistent management were compared with those children whose parents were not firm and consistent.* (Children with moderate and severe congenital heart disease were excluded from this analysis.) Table VII shows that the ponderal indices at 36 months were significantly lower in the former group than in the latter group.

Head Circumference

Descriptive statistics for head circumference of children with Down syndrome are noted in Table VIII as well as in Figures 5 and 6. Compared with the control group, the differences were significant at all intervals for both boys and girls. Boys with Down syndrome were noted to be more variable than the control subjects, while the opposite was true for girls. These data resemble the findings obtained on length assessments, and appear to be a function of the greater variability in both Down syndrome boys and Stuart Study girls. Boys had significantly larger head circumferences than girls at all measurements between 3 to 36 months (Table IX).

When mean head circumferences were plotted against mean lengths (see Figures 7 and 8), neither males nor females could be classified as microcephalic; i.e., at no time were head circumferences two standard deviations below the mean, once length was taken into account.

Children who were born prior to 38 weeks of gestation, and those who were born at 38 weeks of gestation or later had similar head cir-

---

*A definition of this variable is provided in the chapter on Social Development and Feeding Milestones.

TABLE VII

PONDERAL INDICES AT 12, 24 AND 36 MONTHS FOR CHILDREN WHOSE PARENTS
WERE FIRM AND CONSISTENT (GROUP I) AND THOSE WHOSE PARENTS DID NOT
PROVIDE FIRM AND CONSISTENT MANAGEMENT (GROUP II)

Ponderal index at	Group	N	$\bar{X}$	SD	t	p
12 months	I	23	230.6	21.0	.007	NS
	II	46	231.2	22.2		
24 months	I	25	195.5	29.0	.206	NS
	II	42	198.7	25.8		
36 months	I	22	175.6	9.7	5.225	<.05
	II	44	188.2	24.6		

cumference between 3 and 36 months. Moreover, there were no differences in head-circumference measurements between the group of children with moderate or severe congenital heart disease (Table X). Table XI as well as Figures 9 and 10 provide percentile charts for head circumference of girls and boys with Down syndrome respectively.

Bone Age

Bone-age assessments were carried out at 24 and 36 months. At the chronological age of 24 months the mean bone age was 17 months, while at 36 months' chronological age the average bone age was 27½ months. The delay in bone maturation was similar for boys and girls, although at 36 months there was greater variability in boys (standard deviation 9.2 months) than girls (standard deviation 6.8 months) (see Table XII). At the chronological ages of 24 and 36 months, a number of children showed a bone age retarded by 3 to 21 months and some other children's bone age was advanced by 4 to 12 months (see Table XIII). Seventeen percent of children had a normal bone age at 24 months and 15% of children had a normal bone age at 36 months.

TABLE VIII

MEANS ($\bar{X}$) AND STANDARD DEVIATIONS (SD) OF HEAD CIRCUMFERENCÉS (cm)

FOR BOYS AND GIRLS WITH DOWN SYNDROME FROM 3 TO 36 MONTHS

AND COMPARABLE DATA FROM THE STUART STUDY POPULATION

BOYS

Age	N	Down Syndrome $\bar{X}$	SD	N	Stuart Study $\bar{X}$	SD	t	p<
3 months	48	38.585	1.397	96	40.814	1.245	9.35	0.01
6 months	46	41.365	1.511	96	43.913	.999	10.40	0.01
9 months	45	43.053	1.132	96	45.798	1.115	13.49	0.01
12 months	45	44.189	1.236	96	47.077	1.065	13.50	0.01
18 months	47	45.462	1.182	96	48.55	1.100	15.00	0.01
24 months	44	46.314	1.190	96	49.592	1.103	15.00	0.01
30 months	49	46.961	1.263	96	50.018	1.109	14.90	0.01
36 months	47	47.468	1.400	96	50.365	1.140	12.33	0.01

GIRLS

Age	N	Down Syndrome $\bar{X}$	SD	N	Stuart Study $\bar{X}$	SD	t	p<
3 months	39	37.433	1.159	93	39.674	1.327	9.70	0.01
6 months	38	40.024	.992	93	42.650	1.331	12.39	0.01
9 months	34	41.374	1.027	93	44.452	1.338	13.73	0.01
12 months	37	42.589	1.211	93	45.713	1.353	12.83	0.01
18 months	35	43.777	1.117	93	47.165	1.383	14.29	0.01
24 months	34	44.632	.993	93	48.050	1.414	15.21	0.01
30 months	38	45.316	1.011	93	48.766	1.391	15.80	0.01
36 months	34	45.751	1.025	93	49.198	1.366	15.66	0.01

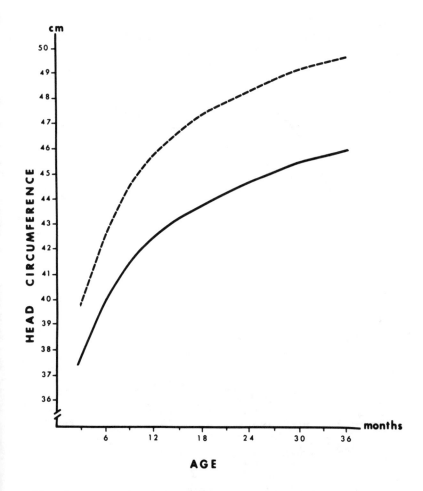

Figure 5:   Mean head circumference of girls with Down syndrome (──────) and
comparative measurements from the Stuart Study population (──────).

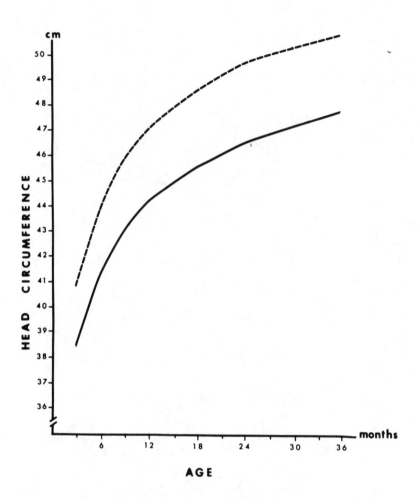

Figure 6: Mean head circumferences of boys with Down syndrome (———)
and comparative measurements from the Stuart Study population (– – – – –).

TABLE IX

MEANS (X) AND STANDARD DEVIATIONS (SD) OF HEAD CIRCUMFERENCES (cm)

COMPARING GIRLS (♀) AND BOYS (♂) FROM BIRTH TO 36 MONTHS

Age	Group	n	X̄	SD	t	p
Birth	♀	16	34.1	1.2	1.4	NS
	♂	18	34.8	1.5		
3 months	♀	39	37.4	1.2	4.1	.01
	♂	48	38.6	1.4		
6 months	♀	38	40.0	1.0	4.6	.01
	♂	46	41.4	1.5		
9 months	♀	34	41.4	1.0	6.9	.01
	♂	45	43.1	1.1		
12 months	♀	37	42.6	1.2	5.8	.01
	♂	45	44.1	1.2		
18 months	♀	35	43.8	1.2	6.3	.01
	♂	47	45.5	1.2		
24 months	♀	34	44.6	1.0	6.6	.01
	♂	44	46.3	1.2		
30 months	♀	38	45.3	1.0	6.5	.01
	♂	49	47.0	1.3		
36 months	♀	37	45.8	1.0	6.2	.01
	♂	47	47.5	1.4		

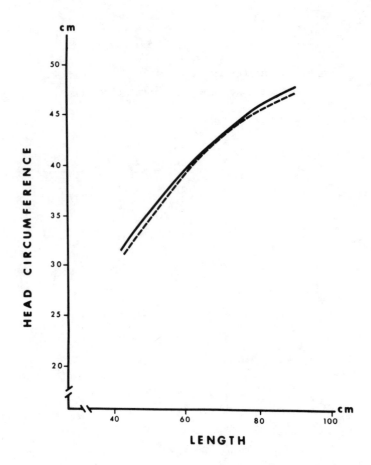

Figure 7: Mean head circumferences plotted against mean lengths of boys with Down syndrome.

———————— Boys with Down syndrome
– – – – – Normal boys - 3rd percentile curve (head circumference measurements below this curve are considered to be within the microcephalic range).

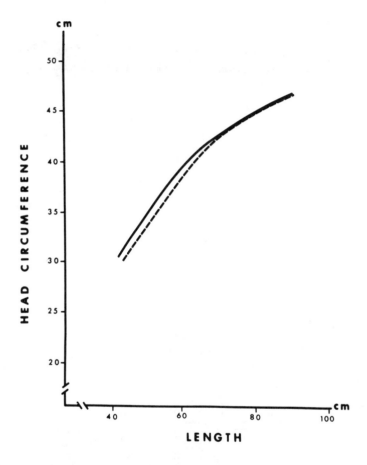

Figure 8: Mean head circumferences plotted against mean lengths in girls with Down syndrome.

Girls with Down syndrome
Normal girls - 3rd percentile curve (head circumference measurements below this curve are considered to be within the microcephalic range).

TABLE X

MEAN (X) AND STANDARD DEVIATIONS (SD) OF HEAD CIRCUMFERENCES (cm)

COMPARING THOSE CHILDREN WITHOUT AND WITH ONLY MILD CONGENITAL HEART DISEASE (GROUP I)

WITH THOSE WHO HAD MODERATE AND SEVERE CONGENITAL HEART DISEASE (GROUP II)

Age	Group	N	$\overline{X}$	SD	t	p
3 months	I	71	38.1	1.3	.53	NS
	II	16	37.9	1.7		
6 months	I	69	40.8	1.5	.4	NS
	II	15	40.6	1.1		
9 months	I	64	42.3	1.4	.06	NS
	II	15	42.3	1.2		
12 months	I	67	43.5	1.5	.00	NS
	II	15	43.5	1.2		
18 months	I	68	44.7	1.5	.5	NS
	II	14	44.9	1.2		
24 months	I	64	45.6	1.4	.08	NS
	II	14	45.5	1.1		
30 months	I	71	46.3	1.5	.43	NS
	II	16	46.1	1.2		
36 months	I	67	46.7	1.6	.19	NS
	II	17	46.7	1.2		

TABLE XI

CENTILE LEVELS* FOR HEAD CIRCUMFERENCE IN DOWN SYNDROME CHILDREN

GIRLS

Age	3	10	25	50	75	90	97
3	35.1	35.8	36.6	37.4	38.2	39.0	39.7
6	38.1	38.7	39.3	40.0	40.7	41.3	41.9
9	39.5	40.1	40.7	41.4	42.1	42.7	43.3
12	40.3	41.0	41.8	42.6	43.4	44.2	44.9
18	41.5	42.2	43.0	43.8	44.6	45.4	46.1
24	42.7	43.3	43.9	44.6	45.3	45.9	46.5
30	43.4	44.0	44.6	45.3	46.0	46.6	47.2
36	43.9	44.5	45.1	45.8	46.5	47.1	47.7

BOYS

Age	3	10	25	50	75	90	97
3	35.9	36.8	37.6	38.6	39.6	40.4	41.3
6	38.6	39.5	40.4	41.4	42.5	43.4	44.3
9	41.0	41.7	42.3	43.1	43.9	44.5	45.2
12	41.8	42.5	43.3	44.1	44.9	45.7	46.4
18	43.2	43.9	44.7	45.5	46.3	47.1	47.8
24	44.0	44.7	45.5	46.3	47.1	47.9	48.6
30	44.5	45.3	46.1	47.0	47.9	48.7	49.5
36	44.8	45.9	46.5	47.5	48.5	49.3	50.2

*Estimated from Standard Deviation values.

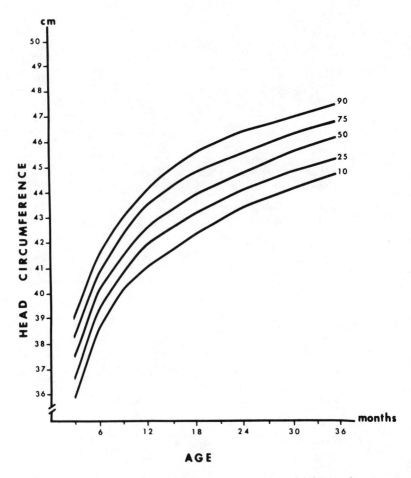

Figure 9: Head circumference percentile chart of girls with Down syndrome.

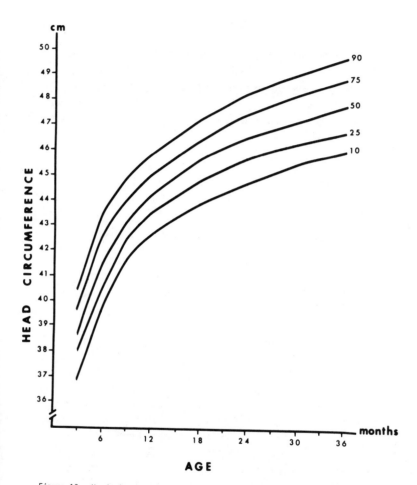

Figure 10:   Head circumference percentile chart of boys with Down syndrome.

Thirty-six children with Down syndrome had two serial bone-age assessments, and seven children had three examinations at yearly intervals. Of the children with two bone-age examinations, 11 showed normal velocity of skeletal maturation, 21 revealed delayed velocity, and five had accelerated velocity of bone maturation.

Of the seven children with three bone-age assessments, four caught up in skeletal maturation, one showed first normal and later delayed velocity, one displayed initially advanced and subsequently normal bone maturation, and another child had retarded bone-age development throughout the study.

An increased heterogeneity of skeletal age in children with Down syndrome was manifest at both 24 and 36 months (34). Comparing skeletal maturation in children without or with mild congenital heart disease, with those who have moderate and severe congenital heart disease, the latter group's bone age is significantly more delayed (Table XIV).

Intercorrelations Of Anthropometric Variables

Correlation matrices of length, head circumference, and bone-age assessments at 24 adn 36 months were analyzed. The correlations for length ranged from about .5 to .95. These correlations were generally slightly lower for girls than for boys. The correlation matrix for the Stuart Study lengths indicated higher correlations than were apparent for the children with Down syndrome. A contrast between the two groups was most striking for girls' length in the first year of life.

Correlations among measures of head circumference at different ages ranged from .8 to .95. These were comparable to those observed in normal children (36). Correlations of head circumference and length were between .3 and .5 for the entire group of children with Down syndrome. Boys showed higher correlations than girls for these interrelationships.

Bone-age assessments at 24 and 36 months revealed a .6 correlation for the entire sample, excluding those children who had moderate and severe congenital heart disease. For boys the correlation coefficient was .73, while in girls it was .44. For normal children, correlations were generally higher and there were no significant sex differences.

TABLE XII

MEANS (X) AND STANDARD DEVIATIONS (SD) OF BONE AGE ESTIMATES

IN GIRLS (GROUP I) AND BOYS (GROUP II) WITH DOWN SYNDROME

Age	Group	N	$\bar{X}$	SD	t	p
24 months	I	30	18.8	5.6	1.9	NS
	II	40	16.3	5.3		
36 months	I	20	27.2	6.8	.4	NS
	II	28	28.1	9.2		

Length and bone age for the entire sample showed correlations of about .4 beginning at 12 months. For girls a -.5 correlation was observed between 36 months' bone-age assessments and their length at the time of birth. For boys, a significant birth length/bone-age association was not observed. Correlations at later ages were slightly higher in boys than in girls.

Intercorrelations Of Anthropometric And Other Variables

The relationships of growth parameters to illnesses, muscle tone, parents' ability to follow through with furnished guidance, cognitive, language and social development, and socioeconomic scores were examined by correlation analysis. Significant correlations were observed for the entire Down syndrome study group between birth length and weight, length at three months, and initial muscle-tone ratings, between length at 24 and 36 months, and muscle-tone ratings during the three-year study, and between length at 24 and 36 months and the combined Receptive-Expressive Emergent Language Scale scores. Most of these correlations were between .25 and .35. For girls, correlations of .4 to .5 were observed between head circumference (6 to 36 months) and both initial muscle-tone ratings, initial scores on the Bayley Scales of Infant Development (motor and mental scales) and the Vineland Social Maturity Scale. Lengths at 6 months were significantly related to early development, later mental-scale scores, and the Receptive-Expressive Emergent Language Scale scores. The relationship to later motor/social development was at a

TABLE XIII

BONE AGE CLASSIFICATION IN CHILDREN WITH DOWN SYNDROME

Age	Bone Age	N	%
	Advanced	4	6
24 months	Normal	12	17
	Retarded	54	77
	Advanced	5	10
36 months	Normal	7	15
	Retarded	36	75

similar level (.33), but fell short of statistical significance. Later motor-social development was also significantly associated with length at 36 months (.42). Within the group of boys with Down syndrome, no relationships reaching the level of statistical significance were observed.

Relationships between the initial muscle tone, early mental development, and later motor-social development were noted with bone age, particularly at 24 months. A similar pattern of relationships was found in the analysis by sex, but none of the relationships reached statistical significance.

DISCUSSION

Data reported concerning length indicate that birth size is close to normal. This impression is reinforced when low gestational-age children are removed from the sample. The greater variability around the mean of the Down syndrome sample when compared to normal controls and the variation of growth velocity across the different age intervals suggest a decreased regulation of the growth process in the study sample. This finding in association with the lower correlation of lengths of this sample with those of their family members

TABLE XIV

BONE AGE ASSESSMENT AT 24 AND 36 MONTHS COMPARING CHILDREN

WITH DOWN SYNDROME WHO HAD NO OR ONLY MILD CONGENITAL HEART DISEASE

(GROUP I) WITH THOSE WHO DISPLAYED MODERATE AND SEVERE CONGENITAL HEART DISEASE (GROUP II)

Age	Group	N	$\bar{X}$	SD	t	p
24 months	I	58	18.12	5.5	3.7	.01
	II	12	13.83	3.2		
36 months	I	42	28.5	8.2	2.27	.01
	II	6	22.3	5.9		

indicates that growth in children with Down syndrome is poorly canalized (less well genetically controlled) (37). The greater variability in boys than in girls and the lower correlations of their lengths with the heights of other family members indicates that the presence of the additional chromosome 21 has a slightly more uniform effect on girls. This further suggests that boys are more poorly canalized than girls.

The effect of significant congenital heart disease on growth has been reported for otherwise normal children. It is of note that the children who underwent cardiac surgery or in whom the ventricular septal defect closed spontaneously showed varying amounts of catch-up growth. This phenomenon is evident in the relatively smaller mean length for the cardiac groups at later ages.

The contrast between the data from earlier studies and this investigation suggests that the children in the present sample are taller at most ages. This may be attributable to one of several sources: secular trend, difference in sample population on a geographical basis, or environment of upbringing. Ikeda and coworkers demonstrated absence of a secular trend in their sample of Japanese children with Down syndrome (21). Numerous studies have shown small advantages for home-reared versus institutionalized children with Down syndrome (38-40). It should be noted that Oster's data, in which length of children sometimes exceeded that of our study population, were based on home-reared children; while Roche's sample, where the length of children were always less than those of our children, were drawn from an institutionalized population.

Both the parent/proband and sibling/proband correlations for the Down syndrome sample are less than expected for normal individuals, though it is important to note that the level of correlations for parent/proband by sex association is that expected for normals. The lengths of girls with Down syndrome showed a significant relationship to that of their siblings, while the relationship in boys is weaker and does not reach statistical significance at the .05 level of confidence. Because of the small numbers these results must be interpreted cautiously. However, they suggest that growth in girls conforms better to that of their genetically predisposed pattern than growth of boys.

The findings concerning the children who are overweight had not been documented previously. The negative association between ponderal index and length suggests that smaller children tend to be more overweight than taller ones. The muscle tone/ponderal index relationship indicates that in girls reduced muscle tone is associated with a tendency to become overweight. This may be related to the lower activity level and associated lower caloric expenditure of the girls in this sample.

Although reduction in head size was observed, the head circumference of the children were not in the microcephalic range once correction was made for length. The correlation between head circumference and length is approximately the same as that noted in normal children. These two findings suggest that reduction in head size is largely a consequence of global growth retardation rather than an exceptional deficiency in brain growth. This is corroborated by the frequently noted deficient growth of the cranial base resulting in unusually short head length (antero-posterior diameter) but normal head breadth.

The data discussed herein do not resolve the discrepancies in the literature concerning bone age. However, it is likely that at least two phenomena are responsible for the differences among studies. The extra chromosome 21 may have effects that are highly individually conditioned by the rest of the genome, and depending on these, bone maturation will be delayed, advanced or normal. It is also possible that the ossification sequence may vary sufficiently in this population of children that bone age determinations for the entire hand and wrist result in discrepant bone-age assignment. A more careful study of this needs to be carried out.

The negative correlation of early muscle tone assessments and scores on cognitive and social development with head size in girls is unexpected. Its validity is supported by the nonsignificant though similar direction and order correlation coefficients for length at six months and these variables, and for both later muscle tone, motor-social scores and head circumference. While it is difficult to interpret the direction of this association, its presence suggests a stable synchrony of developmental processes in girls that does not character-ize that for boys in this sample.

Summary

The following points concerning growth of children with Down syndrome were evident in this study:

1. The mean length of children with Down syndrome is slightly smaller than that of normal children at birth. When children with low gestational age are removed from the sample, birth size approximates the normal mean.

2. Growth velocity for length was deficient during the entire study period, being about 14% less than expected for normal individuals. The greatest deficiency in growth velocity occurred between 6 and 24 months, when the growth rate was reduced by 20%.

3. There was a great deal of variation of longitudinal growth. A few children grew normally while others showed persistent deficiencies across the entire period.

4. Children in this cohort were taller than those reported from institutions, though similar in size to children with Down syndrome who were also home-reared.

5. The relationship between size of parents and siblings to children in this sample was weaker than that expected for normal individuals. Intercorrelations between siblings' size and size of

girls with Down syndrome were significant, while those for boys were not.

6. Weight gain was deficient relative to normal mean weight velocity from birth through about 18 months, after which it was normal. Because many children had normal weight gain in combination with deficient growth after 18 months, they were overweight by the end of the study period. There was a tendency for overweight girls to be those who were smaller and who had poorer muscle tone.

7. Head circumference gains showed deficiency throughout the study period. When mean head circumference was plotted against length, head size fell within the lower normal range. This finding indicates that deficiency in head size is most likely a consequence of global growth retardation, and not due to a specific deficiency in brain growth.

8. Average boneage was reduced relative to standards at 24 and 30 months. In addition, boneage variability was greater than normal. While most children had retarded boneages, some showed normal or advanced skeletal maturation.

9. There was significant correlation between measurements of head circumference and muscle tone assessments and cognitive adaptive scores in girls with Down syndrome but no such relationships were observed for boys.

REFERENCES

1. Smith, A., and McKeown, T. Pre-natal growth of mongoloid defectives. *Archives of Diseases in Childhood*, 30:257–279, 1955.

2. Pueschel, S.M., Rothman, K.J., and Ogilby, J.D. Birth weight of children with Down's syndrome. *American Journal of Mental Deficiency*, 80:442–445, 1976.

3. Kucera, T. and Dolezalova, V. Prenatal development of malformed fetuses at 28–42 weeks of gestational age. *Biologia Neonatorum*, 22:319–324, 1973.

4. Gustavson, K.H. *Down's syndrome: a clinical and cytogenetical investigation.* Uppsala: Almquist and Wiksell, 1964.

5. Oster, J. *Mongolism*. Copenhagen: Danish Science Press Ltd., 1953.

6. Polani, P.E. Incidence of developmental and other genetic abnormalities. *Proceedings of the Royal Society of Medicine*, 66:1118-1119, 1973.

7. Talbot, F.B. Studies in growth. III. Growth of untreated mongoloid idiots. *American Journal of Diseases of Children*, 27:152, 1924.

8. Benda, C.E. Studies in mongolism. I. Growth and physical development. *Archives of Neurology and Psychiatry*, 41:83, 1939.

9. DeToni, G. L'accrescimento somatico dei mongologidi. *Minerva Pediatrica*, 25:1, 1973.

10. Brousseau, K. and Brainerd H.G. *Mongolism: A study of physical and mental characteristics of mongolian imbeciles*. Baltimore: The William and Wilkins Company, 1928.

11. Roche, A.F. The stature of mongols. *American Journal of Mental Deficiency*, 9:131, 1965.

12. Thelander, H.E. and Pryor H. Abnormal growth patterns and development in mongolism. *Clinical Pediatrics*, 5:493, 1966.

13. Hass, B. Follow-up investigation of newborn mongoloids with respect to growth retardation. *Hereditas*, 56:99-108, 1966.

14. Benda, C.E. *Mongolism and Cretinism*. New York: Grune and Stratton, 1946.

15. Benda, C.E. *The Child with Mongolism*. New York: Grune and Stratton, 1960.

16. Roche, A.F. Skeletal maturation and elongation in Down's disease (mongolism). *Eugenics Review*, 59:11, 1967.

17. Dutton, G. The physical development of mongols. *Archives of Disease in Childhood*. 34:46, 1959.

18. Rarick, L. and Seefeldt, V. Observations from longitudinal data on growth in stature and sitting height of children with Down's syndrome. *Journal of Mental Deficiency Research*, 18:63, 1974.

19. Chumlea, W.C., Malina, R., Rarick, G. and Seefeldt, V. Growth of short bones of the hand in children with Down's syndrome. *Journal of Mental Deficiency Research*, 23:137, 1979.

20. Bruskin, B.P. Physical development of children and adolescents with Down's syndrome. *Pediatrya*, 11:70, 1976.

21. Ikeda, Y., Higurashi, M., Herayama, M., Ishakawa, N. and Hoshima, H. A longitudinal study of the growth in stature, lower limb

and upper limb length in Japanese children with Down's syndrome. *Journal of Mental Deficiency Research,* 21:139, 1977.

22. Keith, H. Mongolism. *Postgraduate Medicine,* 23:629, 1958.

23. Rundle, A.T. Anthropometry: a ten year survey of growth. In *Mental Subnormality: Modern Trends in Research.* Richards, B.W. (Ed.) London: Pitman Medical and Scientific Publications, 1963.

24. Madsen, A. *Body size as an index of nutrient and kilocaloric needs in young children with Down's syndrome.* University Microfilms, Ann Arbor, Mich., 1979.

25. Engler, M. *Mongolism (peristatic amentia).* Bristol and London: John Wright and Son Ltd., 1949.

26. Roche, A.F., Seward, F.S. and Sunderland, S. Growth changes in the mongoloid head. *Acta Pediatrica* (Uppsala), 50:133–140, 1961.

27. Hall, B. *Mongolism in newborns: a clinical and cytogeneic study.* Lund: Berlingska Boktrigkeriet, 1964.

28. Roche, A.F., Seward, F.S. and Sunderland, S. Growth changes in the mongoloid head. *Acta Pediatrica* (Uppsala), 50:133–140, 1961.

29. Rarick, G.L., Rapaport J.F., and Seefeldt, V. Bone development in Down's disease. *American Journal of Diseases of Children,* 107:7, 1964.

30. Pozsonyi, J., Gibson, D. and Zarfas, D.E. Skeletal maturation in mongolism. *Journal of Pediatrics,* 64:75, 1964.

31. Hefke, H.W. Roentgenologic study of anomalies of the hand in 100 cases of mongolism. *American Journal of Diseases of Children,* 60:1319, 1940.

32. Rundle, A.T. et al. A catch up phenomenon in skeletal development of children with Down's syndrome. *Journal of Mental Deficiency Research,* 16:41, 1972.

33. Menghi, P. Osseroazioni sull 'eta schelectrica mel mongolismo. *Minerva Pediatrica,* 6:81, 1954.

34. Greulich, W.W. and Pyle, S.I. *Radiologic Atlas of Skeletal Development of the Hand and Wrist.* California: Stanford University Press, 1966.

35. Cameron, Noel. The methods of auxological anthropometry. In *Human Growth* Vol. 2. Falkner, F. and Tanner, J. (Eds.) New York: Plenum Press, 1978.

36. Stuart, H.C., Reed, R.B. and Associates. Longitudinal studies of child health development, Series II. *Pediatrics,* 24:5, Part II, 1959.

37. Shapiro, B.L. Amplified developmental instability in Down's syndrome. *Annals of Human Genetics,* 38(4):429–437, 1975.

38. Stedman, D.J. and Eichorn, D.H. A comparison of growth and development of institutionalized and home reared mongoloids during infancy and early childhood. *American Journal of Mental Deficiency*, 69:391–401, 1964.

39. Centerwall, S.A. and Centerwall, W.R. A study of children with mongolism reared in the home compared to those reared away from home. *Pediatrics*, 25:678–685, 1960.

40. Kugel, R.B., Fedge, A., Trebath, J. and Hein H. Analysis of reasons for institutionalizing children with mongolism. *Pediatrics*, 64:68–74, 1964.

Chapter 6

MOTOR DEVELOPMENT

Elizabeth Zausmer
Alice Shea

INTRODUCTION

In the past four decades, motor development scales have been developed by several investigators (1-5). These scales have been based upon studies of normal populations, some of them longitudinal and others cross-sectional in design.

Previously published reports which have dealt with motor development of children with Down syndrome have, in some instances, been concerned with the comparison of home-reared and institutionalized children (6-9). These studies have included both prospective and retrospective investigations focusing on the time of achievement of specific developmental milestones. Cowie has described the motor characteristics and reflex development in children with Down syndrome in greater detail (10).

Since a variety of factors such as decreased muscle strength, hypotonia, increased flexibility of joints, and significant congenital heart disease may affect development of movement and achievement of milestones in young children with Down syndrome, it is important to take these aspects into consideration when studying motor development and function in these children.

The impact of hypotonia upon motor function of children with neurological disorders is well known. Yet its influence upon motor abilities of Down syndrome children with and without congenital heart disease has not been sufficiently explored. Also, the increased flexibility of joints and the decrease in muscle strength in children with Down syndrome which affects all aspects of functional efficiency require further study.

Considering the complexity of genetic, maturational, structural, and environmental influences upon the development of the young child, it is not surprising that hardly any serious attempts have been made to develop methods for motor evaluation which would allow in-depth analysis of factors possibly contributing to motor problems of the child with Down syndrome. Without such analysis, however, it is nearly impossible to set up individually designed and problem-related sensory-motor stimulation programs.

If one takes into account the impact of motor activities and motor skills on almost all aspects of human development and their influence on social and vocational adjustment throughout one's life, the need for continued investigations related to the acquisition of motor proficiency for analysis of performance patterns and effective methods of training children with Down syndrome cannot be over-emphasized.

The primary objectives of the physical therapy component of the Down Syndrome Program were:

—to obtain measurements and documentation of various parameters needed to evaluate the effect of 5–hydroxytryptophan and/or pyridoxine administration upon the motor development and motor performance of young children with Down syndrome;

—to examine and describe motor developmental aspects and motor behavior; and

—to plan and carry out an early intervention program.

The motor function assessment was designed to provide answers to the following questions:

—Does the motor developmental pattern in children with Down syndrome differ from that observed in a normal population?

—Can specific developmental patterns be identified in these children?

—Which deviations from normal motor development and motor behavior seem to influence the child's motor function most?

—What is the impact of decreased muscle strength and increased range of motion in joints on the child's motor competency?

—Since congenital heart disease is present in a large number of children with Down syndrome, is there any indication that this condition may affect their motor development and motor performance?

—How can the child and family be helped best to make optimal use of all potential capacities?

METHODS

All 89 children in the Down Syndrome Program participated in the motor-developmental study. Except for 15 infants who were not seen for the initial examination, the children were scheduled for evaluation shortly after birth and at ages 3, 6, 9, 12, 18, 24, and 36 months. Most assessments were carried out by one investigator (E.Z.). All children were examined in a relaxed and comfortable clinical environment. The parents were present whenever it seemed desirable.

A specially devised protocol focused on muscle strength, range of motion, muscle tone, and developmental attainment. *Muscle strength* was defined as the ability of a muscle to generate a specific degree of tension which is needed to move a given load. Twenty-one muscle groups of the extremities and the trunk were assessed bilaterally. A slightly modified version of the standard test procedure by Williams (11) and the Infant Test by Zausmer (12) was used. Muscle strength was rated as follows: 1. lifts against gravity—no resistance, 2. slight resistance, 3. moderate resistance, and 4. considerable resistance. Good muscle strength was defined as: lifting against gravity with moderate or considerable resistance. Muscle strength as plotted in Figures 1 to 11 combines the latter two categories.

Range of motion was measured by taking an extremity passively through the arc of motion which was expected to be found in a normal joint; this movement was then continued without forcible stretching to a given end point. Procedures most frequently used by physical therapists for the evaluation of range of motion were applied in the course of this study (13). Twenty-five joints were examined bilaterally in this part of the evaluation. The range of motion in Figures 3 and 4 is expressed as the percentage of children who had increased range of joint motion at the time of evaluation.

Muscle tone was assessed by examining the resistance of a muscle to being stretched by passive movement. Resistance to passive stretch was classified as: completely lacking, weak, moderate, strong, and excessive. It was realized that the degree of resistance to stretch is influenced by the flexibility at the joint. Frequently it was possible to assess these two factors separately.

Developmental Attainments were recorded using the motor developmental assessment scale by Zausmer originally devised for examination of children with cerebral palsy (14, 15). It was adapted to the specific requirements of evaluating infants with Down syndrome. This scale is divided into subgroups of tests which are arranged according to the increasing difficulty and complexity of the test items. The scale follows a developmental sequence: head control, rolling over, sitting, crawling, creeping, standing, walking, stair-climbing, grasping, and manipulating objects. This rating scale includes qualitative as well as quantitative criteria. Quantitative refers to the attainment of a given developmental level, while qualitative refers to the degree of independence, the correctness of execution of the motor act, as well as to speed of performance, number of repetitions, etc.

The test items are graded as:

O - no attempt made

T - tries, but abortive attempt

P - partially fulfills test requirements, yet the quality is unsatisfactory

F - fulfills test requirements with satisfactory quality of performance

G - consistent good quality of performance

N - notably good performance

For this presentation the grades listed above were summarized in two categories: children who *partially* attained a specified performance; and children who *fully* attained a given performance with satisfactory or good quality.

During the analysis of the data it became apparent that the group of childen without or with mild congenital heart disease (group I) differed in several aspects of their motor performance from those who had moderate or severe congenital heart disease (group II).* Therefore, the results of the motor evaluations were reported separately for these two main groups. The relationship between cyanotic heart disease and motor deficits had been explored in chromosomally normal children by Silbert et al (16).

The number of children examined without or with mild congenital heart disease ranged from 66 to 72, and the number of children with moderate or severe congenital heart disease ranged from 15 to 17.

---

*Definition of severity of congenital heart disease is provided in Part I of this monograph.

RESULTS AND DISCUSSION

Muscle Strength

During the first few months of life the motor areas of the cerebral cortex which control the movements of trunk, shoulder, and forearm mature earlier, while those regions which correspond to the lower extremities reach maturity later (17). The first postnatal reflex motor responses occur in relation to the intake of food demonstrated by movements of the neck and lips. This phenomenon corresponds to the early intrauterine development of synapses and nerve endings of the face and trunk.

Augmentation of muscle strength is known to occur with increase in the size of muscle fibers. Such enlargement has been related to functional requirements, i.e. the number of fibers which are used, the degree of pull exerted and the amount of resistance presented. Muscles most needed in the neonatal period for vital functions, such as respiration, sucking and swallowing show a considerably larger muscle fiber size than those which control extremity function (18).

Hip Flexion

In the mature newborn, the flexors of the hip are stronger than the extensors. This uterine position of the hip is ordinarily maintained for a short period after birth. It has also been suggested that the gamma muscle spindle, with its earlier gamma efferent innervation of the flexor muscles of the hip, explains the predominantly flexed position of the newborn infant (19).

As can be seen from Figure 1, the flexors of the hip showed good muscle strength in children without and with mild congenital heart disease as well as those with moderate and severe congenital heart disease at the first examination. The "dip" in the curve between 3 to 12 months is considerably more pronounced in the children with significant cardiac defects. This group does, however, show consistent improvement in hip flexor strength after the age of 12 months. Nevertheless, the hip muscles remain weaker in the group of children with moderate and severe congenital heart disease throughout the first three years of life. The position of hip flexion in which the normal neonate remains for a short period of time after birth is found frequently for a more prolonged time span in the child with Down syndrome.

Hip Extension

Normally, hip extensor activity starts to appear at around two to three weeks of age. Its development becomes most evident during the first four to six months of life.

Figure 1 demonstrates the considerable difference shortly after birth between the strength of hip flexors and hip extensors. This holds true for children without and with mild cardiac problems as well as for those with moderate and severe congenital heart disease. Only at about age 3 years do both muscle groups approach similar strength in most children.

The lag in strength of hip extensors, particularly in the group of children with moderate and severe congenital heart disease, is not surprising in view of the fact that the hip extensors play a most important role in maintaining the upright position of the trunk in standing.

Hip Abduction

As noted in Figure 2, children without and with mild congenital heart disease and those with moderate and severe cardiac defects showed markedly low strength of hip abduction at birth. Children in both groups had a decrease in muscle strength at nine months, and their subsequent increase in muscle strength is slow.

The low level of muscle strength obtained in testing the hip abductors could be attributed to three factors: first, this particular muscle group is one of the most difficult to test reliably in infants and young children; the movement of hip abduction is difficult to elicit: thus lower grades are often obtained. Second, children with Down syndrome have been found to have a small pelvis (20). The altered position of the femur in relation to the hip joint (acetabular and iliac angles) (21, 22) is likely to influence the direction and the tension of

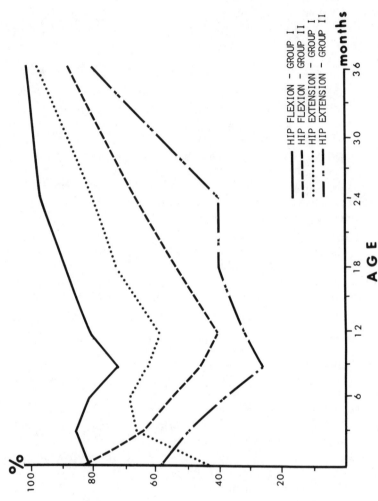

Figure 1:   Percentage of children with "good" muscle strength according to cardiac status.

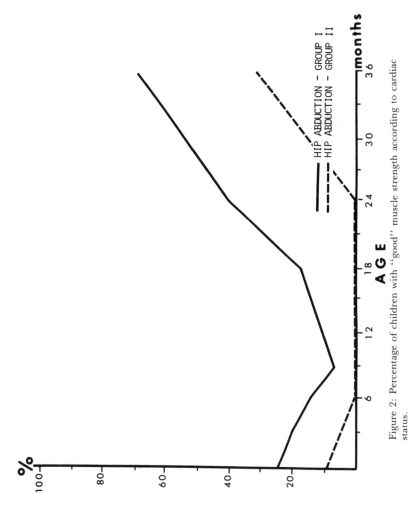

Figure 2: Percentage of children with "good" muscle strength according to cardiac status.

muscles attached to the hip joint, and thus, in turn, their strength is compromised. Third, the hip abductors are used primarily for stabilization of the hip in weight bearing. In children with Down syndrome those muscles are not likely to be called into action or use before the age of 2 to 3 years, the time when most of the children in this program were walking.

Although testing of the hip adductors was not included in the formal muscle evaluations, our informal observations corroborate previous reports indicating that these muscles can only be evaluated with difficulty, and that they are markedly weak in young children with Down syndrome.

Hip Inward and Outward Rotation

The discrepancy in strength between inward and outward rotators of the hip is demonstrated in Figure 3. The "dip" of the curve indicating strength in outward and inward rotation in children without and with mild congenital heart disease as well as in those children with major cardiac defects is quite impressive. We do not have a plausible explanation for the lasting decrease in strength of inward rotation, particularly in children with moderate and severe congenital heart disease. One contributing factor may be the tendency for children with Down syndrome to maintain the position of hip flexion and outward rotation (frog position) for a considerably longer time period than normal children. As can be seen from Figure 1c, the outward rotators eventually develop fairly good strength, while the inward rotators remain weaker. The patterns of distribution of strength in the musculature of the hip later influence posture and ambulation.

Knee Flexion and Extention

An interesting finding (Figure 4) is the remarkable "dip" in the curve depicting muscle strength of the knee extensors (quadriceps) between birth and 12 months in children with moderate and severe congenital heart disease. Only at approximately two years do these children attain the same degree of muscle strength as is displayed at 9 months in children without and with mild congenital heart disease.

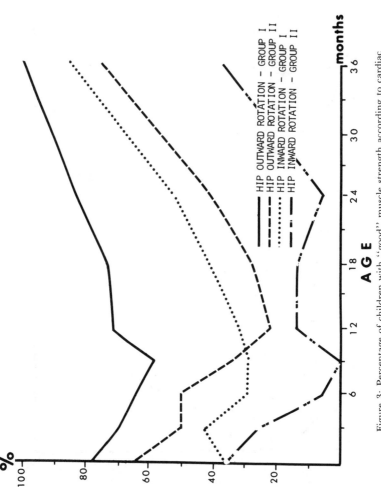

Figure 3: Percentage of children with "good" muscle strength according to cardiac status.

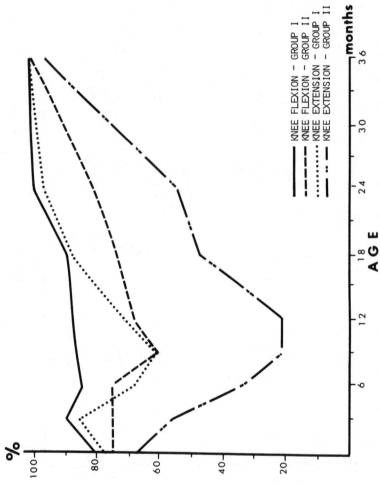

Figure 4: Percentage of children with "good" muscle strength according to cardiac status.

Again, the paucity of movements (such as kicking) at an early age in children with significant cardiac defects may possibly be the reason for the weakness at a later age. It is of note that between 2 and 3 years, when most children stood and walked, the strength of the quadriceps muscles considerably improved. Throughout the first 3 years of life, the flexors of the knee joint maintained a higher level of strength than the extensors of the knee.

Dorsiflexion And Plantarflexion Of The Ankle

Starting at birth, an infant flexes and extends hip and knee in a mass movement of kicking. However, differentiation of movements at the ankle joint such as dorsi- and plantarflexion, as well as inversion and eversion, start at a later stage of development.

There is a difference in strength between dorsiflexors and plantarflexors in the group of children without and with mild congenital heart disease and those with major cardiac problems (Figure 5). It can be assumed that the decreased strength of plantarflexion is related to the limited use of this muscle group in early infancy. During the mass movement of kicking, motion of the ankle lacks drive. It is carried out primarily in the direction of dorsiflexion with a rather passive return to the position of rest in slight plantarflexion. It is only at a subsequent stage of development when the child starts creeping that a "push-off" for propelling the body forward is used, which brings the plantarflexors into action. Considerably later, when the child begins to stand, walk, and raise on toes, these muscles are brought into action more vigorously.

In view of the delayed start of creeping, standing, and walking in children with Down syndrome, the plantarflexors can be expected to remain relatively weak for a longer period of time. Indeed, in our study population plantarflexors seemed never to catch up in strength with other muscle groups during the first three years of life. An interesting finding is the fact that the toe flexors were found to be relatively strong. In children without and with mild congenital heart disease good strength of the toe flexors was recorded at birth and steadily increased to the age of 12 months.

Considering that the toe flexors in normal individuals add considerable strength to the movement of plantarflexion, it seemed

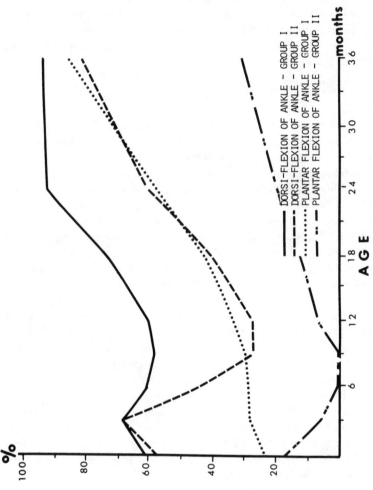

Figure 5: Percentage of children with "good" muscle strength according to cardiac status.

odd that in our children with Down syndrome these muscles did not substantially contribute to plantarflexion. The toe-flexor group acted almost exclusively as flexors of the toes.

Inversion and Eversion

The evertors were consistently a stronger muscle group in the children without or with mild congenital heart disease but this relationship was not consistent in the children with moderate or severe congenital heart disease (Figure 6).

Trunk Flexion and Trunk Extension

During the first few weeks of life, the neonate still maintains the predominantly trunk-flexed position, previously assumed *in utero*. At about 4 weeks of age, trunk extension appears and progresses in a caudal direction.

From Figure 7 it can be seen that trunk strength in flexion, as well as in extension, was considerably greater in the group of children without and with mild congenital heart disease than in children with moderate and severe cardiac problems. In both groups, the trunk extensor strength surpassed the trunk flexor strength.

While the trunk extensors improved consistently between the age of 6 months and 24 months in the group of children without and with mild congenital heart disease, children with moderate and severe congenital heart disease did not attain a satisfactory level of strength within the three-year study period. This lack of strength of the extensors of the trunk was clinically evident in the children's poor sitting position.

Arm Abduction

The functional capacity of arms and hands depends in part on the stability of the bony structures of the shoulder girdle, specifically the scapulae. Not surprisingly, joint stability was found to be lacking in a large number of infants with Down syndrome. Although the muscles which attach to the scapula could not be tested formally, they were noted to be hypotonic and weak. Flatness of the region of the

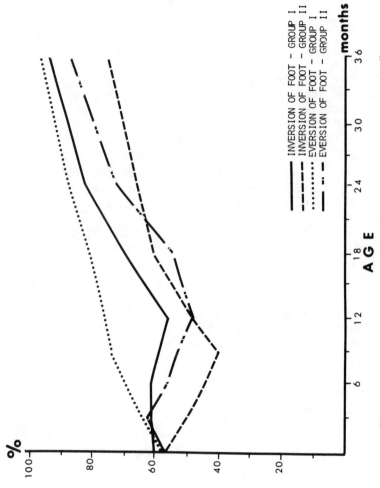

Figure 6: Percentage of children with "good" muscle strength according to cardiac status.

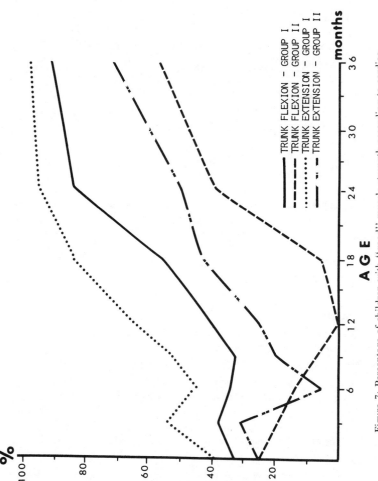

Figure 7: Percentage of children with "good" muscle strength according to cardiac status.

TRUNK FLEXION – GROUP I
TRUNK FLEXION – GROUP II
TRUNK EXTENSION – GROUP I
TRUNK EXTENSION – GROUP II

shoulder girdle was frequently found. Thus the young infant with Down syndrome is not very well equipped for early tasks of reaching and grasping. The strength of the arm abductors (Figure 8) starts at a very low level, and increases by age 2 years in only 50% of children without and with mild congenital heart disease; while many children with significant cardiac problems did not even obtain this level at the age of 3 years.

Elbow Flexion and Extension

As Figure 9 indicates, the elbow flexors in children without and with mild congenital heart disease started out with considerable strength; the elbow extensors caught up at age 12 months, and subsequently surpassed the flexors in strength. One might speculate that through creeping, observed between the age of 9 months and 2 years, the strength of the triceps group may have markedly improved. In contrast, some of the children with moderate and severe congenital heart disease showed reduced strength in these muscle groups up to age 3 years.

Wrist Flexion and Extension

As can be seen in Figure 10, the muscle strength curves for wrist flexion and extension are almost identical. Yet there is a marked difference between the group of children without and with mild congenital heart disease and the group with moderate and severe congenital heart disease. No reason could be found why children in the latter group exhibited such a reduced strength of the musculature of the wrist.

Finger and Thumb Flexion

Normally, the newborn keeps the fingers predominantly flexed, and displays a good grasp reflex in the neonatal period. The grasp reflex is also evident when testing the traction response. Thus, finger strength in the infant can be tested by eliciting this reflex response.

Figure 11 shows that the strength in the muscles of the thumb started to improve slowly at about 12 months in children without and

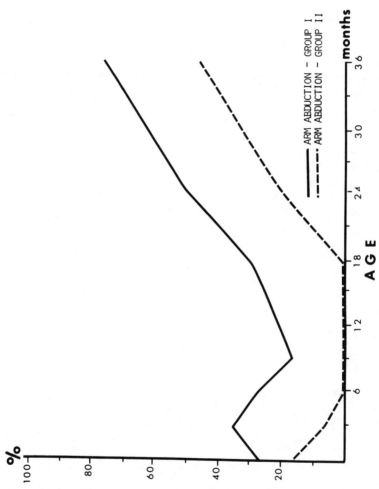

Figure 8: Percentage of children with "good" muscle strength according to cardiac status.

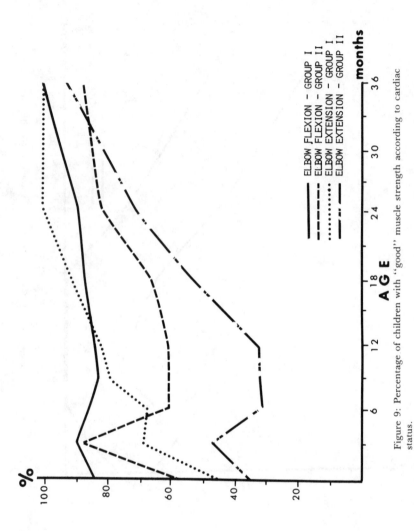

Figure 9: Percentage of children with "good" muscle strength according to cardiac status.

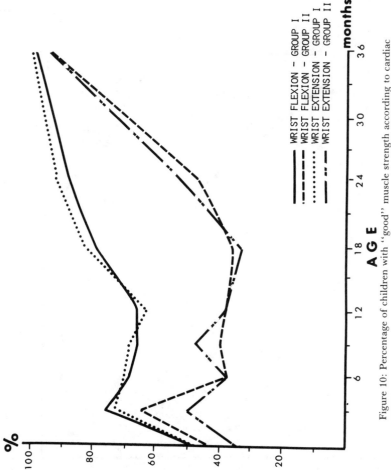

Figure 10: Percentage of children with "good" muscle strength according to cardiac status.

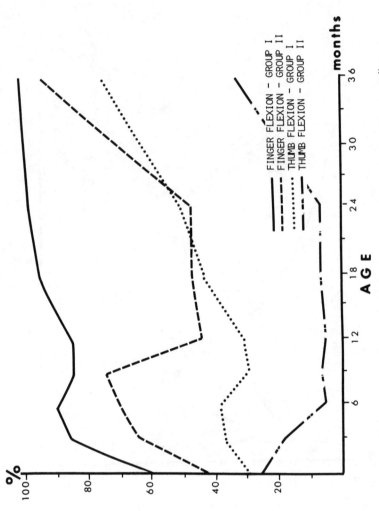

Figure 11: Percentage of children with "good" muscle strength according to cardiac status.

with mild congenital heart disease; yet it remained extremely low in children with moderate and severe cardiac problems until two years of age. Even at age 3 years, thumb flexors remained quite weak in most children of the latter group.

Range of Motion

As expected, the data obtained in this study confirm previous clinical observations that ranges of motion are increased in nearly all joints in children with Down syndrome. The degree of hyperflexibility, as well as the changes taking place throughout the first three years, varied in different joints, which also has been observed in normal children (23). It has been noted that the degree of the observed flexibility differed in some joints between the group of children without and with mild congenital heart disease and the group of children with significant cardiac defects. Children with congenital heart disease who do not have Down syndrome also have hyperflexibility of joints.

Exaggerated abduction and straight leg raising (Figure 12) was observed from age 3 to 12 months in children without and with mild congenital heart defects as well as in children with moderate and severe cardiac problems. An exaggerated degree of range of motion was maintained by both groups thereafter. The increased range of motion in outward rotation and flexion of the hip as compared to inward rotation and hip extension is seen in Figures 13 and 14. While the hyperflexibility in knee flexion was considerably increased in all groups of children with Down syndrome in knee extension it was more pronounced in the group of children with moderate and severe congenital heart disease than in children without and with mild congenital heart disease, as demonstrated in Figure 15.

Figure 16 shows a marked difference in the percentage of increased flexibility in dorsiflexion, as compared to plantar flexion of the ankles. The previously documented better muscle strength of ankle dorsiflexors than that of plantarflexors is possibly reflected in the increased range of motion in dorsiflexion.

Figure 17 illustrates that the increased range of motion in foot eversion is more frequent than that of inversion. This corresponds to the findings of distribution of strength of muscles involved in these movements (Figure 6).

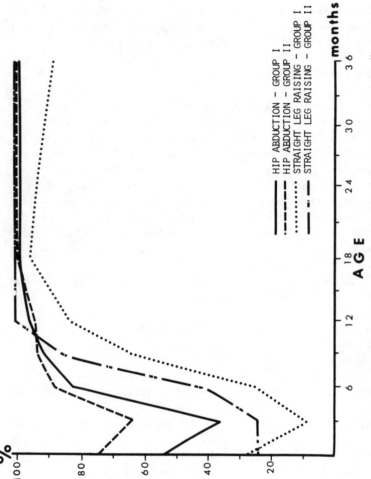

Figure 12: Percentage of children with increased range of motion according to cardiac status.

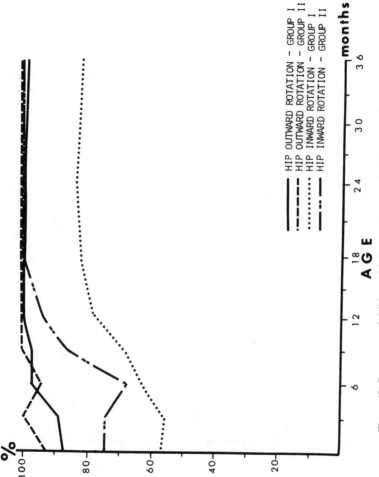

Figure 13: Percentage of children with increased range of motion according to cardiac status.

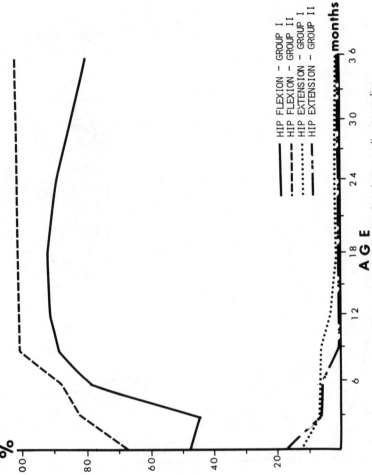

Figure 14: Percentage of children with increased range of motion according to cardiac status.

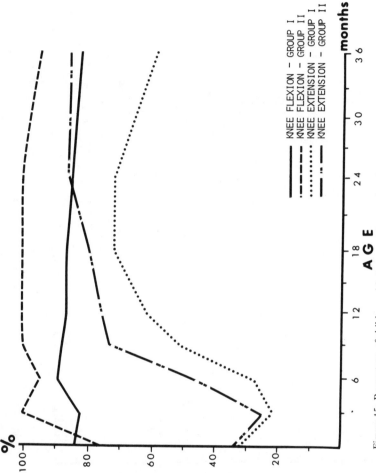

Figure 15: Percentage of children with increased range of motion according to cardiac status.

KNEE FLEXION - GROUP I
KNEE FLEXION - GROUP II
KNEE EXTENSION - GROUP I
KNEE EXTENSION - GROUP II

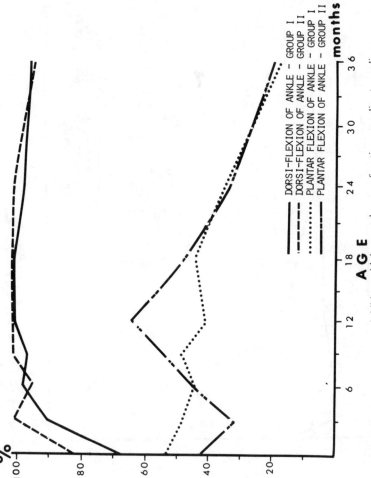

Figure 16: Percentage of children with increased range of motion according to cardiac status.

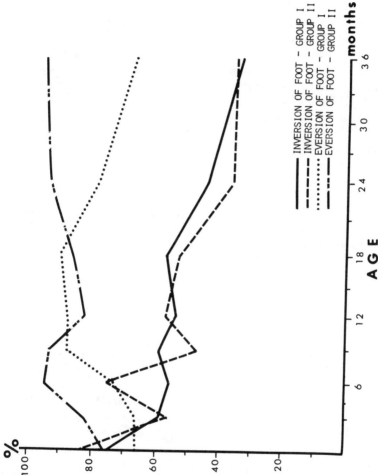

Figure 17: Percentage of children with increased range of motion according to cardiac status.

The increased range of motion in trunk flexion and trunk extension (Figure 18) from age 12 to 36 months in the group of children with moderate and severe congenital heart disease is an interesting observation which merits further analysis.

Hyperflexibility was pronounced in the upper extremities (Figures 19-23). There were minor differences between the group of children without and with mild congenital heart disease and the group of children with moderate and severe cardiac defects. The consistently maintained high degree of increased range of motion in the fingers from age 6 months to 3 years may in part account for the difficulties that the young child with Down syndrome experiences while attempting to perform fine motor skills which demand good stabilization in the joints of the fingers.

Specifically, the increased range of motion in the joints of the thumb (Figure 23) together with the decreased strength of the muscles of the thumb (Figure 11) creates a real handicap in adequately holding and manipulating smaller objects. This fact should be kept in mind when fine motor skill tests are given, in order to avoid an unwarranted reduction in test scores which frequently is regarded as a reflection of the child's intellectual capacity.

Muscle Tone

Resistance to stretch is an important factor in all muscle activity, since stretch on the resting length of a muscle augments the impulses to the muscle which bring about a muscle contraction. Stretch receptors are mainly under the control of the gamma II neurons (24). The degree of decreased muscle tone has an effect on the feedback through the muscle spindle and sensory structures around joints. Such feedback mediates the acquisition of voluntary muscle-control among muscle groups, as well as awareness of body position in space. These factors in turn influence body posture, and the quality of movement.

In hypotonia the resistance of a muscle to passive movement and to stretch is reduced. The effect of hypotonia on the motor development and motor capacity of the child with Down syndrome is of particular interest. It is considered to be one of the causes for the delay in motor development. Specific patterns of deviant movements

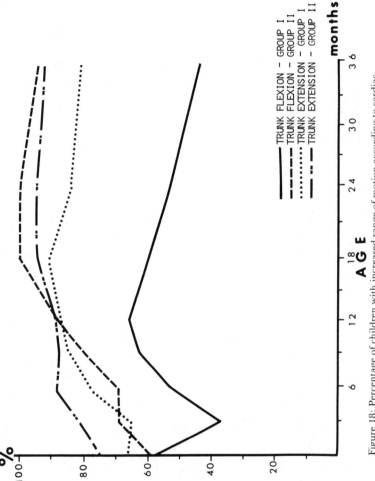

TRUNK FLEXION – GROUP I
TRUNK FLEXION – GROUP II
TRUNK EXTENSION – GROUP I
TRUNK EXTENSION – GROUP II

Figure 18: Percentage of children with increased range of motion according to cardiac status.

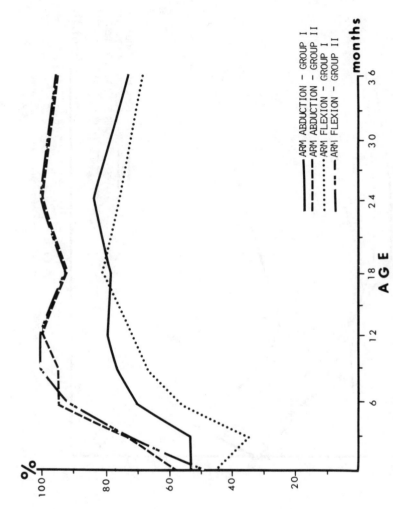

Figure 19: Percentage of children with increased range of motion according to cardiac status.

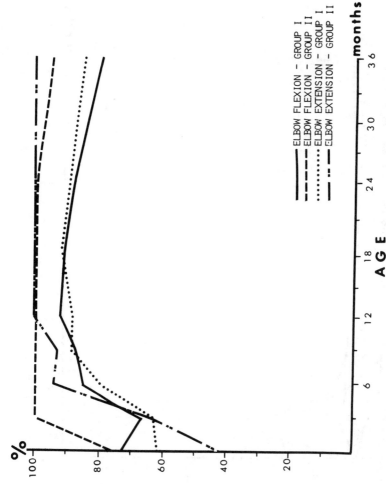

Figure 20: Percentage of children with increased range of motion according to cardiac status.

ELBOW FLEXION – GROUP I
ELBOW FLEXION – GROUP II
ELBOW EXTENSION – GROUP I
ELBOW EXTENSION – GROUP II

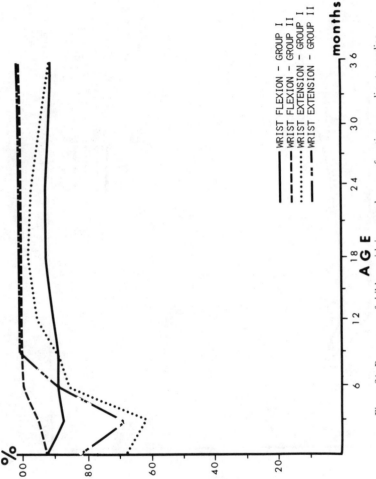

Figure 21: Percentage of children with increased range of motion according to cardiac status.

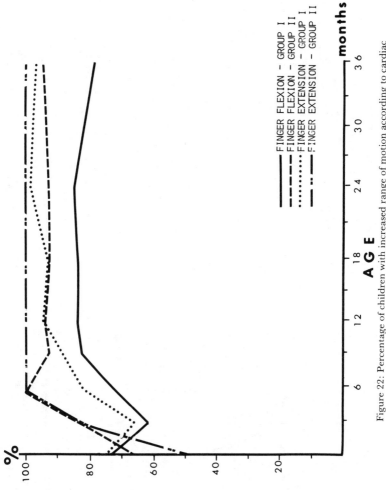

Figure 22: Percentage of children with increased range of motion according to cardiac status.

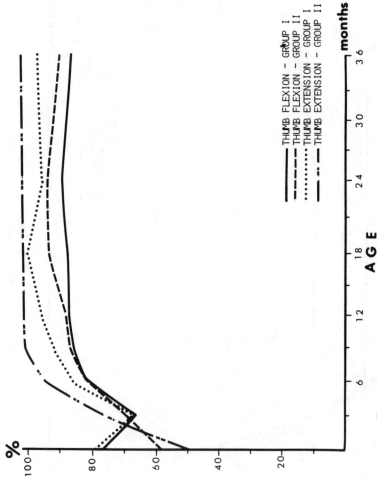

Figure 23: Percentage of children with increased range of motion according to cardiac status.

can be frequently attributed to the lack of muscle tone in given muscles or muscle groups that serve as stabilizers around joints.

The results of the muscle tone testing were combined with muscle-tone data obtained during the pediatric and neurological examinations and have been reported in Part II of this monograph.*

Motor Development Attainments

Head Control Head control is an important prerequisite for later sitting and creeping as well as for standing and walking. The development of head control is closely related to the maturation of neural structures.

The poor postural control of the head and upper back in children with Down syndrome is primarily the result of maturational delay of the central nervous system, laxity of ligaments and hypotonia of muscles. In the course of this study, head control was observed in the prone, supine and sitting positions. From Figures 24 and 25 it can be seen that head extension in prone was partially as well as fully attained considerably earlier than was head flexion (Figure 26). This sequence follows the pattern of development as seen in normal children. When pulled up from the supine to sitting position at age 6 months, less than 50% of the children were able to keep their head in line with the body (Figure 26). The inability to lift the head from supine or to keep it in line with the body when pulled to sitting may be due to the hypotonia of the flexor muscles of the neck. This delay in head control was even more marked in the group of children with moderate and severe congenital heart disease.

Lifting Head and Shoulders in Prone As Figure 27 demonstrates, lifting the head and shoulders in prone position, which is regarded as an important prerequisite for later emerging motor sequences, was well executed at age 6 months by most of the children, except those with moderate and severe congenital heart disease.

Rolling Over Rolling over provides the child with movements around the body axis which are needed to accomplish more complex motor activities later such as creeping and rising to the sitting

*See also chapter on Neurological Investigations

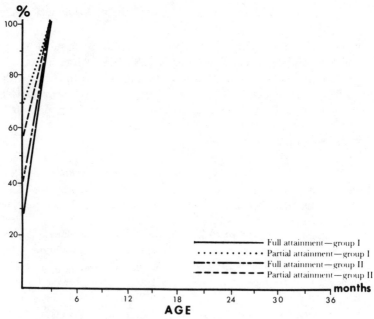

Figure 24: Percentage of children with head control in prone suspension according to cardiac status.

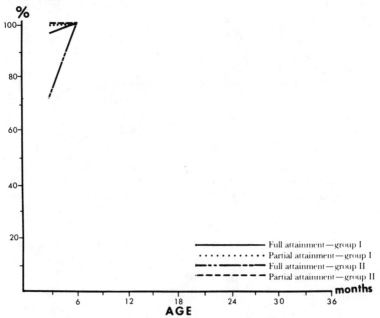

Figure 25: Percentage of children—head lifting in prone position according to cardiac status.

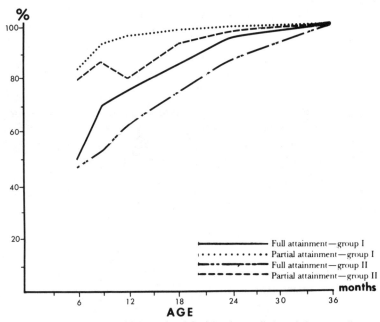

Figure 26: Percentage of children—head flexion when pulled to sitting according to cardiac status.

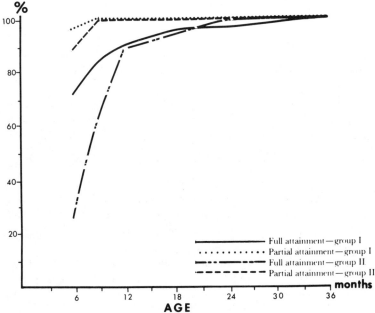

Figure 27: Percentage of children—lifting head and shoulders in prone position according to cardiac status.

181

position. Infants have been observed to roll over within a few days after birth. Such early rolling activity occurs in response to postural righting mechanisms and, therefore, cannot be considered a controlled movement. During our evaluations a special effort was made to exclude motor performances due to reflexive behavior such as turning the body in response to a neck or body righting reflex.

Data on rolling were first collected at age 6 months (Figure 28). At that age many children already used mature patterns of movement by turning parts of their body segmentally. It can be assumed that a fair number of our children had started to roll over before the first evaluation of this motor act took place.

Creeping   Creeping is defined as the ability to carry the weight of the trunk on hands and knees while able to move in various directions. It is generally agreed that creeping represents a difficult and complex motor activity. In this study, three phases of quadruped motor behaviors were rated: coming from prone to hand-knee position, creeping in various patterns, and creeping in reciprocal pattern.

One of the most important prerequisites for creeping is the strength of the antigravity muscles of the arms and legs. Strength of the musculature of the abdomen and back are needed to keep the trunk in appropriate horizontal position. Also to be taken into account is the position of the head in relation to the trunk while in the creeping position. Moreover, the ability to maintain balance while on hands and knees adds to the complexity of this mode of movement. A detailed analysis of various factors involved in creeping can be found in a study by Nathan (25).

The lack of maturational readiness must be considered as one of the main factors in the delay in creeping observed in children with Down syndrome. It could be hypothesized that the continuing presence of hypotonia prevents the execution of the motor act even in children who might be developmentally ready to assume an antigravity position. Reciprocal creeping implies that the weight of the trunk is carried on one hand and the opposite knee while the two other extremities are in motion. It demands more complex

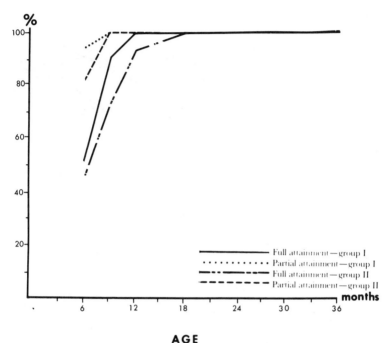

AGE

Figure 28: Percentage of children—rolling over according to cardiac status.

equilibrium reactions. A modified creeping pattern with three-point support was frequently observed in our population. As seen in Figure 29, creeping was accomplished at the age of 24 months by most of the children with Down syndrome without or with mild congenital heart disease.

It was interesting to note that a large number of children with Down syndrome continued to engage periodically in crawling and creeping at a time when they were able to stand and walk. This fact most likely reflects a preference for a more infantile motor behavior pattern which poses fewer physical demands.

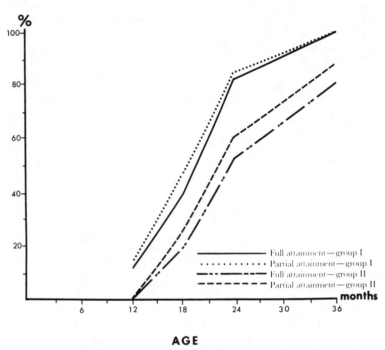

Figure 29: Percentage of children—creeping in reciprocal pattern according to cardiac status.

Sitting In sitting, an infant must for the first time overcome the force of gravity in order to maintain the trunk in the erect position. The hypotonia of the musculature of the trunk may diminish the child's ability to assume or maintain the sitting position, although maturationally the child may be ready for the task.

From the number of different positions included in our investigation (pulled to sitting, sitting on floor—"tailor fashion" sitting with hips and knees flexed, sitting with feet supported, unsupported sitting—legs dangling, sitting and shifting trunk, rising from lying to sitting), selected data are presented here. Following the usual development sequence, the children first sat on the floor with some support on their hands (Figure 30). However, due to the hypotonic musculature of the trunk and to the increased range of motion of the hamstring muscles, the children frequently sat in an exaggerated trunk-flexed position with their legs widely abducted and outwardly rotated.

Sitting on a chair introduces different motoric demands, such as shifting the body weight to the ischia and to a narrower base of support. With the feet on the floor, sitting on a chair does not greatly tax the child's ability to maintain balance. As seen in Figure 31, the majority of children at 1 year of age had attained some ability to sit on a chair. Until the age of 24 months, sitting was difficult for some of the children with moderate and severe cardiac problems. Although sitting on a chair with feet dangling, while engaged in movements of the trunk, was accomplished later (Figure 32), at 2 years of age most children had achieved suffcient truck control and balance to sit totally unsupported.

Normally, children follow a typical sequential motor pattern when moving from a recumbent to a sitting position. They first turn into prone position, then rise onto hands and knees, and with a slight turn of the body push themselves into a sitting position. Children with Down syndrome frequently use an apparently less demanding approach: they abduct the legs widely while lying prone, then arch the back and push up on their arms, thus lifting the trunk to the erect position. Figure 33 shows that this developmental phase was significantly delayed in our population. The majority of children were between 12 and 18 months of age when they could move unassisted from a recumbent to a sitting position. It is assumed that the hypotonia of the musculature of the trunk and the upper extremities significantly limits the child's ability to perform this movement earlier and more efficiently.

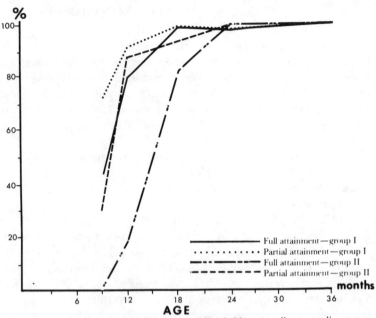

Figure 30: Percentage of children—sitting in tailor fashion according to cardiac status.

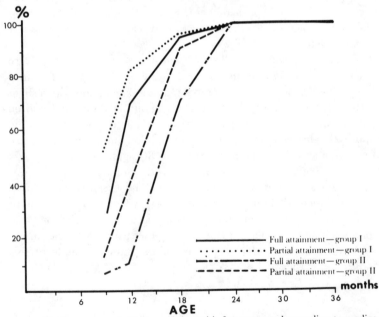

Figure 31: Percentage of children—sitting with feet supported according to cardiac status.

186

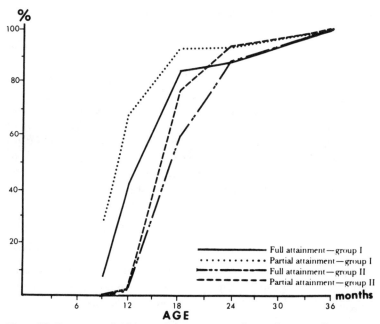

Figure 32: Percentage of children—sitting unsupported according to cardiac status.

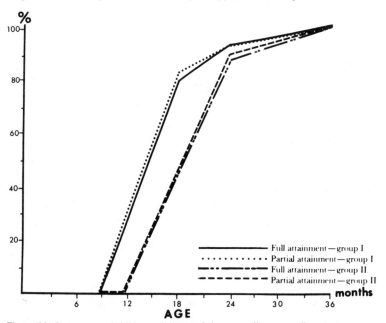

Figure 33: Percentage of children—lying to sitting according to cardiac status.

187

Certain forms of motor behavior are occasionally observed in a number of children during their prewalking stage of development which have been labelled in the literature "hitching, sliding or shuffling"(26). Some of the children with Down syndrome are seen to use such modes of transport mainly at a period in their motor development when they are maturationally ready to explore their environment more actively than had been possible by rolling or crawling. Often, this interim period of moving around on their buttocks may be more prolonged than ordinarily expected. Only six of the children had engaged in this mode of locomotion.

Standing   Generally, children go through a short and transient period of pulling up to stand, followed by standing with support before they stand unsupported. The child with Down syndrome needs more time to progress from one of these phases to the next. Weakness of the upper extremities and the trunk as well as hypotonia may be the primary reasons for the inability to pull to standing at an earlier age. In addition to strength and adequate muscle tone in the upper extremities, a certain degree of initiative and perseverance are also needed for an attempt to pull up to standing.

In Figures 34 and 35 it can be seen that standing with support preceeded pulling up to stand. Up to the age of 18 months, the children were more successful in maintaining the standing position than in pulling up to it. This was particularly true for children with significant cardiac defects, where decreased strength had been observed. The delay in standing unsupported (Figure 36) in contrast to standing with support may in part be attributed to the slow acquisition of effective equilibrium responses, as well as to fear reactions to new situations which are sometimes observed in children with Down syndrome. The competence in standing varied considerably among children of the same chronological age. They were frequently standing with legs widely abducted and with increased outward rotation, their knees hyperextended and their feet pronated. Structural changes of the pelvis in infants with Down syndrome (20-22) may account for some of these abnormal postural patterns in

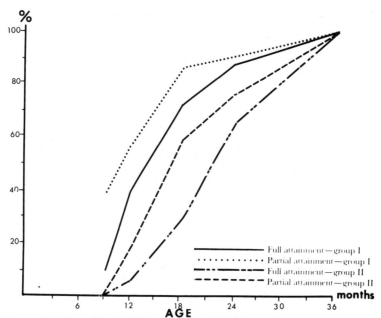

Figure 34: Percentage of children—standing with two-hand support according to cardiac status.

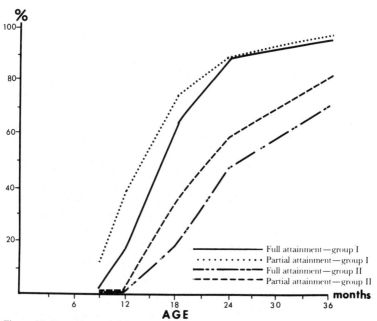

Figure 35: Percentage of children—pulling to standing according to cardiac status.

189

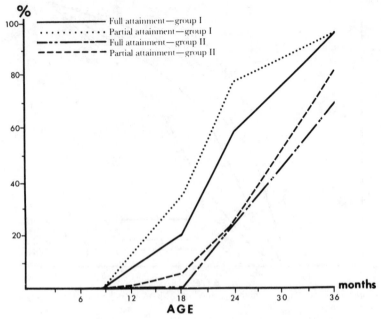

Figure 36: Percentage of children—standing unsupported according to cardiac status.

standing which are also carried over into walking. It is possible that previously uncorrected resting positions such as lying with legs widely abducted and outwardly rotated may result in a faulty habitual postural pattern in children with Down syndrome.

Walking The functional development of locomotion proceeds in a fairly regular sequence. Head control and the ability to sit and stand are prerequisites for the ability to walk. Variations in the rate of development as well as in functional problems of ambulation are related to the stage of neural maturation. In order to assume and maintain the upright position, the neural structures of the cerebellum, the cortico-spinal connections, and other sensory and motor functions of the central nervous system must have reached an adequate degree of maturation. Insufficient development of the brain stem and the cerebellum in children with Down syndrome has been discussed by Benda (27) as well as by Crome and Stern (28). While neuro-pathological observations have mainly been made of brains of older persons with Down syndrome, there are no in-depth studies of correlations between pathological findings of the brain of young children with Down Syndrome and motor developmental course which preceded their death. In addition other factors that may influence the motor behavior in children with Down syndrome have to be considered. Hypotonia presents one of the significant obstacles to the maintenance of the upright posture. This decreased muscle tone as well as muscle weakness were found greatly to affect walking. A correlation of .71 was found between muscle tone ratings and age of walking. Hyperflexibility of the joints which is due to the laxity of the surrounding ligaments and the resulting increased range of motion diminish the stability of joints and thus reduce the child's ability to ambulate effectively.

Figures 37 and 38 demonstrate that almost half of the children without and with mild congenital heart disease could walk with two-hand support at the age of 18 months and approximately 15 percent could walk unsupported. Congenital heart disease presented a major obstacle to achievement of independent walking. While more than 90% of children without and with only mild congenital heart disease walked without support at 36 months, only 60% of children with moderate and severe congenital heart disease were able to do so.*

A tendency to assume atypical postures as described in standing was also observed in walking. Other deviant motor patterns included: insufficient take-off (plantarflexion), resulting in a lack of spring in gait; insufficient tandem (heel-to-toe) gait; increased eversion and pronation of feet with flattening of the arch of the feet, resulting in a "flatfooted" type of gait, and decrease in associative arm swing. It must be emphasized that these deviations from normal gait patterns do not occur always in children with Down syndrome, and may not be seen in a combination of several characteristics in one individual.

A wide-spaced stance in standing and walking is normal in any child's beginning phase of locomotor development. While the average

---

*Similar data on ambulation are also discussed in a slightly different form in the chapter on Neurological Investigations.

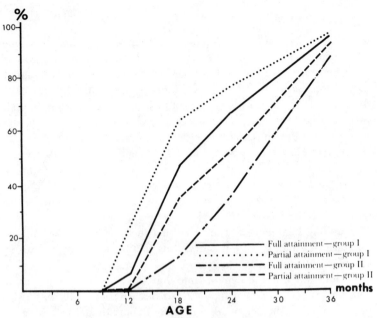

Figure 37: Percentage of children—walking with two-hand support according to cardiac status.

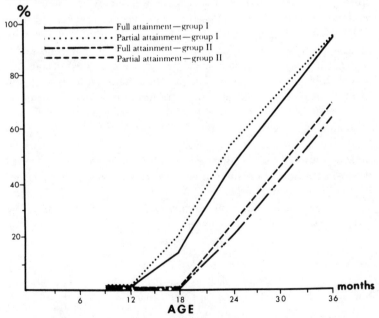

Figure 38: Percentage of children—walking unsupported according to cardiac status.

192

toddler changes from such early and transitory stage of development rather quickly into a more mature pattern of aligning the legs in relation to the rest of the body, the child with Down syndrome may retain a broad-spaced gait pattern. Possibly, the previously described position in lying, sitting and standing, with the hips abducted and outwardly rotated, may be carried over into this broad-based walking pattern unless preventive measures are started early.

Normally, the angle of inclination between the femoral neck and the axis of the shaft of the femur is wide in infancy. It decreases, however, as the child grows older and starts weight bearing. In children with Down syndrome, this angle of inclination frequently remains wide. Because children with Down syndrome generally begin to walk at a later age than the average "normal" child, the hip joint may not be exposed to the positive stresses in weight bearing which affect the coxa valga position.

Hyperextension of the knees in standing and walking is frequently seen in children with Down syndrome, which is thought to be due to a combination of decreased strength of the quadriceps (Figure 4) and the increased range of motion in the knee joint (Figure 15). The frequency of exaggerated eversion of the feet is documented in Figure 17 and can be explained by the difference in strength of the opposing muscle groups around the ankle joint (Figure 6).

The foot of the child with Down syndrome shows an atypical formation of the longitudinal arch. Faulty distribution of the weight of the body upon the sole of the foot, ligament laxity, and the frequently found reduced strength of the gastronemius muscle in plantarflexion (Figure 5) adds to the formation of pronation, with resulting lack of proper "take off" or spring in the gait of the child with Down syndrome.

Stair Climbing and Running   Figures 39, 40, and 41 show the ages of attainment of stair climbing and running. The children were encouraged to develop independence in these areas as soon as developmental and safety factors permitted this. Some of the atypical motor characteristics observed in walking were also seen when the child was running. Running was particularly difficult for children with significant cardiac problems.

Table I lists the median ages of full attainment of the gross motor skills calculated by linear interpolation.

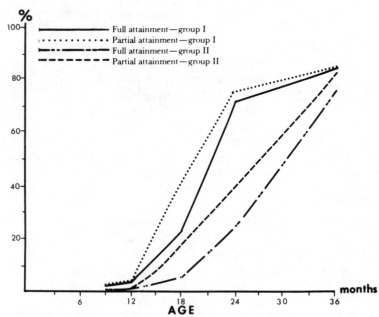

Figure 39: Percentage of children—climbing stairs on hands and knees according to cardiac status.

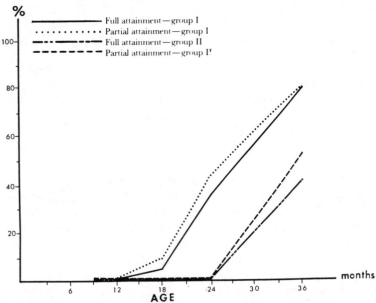

Figure 40: Percentage of children—climbing stairs with two-hand support according to cardiac status.

194

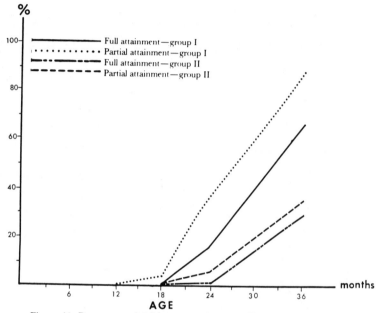

Figure 41: Percentage of children—running according to cardiac status.

Grasp and Prehension As the data in Figure 46 indicate, it appears that reaching for an object began rather early. It can be assumed that a fair number of infants had engaged in this activity before the age of 6 months, when this skill was tested and rated for the first time. Many children had even passed the stage of primitive grasp (Figure 42) at that age and were on the way to using a more mature pincer grasp (Figure 43), which was performed well by more than half of the children at 12 months.

TABLE I

MEDIAN AGE OF FULL ATTAINMENT (IN MONTHS) OF GROSS MOTOR SKILLS
IN YOUNG CHILDREN WITH DOWN SYNDROME ACCORDING TO CARDIAC STATUS

Gross Motor Skills	Month(s) of attainment in Down syndrome children	
	With and without mild congenital heart disease	With moderate and severe congenital heart disease
Controls head in prone suspension	1.3	.7
Lifts head in prone position	*	*
Head flexion in pull to sitting	6	7.5
Lifts head or shoulders to prone	*	7.9
Rolls over	6	6.6
Reciprocal creeping	19.4	22.3
Sitting tailor fashion	9.6	15
Sitting feet supported	10.6	15.9
Sitting without support	13.3	17
Comes from lying to sitting	14.7	19
Stands with two-hand support	14	21.5
Pulls to standing	16.3	25.5
Stands unsupported	22.7	30.6
Walks with two-hand support	18.4	27.4
Walks unsupported	25	32.2
Climbs stairs on hands and knees	21.4	30
Climbs stairs with two-hand support	28	*
Runs	32	*

*Could not be calculated from data because more than 50% of children had achieved the
particular motor skill at the time of initial testing.

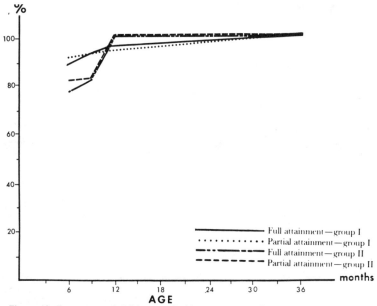

Figure 42: Percentage of children—primitive grasp according to cardiac status.
knees according to cardiac status.

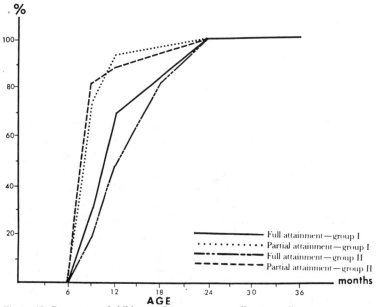

Figure 43: Percentage of children—pincer grasp according to cardiac status.

197

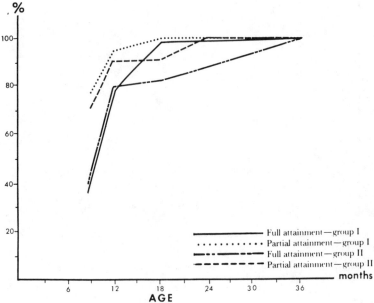

Figure 44: Percentage of children—thumb apposition with cube according to cardiac status.

Holding an object with the thumb in opposition was partially attained at the relatively early age of nine months by a number of children as seen in Figure 44. Obtaining and keeping a small object such as a pellet or piece of cereal between the thumb and index finger puts a great demand on vision, attention, planning of the motor act, and on the muscle strength of fingers. Data in Figure 45 indicate that this skill was accomplished relatively late. The ability to transfer objects from one hand to the other (Figure 47) is dependent on a number of similar factors as noted above. It can be seem from Figure 47 that transfer was achieved at approximately 12 months of age by more than 80% of the children. Transfer was an activity which was encouraged and practiced in the intervention program.

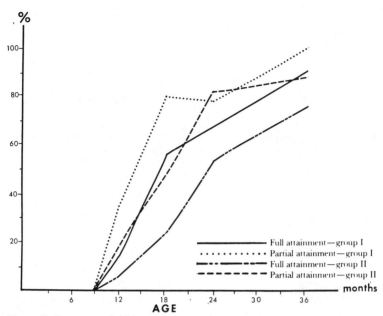

Figure 45: Percentage of children—thumb apposition with pellet according to cardiac status.

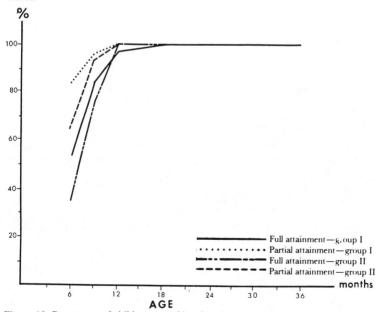

Figure 46: Percentage of children—reaching for object according to cardiac status.

199

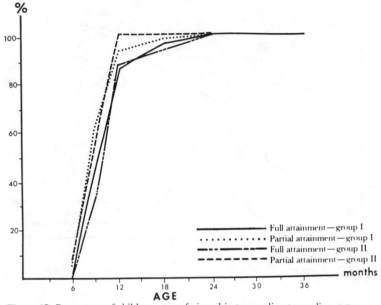

Figure 47: Percentage of children—transfering object according to cardiac status.

Throwing an object was also emphasized, in view of the concomitant values of this movement, such as visually following an object in flight, of observation of distance, aiming at a goal, etc. Figure 48 shows an acceptable level of performance in throwing at age 18 months in our study population.

The association of significant congenital heart disease with greater delay of motor performance is less evident in this area of early grasp and prehension with the exception of grasp of a pellet with the thumb (Figure 45). Perhaps separate organization in the central nervous system of fine and gross movements, as well as the need for strength and endurance in gross motor skills could explain this discrepancy.

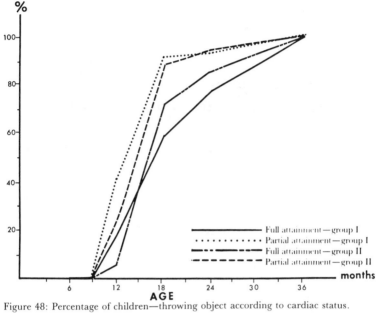

Figure 48: Percentage of children—throwing object according to cardiac status.

From the data presented in Table II it appears that the young child with Down syndrome does not show as extended a delay in all of the areas of prehensile development as one would perhaps have expected, considering the marked delay found in acquiring functional manual skills at a later age. Of course, complex functional skills are more closely related to intellectual abilities than to strict gross motor development.

Early Intervention Program

Concurrent with the motor developmental evaluations, an intervention program was carried out throughout the three years of the

TABLE II

MEDIAN AGE OF FULL ATTAINMENT (IN MONTHS) OF GRASP AND PREHENSION
IN YOUNG CHILDREN WITH DOWN SYNDROME ACCORDING TO CARDIAC STATUS

Fine Motor Skills	Months of attainment in Down syndrome children	
	Without and with mild congenital heart disease	With moderate to severe congenital heart disease
Primitive grasp	*	*
Pincer grasp	*	12.5
Thumb opposition with cube	10	10
Thumb opposition with pellet	17	23.4
Reaches for object	*	7.1
Transfers object	9.3	9.8
Throws cube	16.7	16.1

*Could not be calculated from data because more than 50% of children had
achieved the particular motor skill at the time of initial testing.

study involving all the children in the Down syndrome Program The ability of children with Down syndrome to respond to an enriched environment has been discussed in several publications (30-34) and a description of various techniques used in a carefully planned early intervention program has been detailed previously (35).

SUMMARY

This chapter describes the motor development and movement patterns of 89 children with Down syndrome who were examined at specified ages during the first 3 years of life. Selected areas of muscle strength, range of motion in joints, and developmental attainments have been discussed.

There were changes in strength and flexibility of joints over time. Although an interpretation of specific characteristics was attempted, more definite answers to a number of related questions will need further study. The sequence of motor development was similar to that observed in a normal population. Delay in development was noted in all areas of motor function. Definite differences were found in gross motor development between the group of children without and with mild congenital heart disease and those with moderate and severe congenital heart disease. The difference was less obvious or nil in areas of grasp and manipulation. Significant congenital heart disease seemed to cause additional delay in gross motor development.

Observations of the results of the three-year intervention program strengthened our impression that early stimulation and environmental enrichment geared to the individual needs of the child will influence positively the motor development and motor behavior of infants and young children with Down syndrome, and will also be of benefit to their families.

It is hoped that the various observations and data obtained during the course of this study will lead to a better understanding of some of the mechanisms which underlie specific atypical patterns of motor development and motor behavior in young children with Down syndrome.

REFERENCES

1. Bayley, N. *Bayley Scales of Infant Development.* New York: Psychological Corporation, 1969.
2. Gesell, A. and Amatruda, C. S. *Developmental Diagnosis: Normal and Abnormal Child Development.* New York: Paul Hoeber Inc., 1941.
3. Griffiths, R. *The Abilities of Babies.* London: University of London Press Ltd, 1973.
4. Milani-Comparetti, A. and Gidoni, E. A. Routine developmental examination in normal and retarded children. *Developmental Medicine and Child Neurology,* 9:631-638, 1967.
5. Zdanska-Brincken, M. and Wolanski, N. A graphic method for the evaluation of motor development in infants. *Developmental Medicine and Child Neurology.* 11:228-241, 1969.
6. Carr, J. Mental and motor development in young mongol children. *Journal of Mental Deficiency Research,* 14:205-222, 1970.
7. Centerwall, S. A. and Centerwall, W. R. A study of children with mongolism reared in the home compared to those reared away from home. *Pediatrics,* 25:678-685, 1960.
8. Melyn, M. A. and White, D. T. Mental and developmental milestones of noninstitutionalized Down's syndrome children. *Pediatrics,* 52:542-545, 1973.
9. Shipe, D. and Shotwell, A. Effect of out-of-home care on mongoloid children: a continuation study. *American Journal of Mental Deficiency,* 69:649-656, 1956.
10. Cowie, V. A. *A Study of the Early Development of Mongols.* Oxford: Pergamon Press, 1970.
11. Williams, M. Manual muscle testing: development and current use. *Physical Therapy Review.* 36:797-805, 1956.
12. Zausmer, E. Evaluation of strength and motor development in infants. *Physical Therapy Review,* Part I 33:575-581, Part II 33:621-629, 1953.
13. Moore, M. Measurement of joint motion. *Physical Therapy Review,* Part I 29:256-264, 1949.
14. Zausmer, E. Evaluation of motor development in children. *Physical Therapy,* 44:247-250, 1964.
15. Zausmer, E. and Tower, G. A quotient for the evaluation of motor development. *Physical Therapy,* 46:725-728, 1966.

16. Silbert, A., Wolff, P.H., Mayer, B., et al: Cyanotic heart disease and psychological development. *Pediatrics,* 43:192-200, 1969.
17. Conel, J. L. *The Postnatal Development of the Human Cerebral Cortex.* Vol. I, 1939, Vol. II, 1941. Harvard University Press.
18. Mastaglia, F. L. The Growth and Development of the Skeletal Muscles. In: *Scientific Foundations of Pediatrics.* Davis, J. A. and Dobbing, J. (Eds.) Philadelphia: W. B. Saunders Company, 1974.
19. Schulte, F. J. The Neurological Development of the Neonate. In: *Scientific Foundations of Pediatrics.* Davis, J. A. and Dobbing, J. (Eds.) Philadelphia: W. B. Saunders Company, 1974.
20. Smith, G. F. and Berg, J. M. *Down's Anomaly,* 2nd Edition, Edinburgh, London and New York: Churchill Livingston, 1976.
21. Andren, L. and Hall B. Increased curvature of the ilium: a new roentgenological sign of mongoloid pelvis. *Developmental Medicine and Child Neurology,* 10:781-783, 1968.
22. Caffey, J. and Ross, S. Mongolism (Mongoloid Deficiency) during early infancy: Some newly recognized diagnostic changes in the pelvic bones. *Pediatrics,* 17:642-650, 1956
23. Vlach, V., Zezulakova, J., Ciperova, V., et al. Evolutive changes of muscle extensibility in children. *Acta Universitatis Carolinae Medica Monograph,* 75:23-28, 1976.
24. Rabe, E. The clinical evaluation of the hypotonic infant. *Medical Times,* 95:1134-1151, 1967.
25. Nathan, D. L. *Development of Creeping in a Normal and a Down Syndrome Infant.* Thesis, Boston University Sargent College of Allied Health Professions, Boston, 1976.
26. Robson, P. Shuffling, hitching, scooting, or sliding: Some observations in thirty otherwise normal children. *Developmental Medicine and Child Neurology,* 12:603-617, 1970.
27. Benda, C. E. *The Child with Mongolism.* New York: Grune and Stratton, 1960.
28. Crome, L. and Stern, Y. *Pathology of Mental Retardation.* London: Churchill Livingston, 1972.
29. Kuypers, H. G. J. M. Organization of the motor system. *International Journal of Neurology,* 4:78-91, 1963.
30. Aronson. N. and Fallstrom, K. Immediate and long-term effects of developmental training in children with Down syndrome. *Developmental Medicine and Child Neurology,* 19:489-494, 1977.

31. Bidder, R. T. Benefits to Down's syndrome children through training their mothers. *Archives of Diseases of Childhood*, 50:383-386, 1975.

32. Connolly, B. and Russell, F. Interdisciplinary early intervention program. *Physical Therapy*, 56:155-158, 1976.

33. Zausmer, E., Pueschel, S. and Shea, A. *A Sensory-Motor Stimulation Program for the Young Child with Down's Syndrome*. Maternal-Child Health Exchange, Department of Health Care Administration, Report 2(4). Washington, D.C.: George Washington, 1972.

34. Zausmer, E. Principles and Methods of Early Intervention. In: *Down's Syndrome: Research, Prevention and Management*. New York: Koch, R. and de la Crux, F.F. (Eds.) New York: Brunner/Mazel, 1975.

35. Zausmer, E. *Early Developmental Stimulation*. In *Down Syndrome: Growing and Learning*. Pueschel, S. M. (Ed.) Kansas City: Sheed, Andrews and McMeel, 1978.

Chapter 7

PSYCHOMOTOR DEVELOPMENT

Richard R. Schnell

INTRODUCTION

Research concerning cognitive development in Down syndrome demonstrates that the majority of children with this chromosomal disorder are likely to be retarded. There are controversies in the literature about the change of the cognitive deficit with age, the effects on specific intellectual abilities, the influence of biological and environmental variables, and the degree of impairment. A number of studies have raised the issue of progressive retardation in children with Down syndrome. Earlier investigations have described nearly normal cognitive development during the first six months of life and a slow decline thereafter (1-4). However, employing the Gesell Development Scale, both Dicks-Mireaux and Dameron, found that at three months of age the developmental quotients were already below average (5,6). More recent studies used the Mental Scale of the Bayley Scales of Infant Development and reported relatively normal skills in the first 6 months, with progressive mental retardation then ensuing (7,8). Share and co-investigators described the longitudinal development of a group of 50 young children with Down syndrome as demonstrating a 1.4 month deceleration per year in mental age from 2 to 36 months (9-12). They reported a plateauing of this effect at 36 months of age. Carr on the other hand found a decline in scores on both the Mental and Motor Scales of the Bayley Scales of Infant Development from birth until 10 months, when the decline became more gradual to 24 months (13).

Some investigators used decreasing developmental quotients over longitudinal testing to demonstrate that intellectual deterioration was inherent in Down syndrome (2). Carr has suggested that this apparent decline is an artifact derived from the formula $IQ = MA/CA \times 100$, which assumes a linear relationship between development and chronological age (13).

An additional issue is that investigators tend to stress the first 6 months of development when most assessment tasks are strongly related to reflexive behavior, sensory development and the state of alertness of the child, rather than problem solving behaviors. Cornwell and Birch, studying children 4 to 17 years old, described a decline in IQ development which they related to limitations in the development of language and abstract skills (14). These skills become increasingly more important in cognitive tests for older children.

Sex differences have also been reported. Wallin noted the IQs of girls with Down syndrome to be 5 points higher than those of boys (15). Similarly, Carr found girls to have significantly increased scores on the Mental Scale of the Bayley Scales of Infant Development (13), while LaVeck and LaVeck observed significantly higher scores for girls on the Motor Scale of the Bayley Scales for Infant Development when compared with those for boys (16). Girls have also shown earlier achievement of developmental milestones such as sitting, standing, walking, and the use of a first word (17).

In examining parental genetic contributions Fraser and Sadovnick found a correlation of about .5 between the IQs of non-institutionalized children and their first-degree relatives (18). Studies seeking to relate the number and/or severity of physical stigmata to cognitive level have not been successful (19,20). Studies of the different types of Down syndrome have in general demonstrated that children with mosaicism have better cognitive development than those with trisomy and translocation karyotypes (29-33).

Most early data on the development of children with Down syndrome had come from institutional populations where the lack of stimulation and even deprivation obviously lead to a decrement of cognitive development (13,21-23). Studies of such populations, not surprisingly, generally found the child with Down syndrome who had been institutionalized soon after birth to be at a severely retarded level. Yet children who had been reared at home had a more advanced cognitive development, which lasted three years after their subsequent placement in institutions (24,25). Other studies have noted the majority of children reared at home to be functioning in at least the moderately retarded range (26).

The influences of early intervention programs and new educational programs are beginning to be evaluated. Two recent studies have reported significant effects of early intervention on IQ and language development (27,28).

Much of previous research has assumed that all abilities in children with Down syndrome are equally affected (36). Several investigators, however, have described specific deficits in verbal and abstract skills, which become more important with age (14,38,39,40). Deficits on some aspects of performance can in part be related to the hypotonia that is observed in many children with Down syndrome, although the degree differs from individual to individual. Significant congenital heart disease, a frequent concommitant of Down syndrome, can result in decreased motor activity, thereby impeding development (40). Melyn and White posited a relationship between hypotonic oral musculature and linguistic deficiencies while Cicchetti and Stroufe described a possible association between extreme hypotonia and marked delays in affective behaviors (17,41). Others have related the effects of hypotonia to more general cognitive deficits (42).

As discussed above, early studies found children with Down syndrome to be severely retarded while later many of the children were described as moderately retarded, but demonstrating a deceleration in development during the first 3 years of life. Rarely, however, have important variables such as cardiac status, muscle tone, and stimulation been taken into consideration. In our program, we had the opportunity to study the longitudinal psychological development of children with Down syndrome from age 6 months to age 36 months, and to evaluate developmentally these important variables.

METHODS

The Bayley Scales of Infant Development were used as the main measure of psychomotor development (34-35). They have more up-to-date norms than other similar measures, and age placement of test items appears more accurate than in other tests. The scales yield norms for each month of development from 2 to 30 months for both a mental development scale and a motor development scale. These two scales are made to complement each other.

Each child in the study was assessed by both scales of the Bayley Scales of Infant Development, at semiannual intervals beginning at 6 months, and continuing through 36 months. The assessments were done primarily by two psychologists, Dr. Patricia Boyle and Dr. Betsy Kammerer. Both examiners had been trained by this author in the administration of the Bayley Scales. Appropriate between-tester reliability was established.

The means and standard deviations describing the results of the Bayley Scales assessments are expressed in developmental ages and raw scores. Developmental ages were used because they allow an easy comparison to normal age level development. As recommended by Bayley, each raw score obtained by a child was converted to a developmental age equivalent by using the age in months from the Bayley Scales norms (34). Mental and psychomotor development indices were determined where possible from the mean raw scores for each six-month interval. To give a rough comparison with other research results, developmental quotients were calculated by dividing the mean developmental score at each six-month level by the appropriate age, and multiplying by 100. A number of children obtained index scores below the lowest index score in the norms and there is no satisfactory way of trying to estimate scores below 50.

Since significant congenital heart disease appears to influence many aspects of development, children with moderate and severe congenital heart disease* were placed in one group and children

---

*A definition of the various degrees of severity of congenital heart disease is provided in Part I of this monograph.

without and with mild congenital heart disease were placed in another group.

The muscle tone of the children was rated independently by a physical therapist, neurologist, and pediatrician in the course of their examinations, as mentioned in Parts I and II of this monograph. The muscle-tone ratings were factor-analyzed, and the factor scores were used to assign children to a specified muscle-tone group.

A follow-through rating was developed to serve as an index of parental ability to follow through at home on instructions regarding various aspects of care and stimulation of their child, especially feeding-guidance offered by a nurse.**

RESULTS

The results obtained from assessments on the Mental and Motor Scales of the Bayley Scales of Infant Development are presented in Table I. As noted, children with Down syndrome score at a level slightly higher than half of what would be expected for a normal child at each age tested. The rate of performance on the Mental Scale falls between 55 to 58% of chronological age norms. More variability is apparent on the Motor Scale, with the rate of performance varying between 53 and 67% of chronological age norms. Half of this variability is related to the performance at 6 months, which is 67% of normal, while the next highest percentage is 60% at 12 months. The decreasing percentage of normal for motor development is about ⅔ of normal (67%) at 6 months, falling off through 36 months to 53%. Similarly, the Psychomotor Development Indices demonstrate this phenomenon, while the developmental age progression on the Mental Scale appears stable, with no systematic changes evident. This relative stability also becomes apparent in the Mental Development Indices.

The initial decrease in motor performance of the children may be an artifact of the Bayley Motor Scale, since half of its items between the 6 and 12 months involve the skill of sitting. From the 12 months' level of performance (mean 7.2 months, raw score mean 3.2) 43 of the remaining 49 items of the scale involve only walking activi-

---

**A definition of the follow-through variable is provided in Part II of this monograph.

TABLE I

MEANS AND STANDARD DEVIATIONS OF DEVELOPMENTAL AGES AND RAW SCORES OBTAINED FROM

YOUNG CHILDREN WITH DOWN SYNDROME AT SIX MONTH INTERVALS ON THE

BAYLEY SCALES OF INFANT DEVELOPMENT

Mental Scale

Age in months	N	Developmental Age(months) Mean	S.D.	Raw Score Mean	S.D.	Mental Development Index for the Raw Score Mean	Developmental Quotient from the Mental Age Mean
6	81	3.3	1.1	39.8	11.6	54	55
12	88	6.7	1.7	73.9	11.2	54	56
18	75	10.5	2.3	94.6	9.9	>50	58
24	80	13.6	2.6	108.2	10.4	>50	57
30	80'	16.7	3.0	119.6	10.9	>50	56
36	75	20.6	4.6	133.0	13.7	—	57

Motor Scale

Age in months	N	Developmental Age(months) Mean	S.D.	Raw Score Mean	S.D.	Psychomotor Development Index for the Raw Score Mean	Developmental Quotient from the Motor Age Mean
6	81	4.0	1.2	17.2	4.2	67	67
12	83	7.2	1.6	31.9	6.0	60	60
18	75	10.4	2.6	41.8	5.4	55	58
24	80	13.1	3.4	46.9	5.0	>50	55
30	80	16.6	4.4	52.0	5.9	54	55
36	75	19.0	5.2	55.2	6.5	—	53

ties, to the relative exclusion of other motor skills. In general, children with Down syndrome appear to have more difficulty in learning to sit and walk than would be expected from their other development accomplishments. This delayed ability to sit and walk independently may contribute to the apparent deceleration of development on the Motor Scale.

Table II presents the Pearson product-moment correlation coefficients for each of the scales with itself and those between the two scales. All correlations are significant at least at the .01 level. As the child with Down syndrome gets older, the correlation between the immediate past score and the present score on the Mental Scale becomes progressively larger, reaching a high correlation by 18 months and not appreciably changing thereafter, with about 70% of the variance in common between scores. The ability of each test to predict performance at 36 months also progressively increases from accounting for about 28% of the variance from the 6 months assessment, to accounting for 69% of the variances from the 30 months' assessment.

On the Motor Scale the correlation between the immediate past score and the present score reaches its highest value at the 24 months level, accounting for 69% of the variance. The 30 months' score only accounts for 67% of the variance, while the 12 and 18 months' scores account for 53 to 66% of the variance, respectively. Predictability of performance at 36 months at each testing increases from accounting for about 26% of the variance at 6 months, until about 67% of the variance is accounted for at 30 months.

Correlations between the Mental and Motor Scales given at the same time increase until they reach their highest level at 18 months, accounting for about 46% of the variance, and then slightly decrease to 36 months. Even if adjusted for the different developmental age of the Down syndrome group, correlations between Mental and Motor Scales for normal children demonstrate a lesser relationship than found for the children with Down syndrome. Predictability of the Motor scale score at 36 months at each testing with the Mental Scale increases to a high at 18 and 24 months, accounting for 42% of the variance, and then decreasing to 36 months, where 35% of the variance is accounted for. The Motor Scale's success in predicting the Mental Scale score at 36 months progressively increases from 6

TABLE II

CORRELATION COEFFICIENTS FOR THE BAYLEY SCALES OF INFANT DEVELOPMENT

ADMINISTERED AT SIX MONTH INTERVALS

Mental Scale

	Age in Months	6	12	18	24	30	36
	6						
	12	.43					
Mental	18	.44	.72				
Scale	24	.34	.58	.85			
	30	.48	.64	.78	.84		
	36	.53	.60	.72	.74	.83	

Motor Scale

	Age in Months	6	12	18	24	30	36
	6						
	12	.57					
Motor	18	.53	.73				
Scale	24	.58	.71	.81			
	30	.51	.59	.70	.83		
	36	.51	.68	.72	.79	.82	

Motor Scale

	Age in Months	6	12	18	24	30	36
	6	.53(.78)* (.63)**	.40	.40	.35	.44	.39
	12	.38	.57(.24)* (.78)**	.65	.55	.57	.54
Mental	18	.35	.56	.68(.44)* (.47)**	.55	.62	.65
Scale	24	.40	.54	.60	.61(.34)* (.24)**	.61	.65
	30	.42	.52	.64	.53	.60(.24)* (.44)**	.63
	36	.42	.44	.54	.50	.55	.59(--) (.29)**

* These correlations for normal children are taken from the Bayley Manual (34).

** These correlations represent the Bayley correlations ( )* adjusted for the mental age of the children with Down syndrome.

months to a high at 36 months, where it accounts for 35% of the variance.

Table III demonstrates the Bayley Scales' relationship to other measures given at 36 months of age. All correlations are significant at least at the .01 level. The Mental Scale relationship with the Vineland Social Maturity Scale increases from the 6 months assessment to a high at 18 months, drops slightly, and then returns to almost the 18 months level at 36 months. The Motor Scale increases it relationship from 6 months to a high at 24 months, with a subsequent decrease to 36 months. The heavy dependence on walking items on the Motor Scale beginning around that level (mean developmental age 18 months for the 24 months assessment) may have contributed to this effect.

The Mental Scale at 18 and 36 months predicts about half the variance of the Vineland Social Maturity Scale at those ages while the Motor Scale predicts about 66% of the variance at 24 months, and 41% at 36 months. As would be expected, the Mental Scale at 36 months predicts half the variance of the combined Receptive-Expressive Emergent Language Scale score, while the Motor Scale at 36 months predicts only 27%. The Motor Scale at 24 months is a better predictor than at 36 months.

Table IV presents the means and standard deviations for the Bayley Scales of Infant Development according to sex. No statistically significant differences (.05 level) were found when the t-tests for differences between the means were employed. There does, however, appear to be a trend for girls to have higher scores at most ages. Differences appeared to grow larger with increasing ages, remaining less than one month until two years, and rising to a high of about 1½ months at 36 months. Differences were comparable on both scales. Boys showed a slight advantage in mental scores until 18 months, when the trend reversed. Girls performed better on the Mental Scale after 18 months, and had at least a half a month advantage beginning at 6 months on the Motor Scale. The reversal in the Mental Scale may be due to the appearance of language items around the 18 months' assessment. Differences between the sexes do not appear to have functional significance. A preliminary item analysis of these data suggested that girls have greater continuity in development than do boys. In general, girls appeared slightly less compromised than

TABLE III

CORRELATION COEFFICIENTS FOR THE BAYLEY SCALES OF INFANT DEVELOPMENT
ADMINISTERED AT SIX MONTH INTERVALS WITH THE VINELAND SOCIAL MATURITY SCALE
AND THE RECEPTIVE-EXPRESSIVE EMERGENT LANGUAGE SCALE GIVEN AT 36 MONTHS OF AGE

	Age in Months	Vineland Social Maturity Scale	Receptive-Expressive Emergent Language Scale		
			Receptive	Expressive	Combined
	6	.37	.36	.26	.33
	12	.59	.48	.47	.49
Mental	18	.73	.57	.55	.58
Scale	24	.58	.63	.54	.60
	30	.66	.64	.51	.59
	36	.71	.72	.64	.70

	Age in Months	Vineland Social Maturity Scale	Receptive-Expressive Emergent Language Scale		
			Receptive	Expressive	Combined
	6	.37	.35	.32	.35
	12	.62	.43	.43	.43
Motor	18	.75	.42	.45	.44
Scale	24	.81	.59	.55	.59
	30	.68	.60	.50	.58
	36	.64	.50	.52	.52

TABLE IV

MEANS AND STANDARD DEVIATIONS FOR MALE AND FEMALE CHILDREN WITH DOWN SYNDROME

AT SIX MONTH INTERVALS

ON THE BAYLEY SCALES OF INFANT DEVELOPMENT

Mental Scale

Age in Months	Males Developmental Age (months)			Females Developmental Age (months)		
	N	Mean	S.D.	N	Mean	S.D.
6	47	3.4	.9	34	3.2	1.3
12	48	6.8	1.6	37	6.5	1.7
18	41	10.3	2.2	34	10.7	2.2
24	47	13.2	2.4	33	14.2	2.8
30	43	16.5	2.5	37	16.9	3.4
36	41	19.9	4.1	34	21.6	4.9

Motor Scale

Age in Months	Males Developmental Age (months)			Females Developmental Age (months)		
	N	Mean	S.D.	N	Mean	S.D.
6	47	3.9	1.3	34	4.1	1.1
12	48	7.0	1.4	35	7.3	1.7
18	41	10.0	2.7	34	10.9	2.5
24	46	12.7	3.1	32	13.8	3.5
30	43	15.7	3.5	37	17.6	5.1
36	36	18.3	5.1	25	19.8	5.1

boys. Verbal behaviors seemed to develop differently in the two sexes. Early verbal items were usually delayed in boys but not in girls. Later verbal behavior, requiring expressive language, was considerably delayed in both sexes, though less so in girls.

Next, children without and with mild congenital heart disease were compared with children who had moderate and severe cardiac problems, in order to measure the anticipated additional deficit imposed by the latter handicap. Table V shows that differences between the two groups were statistically significant by t-test at 12, 18, 24, and 36 months on the Motor Scale, and only at 12 months on the Mental Scale. The deficit rises from less than one month to nearly four months on the Motor Scale, and from less than one month to about 2½ months on the Mental Scale. Because of the heavy emphasis on walking behaviors on the Motor Scale, this probably means that children with moderate and severe cardiac problems are walking significantly later than those children without and with only mild congenital heart disease (see also chapters on Neurological Investigations and Motor Development).

The children were then separated into two groups on the basis of their muscle-tone ratings. Children with moderate and severe congenital heart disease were excluded from this analysis (Table VI). On a one-way analysis of variance, all differences between means on both scales were significant at the .05 level or less, beginning at the 12 months' assessment. While only a .3 month difference was evident at six months on the Mental Scale, the degree of difference increased until by 36 months there was a 3.7 months difference. Similarly, on the Motor Scale the initial difference was .9 month, but this progressively increased to 4.2 months at 36 months. Correlations between Bayley scores and muscle-tone scores rose from .26 at 6 months to about .5 at 30 to 36 months of age.

Table VII presents data on developmental age scores from the Bayley Scales of Infant Development comparing children according to their parents' ability to follow through on provided guidance. Children with moderate and severe congenital heart disease again were excluded from the comparison. Differences are apparent at 6 months (a .3 to .6 month difference), and grow progressively larger until 36 months when the group with "good" parental follow-through shows a five months' advantage on the Mental Scale and about a 3½

TABLE V

COMPARISON OF DEVELOPMENTAL AGE SCORES ON THE BAYLEY SCALES OF INFANT DEVELOPMENT
AT SIX MONTH INTERVALS FOR CHILDREN WITH DOWN SYNDROME ACCORDING TO CARDIAC STATUS

Mental Scale

Age in months	Children without and with mild congenital heart disease			Children with moderate and severe congenital heart disease				Level of Significance
	Developmental Age (months)			Developmental Age (months)				
	N	Mean	S.D.	N	Mean	S.D.	t	P
6	67	3.3	1.1	14	3.5	.7	.67	N.S.
12	70	6.9	1.7	15	5.8	.13	2.40	<.05
18	64	10.7	3.0	11	9.5	1.6	1.54	N.S.
24	65	13.9	2.6	15	12.5	2.1	1.95	N.S.
30	66	16.8	3.0	14	16.0	2.5	.97	N.S.
36	61	21.1	4.7	14	18.6	2.6	1.89	N.S.

Motor Scale

Age in months	Children without and with mild congenital heart disease			Children with moderate and severe congenital heart disease				Level Significance
	Developmental Age (months)			Developmental Age (months)				
	N	Mean	S.D.	N	Mean	S.D.	t	P
6	67	4.0	1.2	14	3.7	1.4	.80	N.S.
12	69	7.4	1.6	14	5.9	.8	3.37	<.01
18	64	10.7	2.7	11	8.7	1.3	2.37	<.05
24	63	13.8	3.2	15	10.3	2.4	3.89	<.001
30	66	17.0	4.3	14	14.6	4.3	1.89	N.S.
36	48	19.8	4.9	13	15.9	4.8	2.51	<.05

TABLE VI

COMPARISON OF DEVELOPMENTAL AGE SCORES ON THE BAYLEY SCALES OF INFANT DEVELOPMENT
AT SIX MONTH INTERVALS FOR CHILDREN WITH DOWN SYNDROME ACCORDING TO MUSCLE TONE

Mental Scale

	"Poor" Muscle Tone			"Good" Muscle Tone		
Age in	Developmental Age (months)			Developmental Age (months)		
months	N	Mean	S.D.	N	Mean	S.D.
6	12	3.4	1.0	20	3.7	1.1
12	12	6.3	1.6	20	7.7	1.5
18	12	9.6	2.6	20	11.2	1.8
24	11	12.9	2.8	20	14.3	2.5
30	12	15.0	2.4	19	17.9	2.4
36	11	19.2	3.7	18	22.9	4.9

Motor Scale

	"Poor" Muscle Tone			"Good" Muscle Tone		
Age in	Developmental Age (months)			Developmental Age (months)		
months	N	Mean	S.D.	N	Mean	S.D.
6	10	3.6	1.3	20	4.5	1.0
12	11	7.0	1.6	20	8.0	1.4
18	12	9.4	1.8	20	11.9	2.1
24	11	11.6	3.3	20	15.4	2.5
30	12	14.1	4.5	19	19.5	4.0
36	11	18.7	6.4	11	22.9	3.0

TABLE VII

COMPARISON OF DEVELOPMENTAL AGE SCORES ON THE BAYLEY SCALES OF INFANT DEVELOPMENT
AT SIX MONTH INTERVALS FOR CHILDREN WITH DOWN SYNDROME ACCORDING TO PARENTAL FOLLOW-THROUGH

Mental Scale

Age in months	Adequate Follow-Through Developmental Age (months)			Inadequate Follow-Through Developmental Age (months)		
	N	Mean	S.D.	N	Mean	S.D.
6	42	3.4	1.3	25	3.1	.8
12	43	7.5	1.7	27	6.0	1.3
18	40	11.6	2.1	24	9.2	1.7
24	40	15.1	2.2	25	12.0	2.1
30	40	18.0	3.0	26	15.0	2.1
36	37	23.0	4.5	24	18.2	3.4

Motor Scale

Age in months	Adequate Follow-Through Developmental Age (months)			Inadequate Follow-Through Developmental Age (months)		
	N	Mean	S.D.	N	Mean	S.D.
6	42	4.2	1.0	25	3.6	1.2
12	43	8.0	1.5	26	6.5	1.3
18	40	11.5	2.7	24	9.3	2.1
24	38	14.9	2.8	25	12.1	3.0
30	40	18.1	4.2	26	15.3	4.0
36	25	21.6	4.7	23	17.9	4.2

months' advantage on the Motor Scale. Using a one-way analysis of variance, all differences are statistically significant (p .05 to .001) at all ages for both scales. The association between good performance and parental follow-through was also apparent in correlations between Bayley Scale and follow-through scores which rose from .14 at 6 months to .50 at 36 months, with a high of .58 at 24 months.

DISCUSSION

Our data from the Bayley Scales of Infant Development call into question some previous findings by other researchers, as we took into consideration a number of factors that influence cognitive and motor development of children with Down syndrome. Most of the analyses of our results display some of the variability inherent in Down syndrome.

The data for the total group of children with Down syndrome demonstrate a rather linear development on the Mental Scale, while on the Motor Scale some deceleration was observed. The biases of the Motor Scale in its item content leaning heavily on sitting and walking skills to the exclusion of other motor skills has been discussed above.

The correlations between the Mental and Motor Scales appear to indicate a stronger relationship between the two scales for children with Down syndrome than for normal children. The hypotonia observed in children with Down syndrome may have contributed to this effect. With advancing age of the child, each scale becomes increasingly better at predicting future scores on that scale, demonstrating better reliability of the scale and of the children's performance. The Mental Scale at 36 months displays good correspondence with other related measures such as the Receptive-Expressive Emergent Language Scale as well as self-help and socialization skills from the Vineland Social Maturity Scale, emphasizing its usefulness in predicting functionally important behavior for children with Down syndrome.

While the difference between the means of the adequate and the inadequate follow-through groups is large, the child with significant congenital heart disease appears to do the poorest on both scales. Adequate follow-through has the highest mean on the Mental Score at 36 months, followed by the variables of "good" muscle tone, sex (female), and cardiac status (no and mild congenital heart disease). For the Motor Scale, "good" muscle tone has the highest mean at 36 months, followed by adequate follow-through, no and mild congenital heart disease and sex (female). Muscle tone appears to give greater advantages on the Motor Scale. It is not clear whether the follow-through variable is related to parental characteristics that influence their follow-through behavior; the characteristics of the child having an impact on the parents; or a combination of both. Further research on this important variable is needed.

SUMMARY

The results of this part of the Down syndrome program indicate that the average child in this study functioned in the mildly retarded range during the three-year study period. There was no deceleration of mental functioning over time, while some decrease of the mean Developmental Quotients obtained from the Motor Scale of the Bayley Scales of Infant Development was observed. There was good intercorrelation of the Mental Scale with various measures obtained from other assessment instruments used in this study. Children with Down syndrome in this program performed better when they were of female gender, had no or only mild congenital heart disease, had "good" muscle tone, and their parents followed through adequately with provided guidance.

REFERENCES

1. Gesell, A. and Amatruda, C. *Developmental Diagnosis*. New York: Paul Hoeber, Inc. 1941.
2. Masland, R.L., Sarson, S.B. and Gladwin, T. *Mental Subnormality*. New York: Basic Books Inc. 1958.
3. Oster, J. *Mongolism*. Copenhagen: Danish Science Press Ltd. 1953.
4. Penrose, L.S. and Smith, G.F. *Down's Anomaly*. Boston: Little Brown & Company, 1966.
5. Dicks-Mireaux, M.J. Mental development of children with Down's syndrome. *American Journal of Mental Deficiency*, 77:26–32, 1972.

224   THE YOUNG CHILD WITH DOWN SYNDROME

6. Dameron, L.E. Development of intelligence of infants with mongolism. *Child Development*, 34:733–738, 1963.

7. Corri, J. *Young Children with Down Syndrome.* Boston: Buttersworth, 1975.

8. Lodge, A.L. and Kleinfield, P.B. Early behavioral development in Down's syndrome. In *Serotonin in Down's Syndrome,* Coleman, M. (Ed.) New York: American Elsevier Publishing Company, 1973.

9. Share, J., Webb, A. and Koch, R. A preliminary investigation of the early developmental status of mongoloid infants. *American Journal of Mental Deficiency*, 66:238, 1961.

10. Koch, R., Share, J. and Webb, A. The predictability of Gesell developmental scales in mongolism. *Journal of Pediatrics*, 62:93–97, 1963.

11. Share, J., Koch, R., Webb, A., and Graliker, B. The longitudinal development of infants and young children with Down's syndrome (mongolism). *American Journal of Mental Deficiency*, 68:685, 1964.

12. Fishler, K., Share, J. and Koch, R. Adaptation of Gesell Developmental Scales for evaluation of development in children with Down's syndrome (mongolism). *American Journal of Mental Deficiency*, 68:642, 1964.

13. Carr, J. Mental and motor development in young mongol children. *Journal of Mental Deficiency Research*, 14:205–220, 1970.

14. Cornwell, A.C. and Birch, H.G. Psychological and social development in home reared children with Down's syndrome. *American Journal of Mental Deficiency*, 74:341–350, 1969.

15. Wallin, J. Mongolism among school children. *American Journal of Orthopsychiatry*, 14:104, 1949.

16. LaVeck, B. and LaVeck, G.D. Sex differences in development among young children with Down's syndrome. *Journal of Pediatrics*, 91:767–769, 1977.

17. Melyn, M.A. and White, D.T. Mental and developmental milestones of non-institutionalized Down's syndrome children. *Pediatrics*, 52:542–545, 1972.

18. Fraser, F.C. and Sadovnick, N. Correlation of IQ in subjects with Down syndrome and their parents and sibs. *Journal of Mental Deficiency Research*, 20:179–182, 1976.

19. Baumeister, A.A. and Williams, Jr. Relationship of physical stigmata to intellectual functioning in mongolism. *American Journal of Mental Deficiency*, 71:586, 1967.

20. Domino, G. and Newman, D. Relationship of physical stigmata to intellectual subnormality in mongoloids. *American Journal of Mental Deficiency*, 69:541, 1965.

21. Centerwall, S.A. and Centerwall, W.R. A study of children with mongolism reared in the home compared to those reared away from home. *Pediatrics*, 25:678–685, 1960.

22. Kugel, R.B. and Reque, D. A comparison of mongoloid children. *Journal of American Medical Association*, 175:959–961, 1961.

23. Stedman, D.J. and Eichorn, D. A comparison of growth and development of institutionalized and home reared mongoloids during infancy and early development. *American Journal of Mental Deficiency*, 69:391–401, 1965.

24. Shotwell, A.M. and Shipe, D. Effects of out-of-home care on the intellectual and social development of mongoloid children. *American Journal of Mental Deficiency*, 68:693–699, 1964.

25. Shipe, D. and Shotwell, A.M. Effects of out-of-home care on mongoloid children: a continuation study. *American Journal of Mental Deficiency*, 69:649–652, 1965.

26. Bayley, N., Rhodes, L. and Gooch, B. Environmental factors in the development of institutionalized children. In *Exceptional Infant*: Vol. 2: Studies in Abnormalities. J. Hellmuth, ed. New York: Brunner/Mazel, 1971.

27. Canal, T. *A follow-up of assessment project of a multidisciplinary intervention program for children with Down syndrome.* Doctoral Dissertation. Cornell University, 1978.

28. Ludlow, J.R. and Allen L.M. The effect of early intervention and preschool stimulus on the development of Down syndrome children. *Journal of Mental Deficiency Research*, 23:29, 1979.

29. Sachs, E.S. *Trisomy G/Normal Mosaicism.* Leiden: H. E. Stenfert, 1971.

30. Gustavson, K.H. *Down's Syndrome: A Clinical and Cytogenetical Investigation.* Uppsala: Alonqvist & Wicksell, 1964.

31. Zellweger, H. and Abbo, G. Chromosomal mosaicism and mongolism. *The Lancet*, 1:829, 1963.

32. Rosecrans, C.J. The relationship of normal/21-trisomy mosaicism and intellectual development. *American Journal of Mental Deficiency*, 72:562, 1968.

33. Gibson, D. Karyotypic variation and behavior in Down's syndrome: methodological review. *American Journal of Mental Deficiency*, 78:128–133, 1973.

34. Bayley, N. *Bayley Scales of Infant Development*. New York: The Psychological Corporation, 1969.

35. Bayley, N. On the growth of intelligence. *American Psychologist*, 10:805–818, 1955.

36. Lenneberg, E. *Biological foundations of language*. New York: John Wiley and Sons, 1967.

37. Bilovsky, J.E. and Share, J. The ITPA and Down's syndrome: an exploratory study. *American Journal of Mental Deficiency*, 70:78–82, 1965.

38. Kirk, S.A. and Kirk, W.D. *Psycholinguistic learning disabilities—diagnosis and remediation*. Champaign-Urbana: Univ. of Illinois Press, 1971.

39. Evans, D. The development of language abilities in mongols: a correlational study. *Journal of Mental Deficiency Research*, 21:103, 1977.

40. Smith, G.F. and Berg, J.M. *Down's Anomaly*, 2nd Edition. Edinburgh, London and New York: Churchill Livingstone, 1976.

41. Cicchetti, D. and Stroufe, L.A. The relationship between affective and cognitive development in Down's syndrome infants. *Child Development*, 47:920–929, 1976.

42. Cowie, V. *A Study of Early Development of Mongols*. New York: Pergamon Press, 1970.

Chapter 8

SOCIAL DEVELOPMENT AND FEEDING MILESTONES*

Susan M. Cullen
Christine E. Cronk
Siegfried M. Pueschel
Richard R. Schnell
Robert B. Reed

INTRODUCTION

Although a few studies have reported the early development of children with Down syndrome, most have been based upon cross-sectional studies of institutionalized populations (1-3). During the past decades, three principal observations have been made with regard to the social development of the young child with Down syndrome. First, both social and intellectual functioning of home-reared children with Down syndrome have been noted to be superior to those of institutionalized children with this chromosomal disorder

*Part of this paper was published in the American Journal of Mental Deficiency, 1981, Volume 85, pages 410-415 under the title *Social Development of Young Down Syndrome Children* (copyright American Association of Mental Deficiency). Permission to reproduce obtained from publisher.

(4-9). Second, social development as reflected in social-age equivalents appears to be higher than cognitive functioning in children with Down syndrome (10, 11). Third, while an age-related decline in social age has been demonstrated in several studies, it is less than the decline observed in mental age (12-14).

Feeding problems and delay of feeding milestones in children with Down syndrome have been described in only a few studies (15, 16). Calvert found that 43 to 53% of her sample had difficulties in the use of utensils and chewing of table food. Fifteen percent of parents reported problems with regurgitation, sucking, and drinking from a cup (15). Palmer noted poor sucking and swallowing in early infancy, drooling, persistent tongue protrusion, and difficulties in chewing (16). Neither of these studies documented feeding milestones in children with Down syndrome or explored the relationship of feeding difficulties to other physiological or developmental variables.

METHODS

The nursing component in the Down syndrome program focused primarily on two study elements: documentation of social development and recording of feeding milestones. The Vineland Social Maturity Scale was used in the evaluation of social competence (17). The parents were interviewed at six-month intervals concerning the child's social development, including self-help skills, communication, locomotion, and socialization. Since the Vineland Social Maturity Scale does not provide a detailed description of developmental feeding milestones, a selected subset of feeding milestones including gumming, chewing, bottle-holding, finger-feeding, grasping of spoon, holding the cup, bringing the cup to the mouth, independent cup use, bringing the spoon to the mouth, independent spoon use, and weaning from a bottle was chosen for assessment. (18,19,20). A reliability score based on a comparison between the examiner's observation of the child's behavior during clinic visits and parental report on the Vineland Social Maturity Scale and developmental feeding milestones was formulated for evaluations at 6, 12, 18, 24, 30, and 36 months.

In conjunction with these assessments, specific suggestions and techniques for encouraging feeding development were offered to parents. Parental follow-through on this advice was rated on a dichotomous scale. Since no significant change in the ratings occurred throughout the study period, only one score was assigned to each family for the entire course of the study. This rating was used as an index of the parental ability to follow through with furnished guidance (see also Part II of this monograph).

During the nurse's contact with each family at six-month intervals, the child's day-to-day care and management at home were discussed, parent-child interaction was observed, and the child's feeding behavior was recorded. The parents often required assistance concerning their child's feeding problems and were offered guidelines for feeding readiness. Throughout the study period the need and importance of a firm and consistent approach to the overall management of the child was stressed.

The muscle tone of the children was recorded by three participating investigators including the pediatrician, neurologist, and physical therapist (for details on muscle tone see Part I and Part II of this monograph). The pediatrician and neurologist used simple ordinal scales for rating muscle tone, while the physical therapist employed a composite score based on four ordinal ratings of muscle tone in various parts of the body. The muscle tone ratings were factor-analyzed, and the factor scores were used to assign children to one of the two groups: one group included infants with "good" muscle tone and in the other group were infants with "poor" muscle tone. The Bayley Scales of Infant Development were administered semi-annually by two psychologists (see chapter on Psychomotor Development).

Standard descriptive statistics and t-tests were used for most of the comparisons. Linear contrasts as described by Snedecor and Cochran were employed, which allowed more specific segregation of effects of multiple independent variables and the detection of their interactions (22). Pearson product moment-correlation coefficients were computed and used to examine relationships among the outcome variables.

RESULTS

Social Development

In Table I the mean Vineland Social Maturity Scale raw scores from children with Down syndrome are contrasted with the reference data given by Doll (17). At 6 months the mean for children with Down syndrome is 84% of that of the reference population. This mean score falls to about 70% of that for the reference population by 24 to 36 months. This decline, however, is not statistically significant.

Four variables were examined for potential influence on the Vineland Social Maturity Scale scores: sex, cardiac status, parental follow-through, and muscle tone. Sex comparisons indicated that girls scored an average 4.6% (range 1 to 9%) higher at all ages. Yet the difference between the sexes was not statistically significant by t-test.

The mean scores from the Vineland Social Maturity Scale assessments of children without and with only mild congenial heart disease were compared with those scores of children with moderate and severe congenital heart disease (Table II). While the mean scores

Table I

Vineland Social Maturity Scale Raw Scores for Children With Down Syndrome
Obtained In Comparison To Standard Scores At Six Month Intervals

| | Down Syndrome | | | Standard Scores | |
Age in months	N	Mean	Standard Deviation	Mean (Doll 1965)	Mean for Down Syndrome %of standard
6	85	6.7	1.1	8	84
12	81	13.3	2.6	17	78
18	67	18.3	3.4	27	68
24	77	23.1	4.0	33	70
30	71	27.8	4.5	40	69
36	74	32.1	5.0	44	73

TABLE II

MEAN AND STANDARD DEVIATIONS FROM VINELAND SOCIAL MATURITY SCALE ASSESSMENTS

OF YOUNG CHILDREN WITH DOWN SYNDROME ACCORDING TO CARDIAC STATUS

Age in Months	Group*	N	Mean (raw scores)	Standard Deviations	t	p
6	I	68	6.7	1.2	0.4	N.S
	II	17	6.5	0.6		
12	I	64	13.6	2.7	2.7	.01
	II	17	11.8	1.7		
18	I	56	18.8	3.5	2.5	.01
	II	11	16.0	2.3		
24	I	61	23.9	4.0	3.3	.01
	II	16	20.3	2.7		
30	I	56	28.6	4.5	3.0	.01
	II	15	24.8	3.2		
36	I	60	32.9	4.9	2.9	.01
	II	14	28.7	4.5		

*Group I - no or mild congenital heart disease
 Group II - moderate or severe congenital heart disease

at 6 months were nearly the same for both groups, by 12 months and thereafter, there was a statistically significant difference between the two groups. At 36 months there was a 4-point difference which is equivalent to a 3-month deficit in social maturity of children with moderate and severe congenital heart disease. In the analysis of the remaining control variables, children with moderate and severe congenital heart disease were excluded.

Statistically significant differences between the two follow-through groups were observed for all except the 6-month test scores (Table III). A 4-point advantage (3-months age equivalent) for children of parents who were able to follow through adequately was noted at the 36 months' evaluation.

TABLE III

MEANS AND STANDARD DEVIATIONS FROM VINELAND SOCIAL MATURITY SCALE

ASSESSMENTS OF YOUNG CHILDREN WITH DOWN SYNDROME ACCORDING

TO THEIR PARENTS' ABILITY TO FOLLOW-THROUGH WITH FURNISHED GUIDANCE

(children with moderate and severe congenital heart disease are excluded)

Age in Months	Group*	N	Mean	Standard Deviation	t	p
6	I	37	6.9	1.0	1.8	N.S
	II	31	6.4	1.3		
12	I	37	14.3	2.3	2.4	.01
	II	27	12.8	2.9		
18	I	32	19.9	2.9	3.1	.001
	II	24	17.2	3.6		
24	I	35	25.5	2.9	3.5	.001
	II	26	21.7	4.3		
30	I	30	30.5	3.7	3.9	.001
	II	26	26.3	4.3		
36	I	34	34.4	4.1	3.1	.001
	II	26	30.8	5.0		

*Group I - Adequate parental follow-through.
Group II - Inadequate parental follow-through.

When the two muscle-tone groups were compared, the Vineland Social Maturity Scale scores for the "good" muscle-tone group were statistically significantly higher (at the 5% confidence level) than those of the "poor" muscle-tone group at 12, 18, 24, 30, and 36 months' assessments (Table IV).

Because the follow-through and the muscle-tone variables were observed to have a significant correlation (.4) a series of linear contrasts was carried out. However, no significant interaction effects were found. Figure 1 presents a summary statement of the assessments on the Vineland Social Maturity Scale. Raw scores obtained from these evaluations were converted into percentages of

TABLE IV

MEANS AND STANDARD DEVIATIONS FROM VINELAND SOCIAL MATURITY SCALE
ASSESSMENTS ACCORDING TO MUSCLE TONE RATINGS EXCLUDING DOWN SYNDROME CHILDREN
WITH MODERATE AND SEVERE CONGENITAL HEART DISEASE

Age in months	Group*	N	Mean	Standard Deviations	t	p
6	I	25	6.2	1.5	1.0	N.S
	II	43	6.9	1.5		
12	I	22	12.5	2.8	2.6	.02
	II	42	14.3	2.2		
18	I	21	17.1	3.2	3.1	.01
	II	35	19.7	2.8		
24	I	22	21.4	3.7	5.8	.001
	II	39	25.3	2.9		
30	I	20	26.6	4.2	3.0	.01
	II	35	29.9	3.4		
36	I	22	30.2	4.6	3.6	.001
	II	38	34.4	4.0		

*Group I - children with "poor" muscle tone
Group II - children with "good" muscle tone

normal standards and plotted according to age. Children without and with only mild congenital heart disease whose parents "followed through" on furnished guidance performed markedly better on the Vineland Social Maturity Scale than children without and with only mild congenital heart disease whose parents did not follow through with the guidance offered. Those children with moderate and severe congenital heart disease obtained the lowest scores on the Vineland Social Maturity Scale assessments regardless of the follow through category. In all categories the mean scores decreased from 6 to 18 months, while in the remaining study period a slight increase of the mean scores was observed.

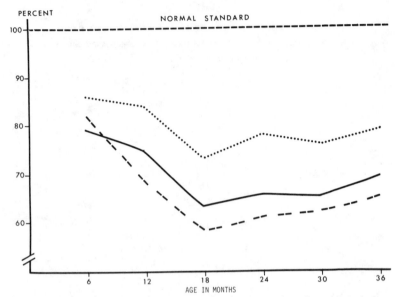

Figure 1 - Mean Vineland Social Maturity Scale raw scores expressed in % of agerage standard scores at six-months intervals

.... Children without or with mild congenital heart disease whose parents followed through adequately.

————— Children without or with mild congenital heart disease whose parents did not follow through with furnished guidance.

— — — Children with moderate and severe congenital heart disease. (Because of the small number this group is not separated into "good" and "poor" follow-through subgroups.

Table V compares social age equivalents with mental age equivalent scores from the Bayley Scales of Infant Development (21). Social age is higher than the mental age at all age periods with a difference of about one month at the 6-months' assessments, and two to three months at the subsequent examinations.

Feeding Milestones

As Table VI demonstrates the developmental sequence of feeding milestones in children with Down syndrome is the same as in normal children (18,19,20,22), though the age of achievement of most feeding skills was delayed. The early feeding milestones were about 35% later than usually observed, while feeding milestones at 12

TABLE V

COMPARISON OF SOCIAL AGE (VINELAND SOCIAL MATURITY SCALE) AND MENTAL AGE (BAYLEY
SCALES OF INFANT DEVELOPMENT) IN DOWN SYNDROME CHILDREN EXCLUDING THOSE WITH
MODERATE AND SEVERE CONGENITAL HEART DISEASE

Age in months	Vineland Social Maturity Scale Social Age	Bayley Scales of Infant Development Mental age	Difference between Social Age and Mental Age
6	4.3	3.3	1.0
12	10.0	6.9	3.1
18	13.1	10.7	2.4
24	16.6	13.9	2.7
30	20.2	16.9	3.3
36	23.1	21.1	2.0

to 18 months were delayed by about 10%; after 18 months a delay of 20 to 30% was noted.

Feeding milestones were analyzed by sex, cardiac status, follow-through variable, and muscle-tone ratings. While girls were earlier in all feeding skills, the differences were usually less than two months and were not statistically significant (Table VI). Mean feeding milestones of children with moderate and severe congenital heart disease were more delayed than those of children without or with only mild congenital heart disease (Table VII). The differences between these two groups reached statistical significance for chewing, finger-feeding, and independent spoon use.

As observed above on the Vineland Social Maturity Scale assessments, children of parents who were able to follow through achieved feeding milestones significantly earlier (5% confidence level) than those children whose parents were unable to follow through with provided guidance (Table VIII). Figure 2 contrasts mean ages and standard errors (± 2) of nine feeding milestones for the "good" follow-through group with those of the "inadequate" follow-through group.

TABLE VI

FEEDING MILESTONES ACCORDING TO SEX

(in months)

Feeding Milestones	Group*	N	Mean	Standard Deviation	t	p
Gumming	I	38	10.7	3.1	.1	N.S.
	II	32	10.6	4.5		
Chewing	I	39	11.2	4.3	.4	N.S.
	II	32	10.8	5.0		
Bottle Holding	I	39	14.2	11.1	1.4	N.S.
	II	30	11.0	6.7		
Finger Feeding	I	38	11.8	6.5	.7	N.S.
	II	32	10.9	4.3		
Grasping of Spoon	I	39	10.9	2.8	1.9	N.S.
	II	32	12.6	4.8		
Holding of Cup	I	40	16.2	6.1	.2	N.S.
	II	32	16.0	6.2		
Cup to Mouth	I	38	19.1	5.9	.2	N.S.
	II	32	18.9	7.1		
Spoon to Mouth	I	40	19.8	5.6	.9	N.S.
	II	32	18.5	6.9		
Independent Cup Use	I	38	26.3	7.0	.5	N.S.
	II	32	25.5	7.3		
Independent Spoon Use	I	38	27.0	6.2	.7	N.S.
	II	32	25.9	7.3		
Weaning	I	31	26.0	9.7	1.0	N.S.
	II	31	28.3	9.1		

*Group I -- Boys; Group II -- Girls

TABLE VII

FEEDING MILESTONES OF YOUNG CHILDREN WITH DOWN SYNDROME

ACCORDING TO CARDIAC STATUS

(in months)

Feeding Milestones	Group*	N	Mean	Standard Deviation	t	p
Gumming	I	70	10.7	3.8		
	II	17	12.4	4.6	1.5	N.S.
Chewing	I	70	11.0	4.7		
	II	17	16.3	9.1	3.3	.001
Finger Feeding	I	70	11.4	5.6		
	II	17	15.8	7.6	2.7	.01
Grasping of Spoon	I	71	11.7	4.0		
	II	17	12.1	4.1	0.4	N.S.
Holding of Cup	I	72	16.1	6.2		
	II	17	18.7	5.1	1.6	N.S.
Cup to mouth	I	72	17.7	6.3		
	II	16	20.2	6.1	1.5	N.S.
Spoon to mouth	I	70	19.0	6.5		
	II	17	22.2	4.8	1.9	N.S.
Independent Cup Use	I	70	25.9	7.2		
	II	16	28.1	7.0	1.1	N.S.
Independent Spoon Use	I	70	26.5	6.8		
	II	17	31.4	5.4	2.7	.01
Weaning	I	65	27.0	9.5		
	II	14	33.9	6.2	3.4	.001

*Group I -- mild or no congenital heart disease
 Group II -- moderate or severe congenital heart disease

TABLE VIII

FEEDING MILESTONES OF YOUNG CHILDREN WITH DOWN SYNDROME ACCORDING TO
THEIR PARENTS' ABILITY TO FOLLOW THROUGH UPON FURNISHED GUIDANCE IN MONTHS
(Children with moderate or severe congenital heart disease are excluded)

Feeding Milestones	Group*	N	Mean	Standard Deviation	t	p
Gumming	I	43	9.7	2.5	2.8	.01
	II	27	12.2	4.9		
Chewing	I	43	9.6	2.9	3.3	.001
	II	28	13.2	5.9		
Finger Feeding	I	43	9.2	2.3	4.4	.001
	II	27	14.5	7.1		
Grasping of Spoon	I	43	10.3	2.6	4.1	.001
	II	28	13.8	5.0		
Holding of Cup	I	43	14.2	5.6	3.4	.001
	II	29	18.9	5.9		
Cup to Mouth	I	43	15.6	5.6	3.8	.001
	II	29	21.1	6.6		
Spoon to Mouth	I	42	17.1	5.7	3.3	.001
	II	27	22.2	7.0		
Independent Cup Use	I	43	15.6	5.6	2.7	.01
	II	29	21.4	6.6		
Independent Spoon Use	I	43	24.2	6.1	3.9	.001
	II	27	30.2	6.2		

* Group I -- adequate parental follow-through
  Group II -- inadequate parental follow-through

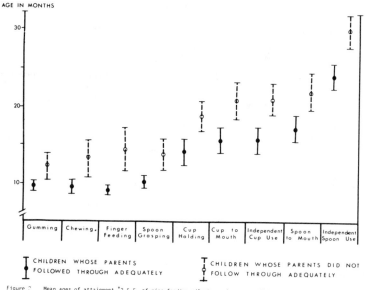

AGE IN MONTHS

| Gumming | Chewing. | Finger Feeding | Spoon Grasping | Cup Holding | Cup to Mouth | Independent Cup Use | Spoon to Mouth | Independent Spoon Use |

⊥ CHILDREN WHOSE PARENTS
● FOLLOWED THROUGH ADEQUATELY

⊥ CHILDREN WHOSE PARENTS DID NOT
φ FOLLOW THROUGH ADEQUATELY

Figure 2   Mean ages of attainment ±2 S.E. of nine feeding milestones in young children with Down syndrome according to their parents ability to follow through with furnished guidance.

The effect of muscle tone on the age of accomplishment of feeding skills was examined in the same way as the muscle-tone effects on the Vineland Social Maturity Scale scores. Significant differences were observed for chewing, finger-feeding, spoon-grasping, and independent spoon use (Table IX).

As with the Vineland Social Maturity Scale scores, no significant interaction effects of follow-through and muscle tone were noted for feeding milestones. Children accomplished independence in holding their bottle by 9 to 10 months. The distribution of this variable, however, was skewed to the right since eight children (seven boys, one girl) had not accomplished bottle holding by 36 months of age. All other children had achieved this milestone by 23 months of age. The mean age for weaning from breast or bottle was 27 months. Fourteen children accomplished this milestone by 15 months, which is the age of attainment for normal children; 35% of the children had not been weaned by the end of the study period at 36 months.

TABLE IX

FEEDING MILESTONES OF YOUNG CHILDREN WITH DOWN SYNDROME

ACCORDING TO MUSCLE TONE RATINGS IN MONTHS

(Children with moderate or severe congenital heart diseases are escluded)

Feeding Milestones	Group*	N	Mean	Standard Deviation	t	p
Gumming	I	24	11.6	5.0	1.5	N.S
	II	45	10.1	2.8		
Chewing	I	25	12.5	6.3	2.1	.05
	II	45	10.1	3.1		
Finger Feeding	I	24	13.8	7.2	3.0	.01
	II	44	9.8	3.7		
Grasping of Spoon	I	25	13.7	4.7	3.5	.01
	II	45	10.5	3.0		
Holding of Cup	I	26	17.2	5.9	1.2	N.S
	II	45	15.4	6.2		
Cup to Mouth	I	26	19.3	6.5	1.7	N.S
	II	45	16.6	6.0		
Spoon to Mouth	I	25	20.1	7.2	1.4	N.S
	II	44	18.1	5.7		
Independent Cup Use	I	26	26.7	8.2	0.8	N.S
	II	43	25.3	6.5		
Independent Spoon Use	I	25	29.1	7.2	2.5	0.2
	II	44	25.0	6.0		

*Group I – children with "poor" muscle tone
 Group II – children with "good" muscle tone

In order to provide more detailed information on the age of accomplishment of specific feeding skills, attainment curves were developed on six feeding milestones (Figures 3 and 4). These charts allow determination of the percentage of children who accomplished a

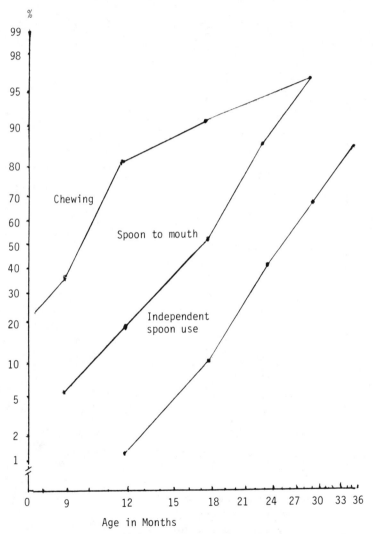

Figure 3: Attainment (%) of three feeding milestones

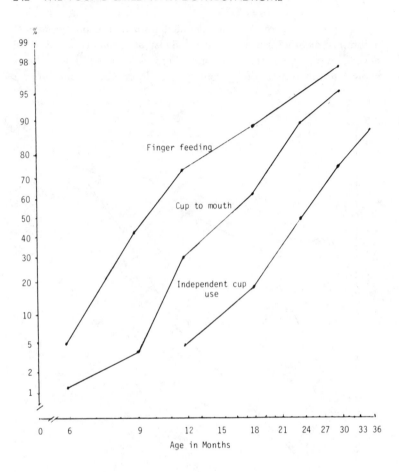

Figure 4: Attainment (%) of three feeding milestones according to age.

given feeding milestone at a certain age. An individual child's percentile position for a given feeding milestone can be located by finding the age at which the milestone was achieved, following this up to the curve for that feeding milestone and then proceeding horizontally to the left where the appropriate point on the percentile scale of the vertical axis can be identified. The charts may also be used as an aid to the assessment of the individual child's progress in feeding development relative to that typical of young children with Down syndrome.

Parental Management

Table X presents the result of a dichotomous rating (yes/no) according to parental management and cardiac status. Approximately 1/3 of parents whose children were in Group I (children

TABLE X

PARENTAL MANAGEMENT ACCORDING TO CARDIAC STATUS

Group *	Parents are firm and consistent			
	Yes		No	
I	26	(36%)	46	(63%)
II	3	(18%)	14	(82%)

	Parents are overprotective			
	Yes		No	
I	20	(28%)	52	(72%)
II	7	(41%)	10	(59%)

	Parents follow through adequately			
	Yes		No	
I	43	(60%)	29	(40%)
II	6	(35%)	11	(65%)

*Group I includes children without and with mild congenital heart disease.

Group II includes children with moderate and severe congenital heart disease.

without and with mild congenital heart disease) and only 1/6 of parents whose children were in Group II (children with moderate and severe congenital heart disease) were rated as being firm and consistent.

Twenty-eight percent of the parents whose children were in Group I, and even more parents (41%) whose children were in Group II, were considered to be overprotective. Table X indicates that parents of children in Group I have a higher compliance rate (60%) than those parents in Group II (35%). As noted, children with significant congenital heart disease were less likely to have firm and consistent parental management, their parents were more overprotective, and follow-through was often compromised.

Intercorrelations among management variables are presented in Table XI. Significant positive correlations were noted between adequate follow-through and firm and consistent management, as well as between permissiveness and overprotectiveness. Table XII shows the relationship between follow-through and parental management variables. The results indicate that those parents who were firm and consistent as well as those who were not overprotective displayed a greater ability to follow through on furnished guidance.

The relationships of the Vineland Social Maturity Scale scores, the feeding milestones, and parental-management variables were also analyzed. A Pearson product moment-correlation matrix is presented

TABLE XI

INTERCORRELATION OF MANAGEMENT VARIABLES

	Follow-through	Firm and Consistent	Overprotective	Permissive
Follow-through	1.00			
Firm and Consistent	.617	1.00		
Overprotective	-.397	-.402	1.00	
Permissive	-.636	-.971	.416	1.00

TABLE XII

PARENTAL MANAGEMENT VARIABLES IN RELATION TO THE PARENTS'

ABILITY TO FOLLOW THROUGH WITH FURNISHED GUIDANCE

Parents are firm and consistent

		Yes	No	t	P
Follow-through	Yes	26	17	53.2	< .01
	No	0	29		

Parents are overprotective

		Yes	No	t	P
Follow-through	Yes	7	36	7.03	< 0.01
	No	13	16		

in Table XIII. As noted in this table the strength of the relationships increases for all the variables with age, with the exception of holding the bottle. Correlations between permissiveness as well as firm and consistent parental management with all other variables approach .5. While overprotectiveness shows some correlation with all developmental variables, it is not as strong as with other parent-management variables.

Increased weight gain is often a problem in children with Down syndrome. Because it was of interest to assess whether parental management contributed to this problem, t-tests comparing ponderal index (weight/height^3) for children of parents with and without firm and consistent management were carried out (Table XIV). The ponderal indices at 12 and 24 months were similar when the group of parents who were rated as firm and consistent was compared with those parents who did not display such parental management qualities. However, a statistically significant difference between the latter two groups was apparent at 36 months. The relationship between parental management and ponderal index was also observed in a significant correlation (.321 p<.01) of ponderal index with firmness and consistency in handling the children.

TABLE XIII

INTERCORRELATIONS OF SELECTED VINELAND SOCIAL MATURITY SCALE SCORES, FEEDING MILESTONES,
AND BEHAVIOR MANAGEMENT VARIABLES

	Vineland at 6 months	Vineland at 12 months	Vineland at 24 months	Vineland at 36 months	Chewing	Finger feeding	Bottle holding
Vineland at 6 months	1.000						
Vineland at 12 months	0.494**	1.000					
Vineland at 24 months	0.487**	0.599**	1.000				
Vineland at 36 months	0.298*	0.727**	0.749**	1.000			
Chewing	-0.423**	-0.590**	-0.507**	-0.640**	1.000		
Finger Feeding	-0.319**	-0.584**	-0.590**	-0.548**	0.565**	1.000	
Bottle Holding	-0.165	-0.416**	-0.211	-0.262	0.141	0.322*	1.000
Grasping of Spoon	-0.126	0.443**	-0.419**	-0.458**	0.484**	0.433**	0.195
Independent Spoon Use	-0.227	-0.434**	-0.655**	-0.610**	0.366*	0.285*	0.074
Independent Cup Use	-0.044	-0.417**	-0.564**	-0.467**	0.231*	0.358*	0.056
Firm and Consistent	-0.107	-0.429**	-0.450**	-0.547**	0.270*	0.269*	-0.029
Permissive	0.089	0.453**	0.498**	0.565**	-0.274*	-0.295*	0.008
Overprotective	0.182	0.183	0.381*	0.234	-0.161	-0.320*	0.036
Follow-through	-0.190	-0.365*	-0.443**	-0.453**	0.365**	0.487**	0.110

* $p < .05$

** $p < .01$

Grasping of Spoon	Independent Spoon Use	Independent Cup Use	Firm and Consistent	Permissive	Overprotective	Follow-through
1.000						
0.529**	1.000					
0.456**	0.535**	1.000				
0.358*	0.478**	0.378**	1.000			
-0.361*	-0.499**	-0.383**	-0.971	1.000		
-0.299	-0.420**	-0.409**	-0.402**	0.416**	1.000	
0.452**	0.456**	0.304**	0.617**	-0.636**	-0.313	1.000

TABLE XIV

PONDERAL INDICES ACCORDING TO PARENTAL MANAGEMENT

EXCLUDING CHILDREN WITH MODERATE AND SEVERE CONGENITAL HEART DISEASE

Group*	Age in Months	N	Mean	Standard Deviations	t	p
I	12	23	231	20	.007	N.S.
II	12	46	231	22		
I	24	25	196	29	.459	N.S.
II	24	42	199	26		
I	36	22	176	10	2.286	.025
II	36	44	188	25		

*Group I includes parents who were firm and consistent.

Group II includes parents who were not firm and consistent.

Interrelationships

Correlations between the Vineland Social Maturity Social Scale scores at 12 and 24 months as well as the age of attainment of feeding milestones achieved near these ages were all significant at the .001 level of confidence. Correlations between 12-month Vineland Social Maturity Scale scores and early feeding milestones (gumming, chewing, finger-feeding, and spoon-grasping) were near .5, while the later achieved milestones (independent spoon use and independent cup use) had an average correlation with Vineland Social Maturity Scale scores at 24 months of .6. Correlations between the Vineland Social Maturity Scale scores and feeding milestones were frequently higher than those among the feeding milestones.

DISCUSSION

The results of these investigations indicate that social and feeding competencies in young children with Down syndrome develop more slowly than in normal children (20,22). The slight decline of Vineland Social Maturity Scale scores during the first 18 months of life resembles that of previously reported observations for both social and cognitive development of children with Down syndrome (11,14). Because of the nature of standard tests during infancy, and the optimism expressed in the parents' initial reporting, it is questionable whether the decline of Vineland Social Maturity Scale scores represents a real downward trend.

Since children with moderate and severe congenital heart disease were often in cardiac failure, frequently were hospitalized for cardiac studies and/or significant respiratory infection, and had a slow growth rate, it is not surprising that their scores were lower on the Vineland Social Maturity Scale and that most of their feeding milestones were achieved later than children without or with only mild heart defects.

The significance of the increased function associated with good parental follow-through on both the Vineland Social Maturity Scale and feeding milestones is uncertain. It was noted that the number of children with good muscle tone and those without significant congenital heart disease was greater in the group whose parents were able to follow through with furnished guidance, suggesting an interaction effect of certain biological variables with follow-through. However, linear contrasts demonstrated that parental follow-through had effects independent of muscle tone and cardiac status indicating that the quality of parental follow-through fosters learning of self-help skills.

The difference in delay for early, middle and late feeding milestones is unexpected. The considerable delay in the two earliest feeding skills probably relates to their dependence upon intact oromuscular development and good muscle tone. Grasping of cup and spoon are simple single-step processes that may be learned easily. Finger-feeding, while involving several steps, builds upon skills already well established in the behavioral repertoire at its initiation. In contrast, the later four more complex skills involve good coordination of several multiple-step skills requiring higher cognitive function. Considerable delay of accomplishment of these skills was identified in our children with Down syndrome.

The high correlations between feeding milestones and Vineland Social Maturity Scale scores indicate that a significant proportion of their variance is shared in common. The higher correlations of the later milestones with the Vineland Social Maturity Scale scores, as contrasted with the relatively modest correlations between early and later feeding milestones with the scores from the Vineland Social Maturity Scales, probably reflect the more complicated character of underlying competencies during the third year of life.

The age of achievement for feeding skills offers one comparison with normal developmental progress; yet it should be noted that there are also qualitative differences in feeding skills in children with Down syndrome when compared with normal children. It is assumed that these differences are attributable to the anatomic and functional deficits seen in many children with Down syndrome.

While the development of most of the feeding skills was slow in the majority of children, independent bottle feeding and weaning from the bottle were particularly delayed. Since the children's progress in motor development would have made such activities possible, other factors must have prevented many of the children from achieving these two feeding milestones.

SUMMARY

Since early social and feeding experiences can provide a foundation for the development of positive personal relationships, this component of the Down syndrome program was of particular importance. Longitudinal follow-up of social development of the children with Down syndrome demonstrated an average social quotient of 84 at 6 months, falling to 63 by 36 months. Feeding milestones were delayed by about 2 months in the first year, and by 3 1/2 months in the second and third years. Independence in bottle holding and complete weaning were significantly more delayed, while finger-feeding and spoon-grasping were relatively more advanced.

In the assessment of the data four variables including sex, cardiac status, parental follow-through, and muscle tone were examined for potential influence on the Vineland Social Maturity Scale scores and on a selected subset of feeding milestones. While there was no significant difference between boys and girls, the analysis of the data revealed that young children with Down syndrome attain significantly higher scores on the Vineland Social Maturity Scale and achieve most feeding milestones earlier when they have no or only mild congenital heart disease, their parents follow through appropriately with furnished guidance, and the children exhibit "good" muscle tone.

REFERENCES

1. Brousseau, K. and Brainerd, H. *Mongolism: A Study of Physical and Mental Characteristics of Mongolian Imbeciles.* Baltimore: The William and Wilkins Company, 1928.
2. Benda, C.E. *The Child with Mongolism.* New York: Grune and Stratton, 1960.
3. Oster, J. *Mongolism.* Copenhagen: Danish Science Press, 1953.
4. Centerwall, S.A. and Centerwall, W.R. A study of children with mongolism reared in the home compared to those reared away from home. *Pediatrics*, 25:678–685, 1960.
5. Stedman, D.J. and Eichorn, D.H. A comparison of the growth and development of institutionalized and home-reared mongoloids during infancy and early childhood. *American Journal of Mental Deficiency*, 69:391, 1965.
6. Shotwell, A.M. and Shipe, D. Effect of out-of-home care on the intellectual and social development of mongoloid children. *American Journal of Mental Deficiency*, 68:693–699, 1964.
7. Shipe, D. and Shotwell, A.M. Effect of out-of-home care on mongoloid children. *American Journal of Mental Deficiency*, 69:649–652, 1965.
8. Kugel, R.B. and Reque,D. A comparison of mongoloid children. *Journal of the American Medical Association*, 175:959–96l, 1961.
9. Carr, J. Mental and motor development in young mongol children. *Journal of Mental Deficiency Research*, 14:205–220, 1970.
10. Quaytman, W. The psychological capacities of mongoloid children in a community clinic. *Quarterly Review of Pediatrics*, 8:255–267, 1953.
11. Cornwell, A.C. and Birch, H.G. Psychological and social development in the home-reared children with Down's syndrome. *American Journal of Mental Deficiency*, 74:341–350, 1969.

12. Masland, R.I., Sarason, S.B. and Gladwin, T. *Mental Subnormlity*. New York: Basic Books, 1958.

13. Share, J., Koch, R., Webb, A. et al. The longtitudinal development of infants and young children with Down's syndrome. *American Journal of Mental Deficiency*, 68:685–692, 1964.

14. Melyn, M.A. and White, D.T. Mental and developmental milestones of non-institutionalized Down's syndrome children. *Pediatrics*,52:542–545, 1973.

15. Calvert, S.D., Vivian, V.M. and Calvert, G.P. Dietary adequacy, feeding practices and eating behavior of children with Down's syndrome. *Journal of the American Dietetic Association*, 69:152–156, 1976.

16. Palmer, S. and Ekvall, S. Pediatric nutrition in developmental disorders. Springfield, Illinois: Charles C. Thomas, 1978.

17. Doll, E.A. *The measurement of social competence: A manual for the Vineland Social Maturity Scale*. Minneapolis: Educational Testing Bureau, 1953.

18. Gesell, A. and Ilg, F.L. *Feeding Behavior of Infants*. Philadelphia: J.B. Lippincott, 1937.

19. Gesell, A., Halverson, H.M., Ilg, F.L. et al. *The First Five Years of Life*. New York: Harper and Brothers, 1940.

20. Gesell, A. and Amatruda, CS. *Developmental Diagnosis*. New York: Harper and Row, 1975.

21. Bayley, N. *Bayley Scales of Infant Development*. New York: The Psychological Corporation, 1969.

22. Snedecor, G.W. and Cochran, W.G. *Statistical Methods*. Iowa: The Iowa State University Press, 1967.

Chapter 9

SPEECH AND LANGUAGE EVALUATION

Ann Z. Strominger
Mindy R. Winkler
Linda T. Cohen

INTRODUCTION

The nature of speech and language disorders in children with Down syndrome has been described in the literature (1-17). Since these data derive largely from studies of institutionalized populations, comparisons to home-reared children with Down syndrome must be made with caution. During the sixties several investigators compared cognitive functioning and social development of home-reared and institutionalized children with Down syndrome (18-21). More recent studies of institutionalized and noninstitutionalized retarded children have shown superior language skills in the latter group (22-24).

The present trend towards home care of children with Down syndrome has led to several investigations of the typography of speech in the children's homes. Comparisons of the early maternal linguistic environment of young children with Down syndrome and normal young children have yielded both similarities and differences (25–29). There is general agreement that mothers of children with Down syndrome typically use a shorter mean length of utterances for an extended period of time. Subsequent increases in the maternal mean length of utterances are associated with improvement in the child's use of expressive language (27,29). According to Lombardino (29) these findings suggest a need for changes in mothers' verbalizations "to better facilitate a range of communicative skills in their language-learning children."

Large individual differences in children with Down syndrome, particularly in the use of words and sentences, have been reported (15,30,31). A discrepancy between language comprehension and production abilities also has been noted, with receptive performance being superior to expressive language production (5).

In a controversial study, Lenneberg, Nichols, and Rosenberger concluded that the pattern of language development in children with Down syndrome is identical to that of normal youngsters, but that it proceeds at a slower rate of development, with the former being "more closely controlled by maturational factors than intellectual ability" (3). This finding is supported by Dooley's (32) and Coggins' (33) investigations of the use of two-word utterances by children with Down syndrome who appeared to be at Brown's Stage I of language development (34). These authors found that both normal children and youngsters with Down syndrome at Stage I language development coded similar semantic relations in their two-word utterances.

Thus, despite a large body of literature, there is a need for new information in this area of study that could enhance our understanding of the speech and language development of the young home-reared child with Down syndrome.

METHODS

The purpose of this component of the Down Syndrome Program was to gain knowledge regarding the communicative performance and the language development of young children with Down syndrome enrolled in this program. Parents of children with Down syndrome had participated in periodic educational sessions with a speech therapist who had discussed with parents aspects of speech and language development and had demonstrated language-stimulation techniques. At the third birthday, 81 of the 89 children underwent formal evaluations of their receptive and expressive language skills. Parents were asked to provide information on the age of speech onset, size of vocabulary, and the child's primary means of communication. A judgment regarding the age of speech onset was based upon the emergence of a first word or words used consistently as meaningful utterances. Data on vocabulary-size were gathered through vocabulary lists which were provided by parents. Primary means of communication was specified by the category which best described the child's method of communication: crying, pointing without vocalizing, pointing with vocalizing, gesturing with vocalizing, pointing and gesturing without vocalizing, pointing and gesturing with vocalizing, single words, two-word phrases, or three or more word phrases and sentences. In addition, the children's language development was assessed using the Bzoch-League Receptive-Expressive Emergent Language Scale (15,37,38). This is a developmental scale based upon a "predictive pattern of receptive and expressive language development during the first 36 months of life." Items are scaled at two-month intervals from birth to 12 months, at three-month intervals for ages 13 to 24 months, and four-month intervals from 25 to 36 months of age. Information gathered through parental interview yielded a receptive language age, an expressive language age, and a combined receptive-expressive language age.

RESULT AND DISCUSSION

Onset of Speech and Size of Vocabulary

The heterogeneity of the group of children with Down syndrome was demonstrated in descriptive analyses of such variables as age of speech onset and expressive vocabulary size. Parental recall of the age of speech onset ranged from 10 to 36 months, with two children uttering no single words by age three. The use of first words had been achieved by 85% of the subjects by 30 months of age.

Vocabularies ranged in size from one to 85 words with a mean vocabulary size of 18.5 words. The large standard deviation of 16.6 again reflects the high degree of variability within the population. Forty-three percent of the children were reported to have less than a ten-word vocabulary and 66% had vocabularies of less than 20 words at 36 months of age. Expressive vocabulary size in normal children of the same age is reported to range from 500 to 1500 words (39).

Modes of Communication

Parental ratings of the primary means of communication utilized by their children indicated that 69% of the children favored communicating by combining pointing and/or gesturing with vocalization. While 26% of the children communicated primarily through single-word usage, only one child used word combinations, and two children continued to communicate solely through crying.

Further investigation of the relationship between vocabulary size and primary means of communication showed that for those children who had acquired a vocabulary of 30 words or more, the odds were greater than 50% that communication would be solely through the use of single-word vocalizations. Below that level, the chances for verbal communication diminished, and above it they increased. Such factors as personality and communicative style must be considered when looking at individual results.

Although these findings generally support the existing literature describing the child with Down syndrome as one who favors manual communication, such description in disregard of expressive vocabulary level can be misleading (15,41). Our results suggest that an early language intervention program favoring strong use of natural gesture or American Sign Language in conjuction with expressive speech and language stimulation techniques may benefit the young child with Down syndrome in the early stages of expressive language production .

Receptive and Expressive Language Skills

Further descriptive analyses of our data were in agreement with previously cited studies reflecting a wide individual variation of linguistic performance within the Down syndrome population (30,

31). Receptive language skills in the 36-month-old children ranged in age from 5 to 30 months as measured by the Receptive-Expressive Emergent Language Scale. The mean receptive language age was 18.8 months (S.D. 5.2) or approximately half of the child's chronological age. Similar variations were reflected in expressive language abilities with a mean expressive language age of 16.5 months (S.D. 5.0) and a range from 4 to 34 months.

A significant positive correlation was found between receptive and expressive language skills (r = .78), with a mean difference of only two months (S.D. 3.3) between receptive-language age and expressive-language age. Although 61% of the subjects showed higher receptive than expressive language scores, 86% of these differences were less than 6 months. This finding may arise from an interaction of such independent variables as informed parents, rich linguistic environments and home rearing. Since home rearing itself has already been correlated with improved linguistic performance (18,20-24), it could be further hypothesized that the consistent interactions between a well-informed parent and a child with Down syndrome are particularly important in the early stages of language learning.

Correlates of Language Development

Assessments of the Receptive-Expressive Emergent Language Scale data by sex showed significantly higher mean achievements by the girls than by the boys (t = 1.87, p<.05). Similar male/female discrepancies were found during the evaluation of cognitive and social functionings, reported elsewhere in this monograph. This is of particular interest in light of recent reports of male/female discrepancies in the opposite direction in a population of children with specific language disabilities (40).

Not surprisingly, significant correlations were found between reported language levels on the Receptive-Expressive Emergent Language Scale and performances on the Bayley Scales for Infant Development (r = .79 for the girls; r = .55 for the boys).*

A multiple regression analysis of the data indicated a statistically significant relationship between measures of muscle tone and the

*See also chapters on Psychomotor Development and Interrelationships of Biological, Environmental and Competency Variables.

combined receptive-expressive language age (p<.05). That is, higher general muscle-tone ratings at ages 2 and 3 years were predictive of enhanced receptive-expressive language development at age 3. Similar relationships could not be established between either general muscle tone and oral muscle tone or oral muscle tone and receptive-expressive language performance. These results suggest the importance of sensory-motor maturational factors as precursors to speech and language development in children with Down syndrome (41).

SUMMARY

The analysis of speech and language data of 36-month-old children with Down syndrome revealed that there was great variability, particularly in age of speech onset and vocabulary size. The majority of the children favored a method of communication which incorporated pointing, gesture, and vocalization. Their receptive and expressive language functioning was at about the 18 months' level, or approximately ½ their chronological age. These levels of language functioning were considerably higher than previous reports had indicated. Performance levels of those children whose parents have been involved in educationally-oriented intervention programs, provide support for such an early intervention approach.

The children's cognitive functioning and their general muscle tone showed significant correlations with language skills at 36 months of age. Girls showed significantly better performances on both receptive and expressive language scales than boys.

Further research investigating the role of general muscle tone in speech and language development, particularly as it relates to early use of gestural representation, is needed to insure an appropriate intervention curriculum. In the interim, when intervention is through educating parents, emphasis must continue to be placed on the importance of the parental home linguistic environment and appropriate modifications within this environment.

REFERENCES

1. Strazzula, M. Speech problems of the Mongoloid child: *Quarterly Review of Pediatrics,* 8:268, 1953.

2. Schlanger, B. and Gottsleben, R.H. Analysis of speech defects among the institutionalized mentally retarded. *Training School Bulletin*, 54:5-8, 1957.

3. Lenneberg, E., Nichols, I. and Rosenberger, E. Primitive stages of language development in mongolism. In *Disorders of Communication*, D. McRioch and E. Weinstein (Eds.), Baltimore: Wilkins and Williams, 1964, pp. 119-137.

4. Share, J., Koch, R., Webb, A., and Graliker, B. The longitudinal development of infants and young children with Down's syndrome. *American Journal of Mental Deficiency*, 68:685-692, 1964.

5. Bilovsky, D. and Share, J. The ITPA and Down's syndrome: an exploratory study. *American Journal of Mental Deficiency*, 70:78-82, 1965.

6. McCarthy, J.M. *Patterns of psycholinguistic development of mongoloid and non-mongoloid severely retarded children.* Unpublished doctoral dissertation. Chicago: University of Illinois, 1965.

7. Zisk, P.K. and Bialer, I. Speech and language problems in mongolism: A review of the literature. *Journal of Speech and Hearing Disorders*, 32:228-241, 1967.

8. Greenough, D. *Comprehension and imitation of sentences by institutionalized trainable mentally retarded children as a function of transformational complexity.* Office of Education, Department of Health, Education, and Welfare, Washington, D.C., Bureau of Research, 1968.

9. Semmel, M.I. and Dolley, D.G. Comprehension and imitation of sentences by Down's syndrome children as a function of transformational complexity. *American Journal of Mental Deficiency*, 75:739-745, 1971.

10. Olovsky, L. A communication program for children with Down's syndrome. *Training School Bulletin*, 69:5-9, 1972.

11. Dodd, B.J., Comparison of babbling patterns in normal and Down syndrome infants. *Journal of Mental Deficiency Research*, 16:35-40, 1972.

12. Evans, D. Language development in mongols. *Special Education Forward Trends*, 1:23-25, 1974.

13. Cornwell, AC. Development of language, abstraction, and numerical concept formation in Down's syndrome children. *American Journal of Mental Deficiency*, 79:179-190, 1974.

14. Dodd, B. Recognition and reproduction of words by Down's syndrome and non-Down's syndrome retarded children. *American Journal of Mental Deficiency*, 80:306-311, 1975.

15. Cohen, L. *The infant and young child with Down syndrome: Speech and language development.* Paper presented at the meeting of the International Congress of the Association for Mental Deficiency, Washington, D.C., August, 1976.

16. Ikeda, Y. Speech and language development in Down's syndrome: Analysis of imitation. *Special Bulletin of Facts in Education,* 22:129-138, 1976.

17. Evans, D. The development of language abilities in mongols: A correlational study. *Journal of Mental Deficiency Research,* 21:103-117, 1977.

18. Centerwall, S.A. and Centerwall, W.R. A study of children with mongolism reared in the home compared to those reared away from the home. *Pediatrics,* 24:678-685, 1960.

19. Stedman, D.J., Eichorn, D.H., Griffin, J. and Gooch, B. *A comparative study of growth and developmental trends of institutionalized and non-institutionalized retarded children.* Paper presented at American Association of Mental Deficiency meeting, May, 1962.

20. Shotwell, A. and Shipe, D. Effect of out-of-home care on the intellectual and social development of mongoloid children. *American Journal of Mental Deficiency,* 68:693-699, 1964.

21. Cornwell, A.C., and Birch, H.G. Psychological and social development in home reared children with Down's syndrome. *American Journal of Mental Deficiency,* 74:341-350, 1969.

22. Lyle, J.G. Some factors affecting the speech development of imbecile children in an institution. *Child Psychology and Psychiatry,* 1:121-129, 1960.

23. Montague, J.C., Hutchinson, E.C. and Matson, E. A comparative computer content analysis of the verbal behavior of institutionalized and non-institutionalized retarded children. *Journal of Speech and Hearing Research,* 18:43-57, 1975.

24. McNutt, J.C. and Leri, S. Language differences between institutionalized and non-institutionalized retarded children. *American Journal of Mental Deficiency,* 84:39-45, 1979.

25. Show, C.E. Mothers' speech to children learning language. *Child Development,* 43:549-565, 1972.

26. Marshall, N.R., Hectrenes, J.R. and Goldstein, S. Verbal interactions: Mothers and their retarded children vs. mothers and their non-retarded children. *American Journal of Mental Deficiency,* 77:415-419, 1973.

27. Rondal, J. *Maternal speech to normal and Down's syndrome children matched for mean length of utterance.* Doctoral Dissertation, University of Minnesota. Ann Arbor, Michigan: University Microfilms, 1976.

28. Buckhalt, J., Rutherford, R. and Goldberg, K. Verbal and non-verbal interactions of mothers with their Down's syndrome and non-retarded infants. *American Journal of Mental Deficiency,* 82:334-343, 1978.

29. Lombardino, L. Maternal speech to normal and Down's syndrome children: A taxonomy and distribution. Paper presented at American Association for Mental Deficiency meeting, Miami, 1979.

30. Levinson, A., Friedman, A. and Stamps, F. Variability in mongolism. *Pediatrics,* 16:43-49, 1955.

31. LaVeck, B. and Brehm, S. Individual variability among children with Down syndrome. *Mental Retardation,* 2:135-137, 1978.

32. Dooley, J. *Language acquisition and Down's syndrome: A study in early semantics and syntax.* Unpublished doctoral dissertation, Harvard University, 1977.

33. Coggins, T. Relational meaning encoded in the two-word utterances of stage I Down's syndrome. *Journal of Speech and Hearing Research,* 22:166-178, 1979.

34. Brown, R. *A first language: the early stages.* Cambridge, Mass: Harvard University Press, 1973.

35. Dunn, L. *Peabody Picture Vocabulary Test,* American Guidance Service, Circle Pine, Minnesota, 1959.

36. Zimmerman, I., Steiner, V., and Evatt, R. *Preschool Language Scale,* Columbus: Merrill, 1969.

37. Bzoch, K. and League, R. *The Receptive-Expressive Emergent Language Scale for the Measurement of Language Skills in Infancy.* Gainesville, Florida: The Tree of Life Press, 1970.

38. Bzoch, K. and League, R. *Assessing Language Skills in Infancy.* Gainesville, Florida: The Tree of Life Press, 1972.

39. McCarthy, D. Language development in children. In *Manual of Child Psychology,* 2nd ed., L. Carmichael (Ed.). New York: Wiley, 1954.

40. Strominger, A. *Language delayed children at middle school age: A follow-up study.* Unpublished doctoral dissertation, Boston University, 1980.

41. Shane, H. Personal communication, 1979.

Chapter 10

NEUROLOGICAL INVESTIGATIONS

Liza Yessayan
Siegfried M. Pueschel

INTRODUCTION

Because of the rare occurrence of specific neurological complications in young children with Down syndrome, the neurologist's role has historically been that cf an occasional consultant, rather than of an active participant in the management of the child. Therefore, very few publications are available on clinical neurological aspects, especially those dealing with early neurodevelopmental issues in Down syndrome. To our knowledge, the only longitudinal study that dealt with neurological concerns in the infant with Down syndrome was published by Cowie (1). Otherwise, most of the neurological literature discusses Down syndrome in rather a collective and stereotypic manner (2).

METHODS

The neurological evaluation was designed to assess the standard, age-specific neurological function to study both the evolution and disappearance of primitive and postural reflexes, and to document the acquisition of various neuromotor skills in children with Down syndrome during the first 3 years of life.

All examinations were performed by the same pediatric neurologist (L.Y.) Each child was scheduled for a total of five evaluations during the three-year study period: in the newborn period and at 6, 12, 24, and 36 months of age. Whenever specific concern arose, or when complications such as a seizure disorder developed, the child was seen more often. Although not all children could be examined at each scheduled assessment, approximately ⅔ of them did undergo neurological evaluations at the specified time periods.

There were 66 variables listed in the neurology protocol. While some of the test items changed as the children grew older, the following variables were examined at each session: head circumference, head shape, cry, general motor activity, muscle tone, hyperflexibility of joints, deep tendon reflexes, ankle clonus, auditory response, ophthalmological function, and opticokinetic nystagmus.

During the newborn examination, primitive reflexes and muscle tone were assessed including Moro reflex, traction response, ventral suspension, arm and leg recoil, rooting and sucking, palmar and plantar grasp, placing, stepping, tonic neck reflex, and posture in prone and supine position.

At six months the above-mentioned reflexes were re-examined. In addition, the emergence of developmental milestones and various motor skills were studied. This included motor behavior in prone and supine, head control, rolling over, sitting posture, and hand manipulation.

At ages 1, 2 and 3 years, the children were screened for residual primitive reflexes. The neurological examination then concentrated primarily on observations of gross and fine motor skills, including sitting, crawling, standing, walking, going up and down stairs, running, and appearance of parachute response, as well as finger and hand manipulation.

Since neurology was one of the many disciplines involved in the developmental assessment of the children with Down syndrome, there was some overlap in observations made and data gathered, particularly with disciplines such as pediatrics, physical therapy, ophthalmology, speech and language, and psychology. For this reason not all information obtained from the neurological evaluations will be discussed here. Rather, this presentation will selectively focus on the infant's cry, muscle tone, certain reflex behaviors, ambulation, intercorrelations of specific biological and developmental variables, and seizure activity.

RESULTS AND DISSCUSSION

Cry

Very little is known about the nature of the cry pattern in infants with Down syndrome. Only on rare occasions it has been said that babies with Down syndrome seldom cry and usually have a weak cry (3). In our study we were impressed by the difference in the quality of the infant's cry. While 23 of the 68 newborns examined exhibited a reasonably normal lusty cry, 45 infants had an abnormal cry pattern. The abnormalities ranged from a feeble to a high-pitched cry. Most characteristic, however, was the sudden, explosive, shrill burst of the cry pattern, which was brief, with an almost abrupt cessation, followed by quiescence. Further investigations of structural changes of larynx and hypopharynx, potential neurological and muscular influences, as well as spectrographic voice analysis, should be pursued in order to gain a better understanding of the abnormal cry pattern observed in many infants with Down syndrome.

Muscle Tone*

Diminished muscle tone is the most characteristic neurological finding in the young child with Down syndrome. In fact, most authors have written about hypotonia as *the* neurological abnormality

*See Part II of this monograph for the effect of ''medications'' on muscle tone.

in the child with Down syndrome (3,4). Cowie noted that hypotonia was present in every infant in her study (1); likewise, Hall mentioned reduced muscle tone as a universal finding in his patients (3). McIntyre and coworkers reported that generalized hypotonia was present in 84 of the 86 patients in their series (5). Other investigators observed a lower incidence of hypotonia (6-9). Loesch-Mdzewska found that only 44% of children in the age group of birth to 9 years were hypotonic, while Levinson noted the prevalence of reduced muscle tone in Down syndrome to be 66% (8,9).

Since muscle tone cannot be objectively assessed, and additional factors such as the child's state of alertness, the time of feeding prior to the examination, irritability and crying modify muscle tone, accurate grading of muscle tone is a formidable task. We assessed the muscle tone in the children with Down syndrome using a set of specific clinical criteria, including resistance to passive movements, palpation of the muscle mass for consistency and resilience, and flapping of the distal segments. We rated muscle tone on a scale from 0 to 4 (0-extremely hypotonic, 1-moderately hypotonic, 2-mildly hypotonic, 3-normal muscle tone, and 4 hypertonic) separately in the upper extremities, lower extremities, neck and trunk.

Our results indicate that the muscle tone in the upper extremities rated slightly higher than that in the lower extremities, particularly during infancy. In further analysis of the muscle-tone data we used composite scores which included the different muscle-tone ratings obtained from assessments of upper and lower extremities, neck and trunk. Tables I and II present these muscle tone scores at yearly intervals according to sex and cardiac status respectively. As noted in both tables, the muscle tone in young children with Down syndrome improved gradually over time: most markedly, however, during the first year of life. There was no significant difference in muscle tone between boys and girls except at the 36 months' level ($p < .05$), when the girls displayed better muscle tone than boys (Table I). The reason for this difference is unknown.

As Table II demonstrates, children with moderate and severe congenital heart disease have a markedly reduced muscle tone during the first year of life, when compared with children who have no or only mild congenital heart disease. This difference was significant during the neonatal muscle-tone assessment ($p < .05$), and at the 12

TABLE I

COMPOSITE SCORES* OF MUSCLE TONE ´AT YEARLY INTERVALS
ACCORDING TO SEX

Age	Sex	N	Mean	SD	F	P
Newborn	female	29	1.6	0.84	0.24	NS
	male	39	1.5	0.70		
12 months	female	23	2.5	0.61	1.17	NS
	male	35	2.3	0.65		
24 months	female	25	2.8	0.28	0.45	NS
	male	37	2.7	0.33		
36 months	female	30	2.9	0.38	4.70	$< .05$
	male	46	2.6	0.52		

*Muscle tone was recorded as follows:

    0 - extremely hypotonic

    1 - moderately hypotonic

    2 - mildly hypotonic

    3 - normal muscle tone

    4 - hypertonic

months evaluation ($p < .01$). The difference of muscle tone in the subsequent years was less marked. This could be explained by the fact that some children with severe congenital heart disease had undergone corrective heart surgery, or that their cardiac status had improved considerably.

TABLE II

COMPOSITE SCORES* OF MUSCLE TONE AT YEARLY INTERVALS ACCORDING TO CARDIAC STATUS

Age	Cardiac Status**	N	Mean	SD	F	P
Newborn	Groups 1 and 2	57	1.6	0.78	4.24	<.05
	Groups 3 and 4	11	1.1	0.48		
12 months	Groups 1 and 2	51	2.4	0.62	5.91	<.01
	Groups 3 and 4	7	1.8	0.51		
24 months	Groups 1 and 2	50	2.8	0.32	1.89	NS
	Groups 3 and 4	12	2.6	0.25		
36 months	Groups 1 and 2	62	2.8	0.46	3.56	NS
	Groups 3 and 4	14	2.5	0.52		

*Muscle tone was recorded as follows:

0 - extremely hypotonic

1 - moderately hypotonic

2 - mildly hypotonic

3 - normal muscle tone

4 - hypertonic

**Cardiac status:

Groups 1 and 2 - includes children without and with mild congenital heart disease.

Groups 3 and 4 - includes children with moderate and severe congenital heart dis.

Traction Response

The traction response is obtained by grasping the infant's hands and drawing him/her from supine to a sitting position. The two important observations relative to the traction response involve head control and resistance of the arms to extension at the elbows. There is some controversy as to what duration and degree of head lag during the traction response should be considered normal in the full-term newborn (10). Most authors agree that a slight degree of head lag is acceptable up to 2 to 3 months of age.

As noted in Table III, the majority of newborns and almost one-third of the six months-old children demonstrated various degrees of head lag, while at 12 months only six children displayed poor head control. Similarly, the data concerning resistance of arms show that there is marked improvement in the traction response as the child matures.

Ventral Suspension (Landau Maneuver)

The Landau response is obtained by holding the prone infant aloft. In the normal infant this usually results in the elevation of the head above the horizontal level, extension of back muscles accompanied by some arching of the spine, and partial extension of the lower extremities; while maintaining some flexion posture of the arms.

Most of the newborns demonstrated a ventral suspension pattern that could be considered abnormal according to the above criteria. Eighty percent of children displayed a pathological Landau response, with the spine assuming a convex position and the head and extremities hanging down in a nearly inverted U fashion. Adequate Landau responses were seen in three newborn infants.

Moro Reflex

There are only a few investigations concerning the Moro reflex in infants with Down syndrome. In her monograph (1) Cowie described the Moro reflex in detail. Paulson mentioned that the Moro reflex usually is absent in the newborn with Down syndrome (11).

There are various methods that can be employed to elicit the Moro response. We used the "head drop" maneuver as described by Parmalee (12). Two main observations of the Moro response were recorded: the ease with which it was elicited, and the components of the motor act proper. Ordinarily, the Moro response consists of an initial extension followed by full flexion of both arms. In 61 of 67 children examined in the newborn period, the Moro reflex was obtained

TABLE III

TRACTION RESPONSE IN INFANTS WITH DOWN SYNDROME

Age	Complete head lag	Partial head lag	Brings head in line with body	Maintains head in line with body	Head is anterior to body	Arms fully extended no resistance	No resistance at shoulder slight resistance at elbow	Slight resistance at shoulder and elbow	Moderate resistance at shoulder and elbow	Normal elbow flexion and shoulder assistance
	N	N	N	N	N	N	N	N	N	N
Newborn	42	16	2	4	3	15	16	24	9	3
6 months	3	8	6	12	27	2	4	9	21	20
12 months	0	4	2	10	43	0	6	10	21	20

with ease. In four of the remaining six infants, the Moro reflex was elicited with difficulty, and in two newborns the Moro response could not be obtained. As to the quality of the motor components of the Moro reflex, none of the children had a completely normal Moro response. The best response was full extension of both arms, with only partial subsequent flexion observed in 31 (46.3%) of the 67 newborns examined. Thirty-two children (47.8%) exhibited an extension pattern only, without a flexion component. There were two infants who demonstrated slight arm movements with no consistent pattern, while two children, as noted above, had no Moro response whatsoever. The presence or absence of congenital heart disease did not seem to affect the Moro response. (see Table IV).

At the six months' evaluation, eight of the 57 children still had well-preserved reproducible Moro reflexes; four of these children exhibited partial flexion responses, while the remaining four had extension patterns only. Forty-one children (72%) displayed some residual reaction, mostly in the form of asymmetrical, partial, or incomplete extension patterns. In eight children, the Moro reflex had completely disappeared. At the 12 months' examination the Moro response could not be elicited in any of our children.

Tonic Neck Reflex

The tonic-neck reflex was tested in infants with Down syndrome during the newborn period, at 6 months, and in all nonambulatory children during subsequent scheduled examinations. Except for one infant during the initial assessment, an obligatory tonic-neck reflex was not observed in any of the children at any age level. The tonic-neck reflex that had been noted in this newborn infant was not present at his six months' evaluation.

Deep Tendon Reflexes

None of the children exhibited abnormally brisk or hyperactive deep tendon reflexes which would have suggested pyramidal tract involvement, and no persistent asymmetrical responses were observed. Data in Table V indicate that the patellar reflex gradually becomes less active with increasing age of the child.

TABLE IV

MORO REFLEX IN INFANTS WITH DOWN SYNDROME

Age	Cardiac status*	Normal response, full extension, full flexion N	Full extension, partial flexion N	Full extension, no flexion N	Some arm movements, inconsistent pattern N	No response N	Total N
Newborn	groups 1 and 2	0	5	6	0	0	67
	groups 3 and 4	0	26	26	2	2	
6 months	groups 1 and 2	0	1	0	8	2	57
	groups 3 and 4	0	3	4	33	6	
12 months	groups 1 and 2	0	0	0	1	6	59
	groups 3 and 4	0	0	0	1	51	

*Cardiac status: Groups 1 and 2 - children without and with mild congenital heart disease.

Groups 3 and 4 - children with moderate and severe congenital heart disease.

Ankle Clonus

Only three children in our cohort displayed unsustained ankle clonus. In one infant, ankle clonus was observed during the newborn examination, and in the other two children at the six-month assessment. No ankle clonus was noted in these children during subsequent evaluations.

Parachute Response

The parachute response ordinarily appears late during the first year of life. It consists of symmetrical extension of upper extremities with spreading of fingers elicited by a downward movement while the infant is held from the waist in prone position. Paine and coworkers reported that the appearance of the parachute response in form of an incomplete extension of the upper extremities was observed as early as 2 months in normal infants; by 9 months most of these infants showed some reaction, and the complete parachute response was present in all of the children by the age of 12 months (13).

The results of the parachute response observed in our population are presented in Table VI. Approximately ⅓ of the infants with

TABLE V

PATELLAR REFLEX ACTIVITY IN YOUNG CHILDREN WITH DOWN SYNDROME

Age	Type of Response			
	Normoactive	Hypoactive	Asymmetrical	Total
	N	N	N	N
Newborn	61	6	1	68
6 months	45	10	1	56
12 months	44	14	2	60
24 months	37	24	1	62
36 months	36	36	3	75

Down syndrome exhibited a complete parachute response at the age of 12 months, while in 37 children (62%) no reaction was noted. At 24 months only two children did not respond when we attempted to elicit the parachute reflex, while the majority of children performed normally. No asymmetrical parachute response was seen in any of the children examined.

Walking

Our grading system with respect to ambulation skills included five categories, from no weight bearing to independent walking with a narrow-based gait. Table VII shows the number of children at different age levels who achieved the respective ambulation skills in the categories listed. At 12 months, only two of the 59 children examined could walk short distances. At 24 months of age, about half of the children were walking independently, while ⅓ of them were not able to bear weight. At 36 months all but three children were ambulating.*

Walking Up and Down Stairs and Running

More advanced gross motor skills such as walking up and down stairs and running were examined at the 36 months' evaluation. Of a total of 76 children, 13 could not walk up or down stairs, 4 crawled on stairs, 57 walked up and down stairs with one hand holding on to the railing, and 2 children without holding on. Concerning the children's running skill, 43 children were not able to run, 22 children ran awkwardly and only 11 ran well.

Correlations of Neurodevelopmental Variables

During further analyses of our data we studied correlations of selected biomedical and behavioral variables. Table VIII presents the results of a correlation matrix which includes selected developmental milestones such as independent sitting at 12 months and 24 months; walking at 24 and 36 months; neurology assessments of muscle tone at birth, 12, 24, and 36 months: motor and mental development at 6 months; and motor and social development as well as intellectual functioning during the second and third years of life. It is of interest

TABLE VI

PARACHUTE RESPONSE IN YOUNG CHILDREN WITH DOWN SYNDROME

| Age | Parachute Response | | | Total |
| | Absent | Incomplete | Normal | |
	N	N	N	N
12 months	37	4	19	60
24 months	2	5	55	62

TABLE VII

AMBULATION SKILLS OF CHILDREN WITH DOWN SYNDROME

| Age | Does not bear weight | Walks with support | Walks alone, few steps | Walks alone, wide based | Walks alone, narrow based | Total |
	N	N	N	N	N	N
12 months	52	5	2	0	0	59
24 months	20	13	8	19	2	62
36 months	3	7	8	40	18	76

that with the exception of the initial muscle tone and sitting at 24 months, most of the correlations are highly significant, in particular, those involving walking, muscle tone at 12, 24 and 36 months, and the psychosocial variables. Moreover, the correlation coefficients of the psychosocial variables during the second and third years of life are all above .6. These data indicate that muscle tone and sitting at 12 months are good predictors of subsequent motor development. If the correlations of muscle tone and sitting at 12 months are combined to predict the motor and social development during the second and third years of life, the multiple correlation is only slightly increased (.680). Correlations between muscle tone at 24 months and walking at 24 months with the motor/social development during the second and third years of life, as measured on the Bayley Scales of Infant Devel-

*Similar data on independent walking are discussed in a slightly different form in the chapter on Motor Development.

opment and the Vineland Social Maturity Scales, are slightly higher than those with muscle tone and sitting at 12 months. When the two variables, muscle tone and walking at 24 months, are used together, the multiple correlation again rises only slightly to .787.

As expected, motor milestones such as sitting and walking are all highly associated with each other. It is well known that the child who accomplishes motor milestones, such as sitting, early in life usually will continue to progress at a similar rate of development and will stand and walk at a young age. In contrast, the child who has significant muscle weakness and is slow during the early stages of development may make only slow progress later.

Surprisingly, muscle tone scores obtained during the initial examination show no or very little correlation with sitting or walking and with later muscle tone assessments at 24 months; moreover, initial muscle tone is only moderately correlated with early developmental assessment; yet it shows a high correlation with later muscle tone at 36 months, as well as with motor/social and mental development during the second and third years of life. As noted in Table VIII, muscle tone examinations at 12 months are excellent predictors for sitting at 12 months, walking at 24 months, and motor/social development during the second and third years of life.

Seizures

It is generally assumed that seizures are infrequent in children with Down syndrome. Many previous publications on Down syndrome either did not mention seizures at all, or stated that epilepsy is rare (14,15). More recent reports estimate the frequency of seizures in Down syndrome including all ages to range from 2.6 to 8.8% (16-18). MacGillivray found the occurrence of grand mal seizures to be 8.1% in 102 patients with Down syndrome (17). In his study of 1154 institutionalized patients, Veall observed 5.8% of individuals with seizure disorders. He attributes the difficulty of determining the incidence of seizures in Down syndrome to the imprecise definition of the term "epilepsy," particularly by earlier authors, the small number of patients in certain studies, and the nondefining of the age groups under study (18). Veall included only those patients in his series who met rigid and specific criteria of clinical seizures. In determining the age-specific rates, the incidence was 1.9% for persons with Down syndrome under the age of 20 years, 6% between 20 and 55 years, and 12.2% over the age of 55 years. He raised the possibility of a relationship between Alzheimer disease and late onset of seizures (18). In her series of 128 children, Tangye observed eight patients with a seizure disorder. She followed her study population for six years, and during this time period five more patients developed seizures (19).

During the past decade there has been an increasing awareness of the high prevalence of seizures among individuals with Down syndrome. In addition, specific seizure forms such as infantile spasms have been discussed in the literature (20-23). Coriat and Fejerman reported 14 children who developed infantile spasms with hypsarrhythmic electroencephalographic changes among 1300 children with Down syndrome over an eight-year period (20). Coleman observed infantile spasms in 9 out of 60 patients with Down syndrome to whom had been administered 5-hydroxytryptophan (21). These patients showed reversal of symptoms when 5-hydroxytryptophan was discontinued or the dosage lowered. Among young children with Down syndrome Walcott and Chun found three with myoclonic seizures occuring spontaneously (22). Complete seizure control was achieved in two of the three children. These authors made the interesting observation that none of the patients showed developmental regression usually noted in chromosomally normal children with infantile spasms. Also, Pollack and coworkers described five children with Down syndrome who developed infantile spasms during their first year of life with concommitant hypsarrhythmic electroencephalograms (23). Three of their patients recovered completely with normalization of the electroencephalograms. In one of the remaining two children, there was no appreciable change, while in the other only partial control of seizures was achieved. None of their patients was treated with ACTH (23).

Of the 89 children in our study sample, five infants developed seizures when they were less than one year of age. Three of the five children displayed clinical features of infantile spasms, and had hypsarrhythmic electroencephalograms. The fourth child also had a hypsarrhythmic electroencephalogram, but clinically he presented with grand mal seizures. The fifth infant started with episodes of

TABLE VIII

INTERCORRELATIONS OF SELECTED NEURODEVELOPMENTAL VARIABLES

	Sitting at 12 months	Sitting at 24 months	Walking at 24 months	Walking at 36 months
Sitting at 12 months	1.000 (59)			
Sitting at 24 months	0.227 (40)	1.000 (62)		
Walking at 24 months	0.607*** (40)	0.187 (62)	1.000 (62)	
Walking at 36 months	0.572*** (49)	0.286** (56)	0.630*** (56)	1.000 (76)
Muscle tone at birth	0.178 (46)	0.210 (49)	0.173 (49)	0.264* (58)
Muscle tone at 12 months	0.589*** (58)	0.261* (39)	0.532*** (39)	0.541*** (48)
Muscle tone at 24 months	0.448** (40)	0.213* (62)	0.576*** (62)	0.418*** (56)
Muscle tone at 36 months	0.601*** (49)	0.467*** (56)	0.484*** (56)	0.637*** (76)
General development at 6 months	0.363** (59)	0.332** (62)	0.533*** (62)	0.322** (76)
Motor-social development from 12 to 36 months	0.621*** (57)	0.402*** (59)	0.770*** (59)	0.677*** (73)
Mental development from 12 to 36 months	0.336** (58)	0.357** (60)	0.593*** (60)	0.374*** (74)

Muscle tone at birth	Muscle tone at 12 months	Muscle tone at 24 months	Muscle tone at 36 months	General development at 6 months	Motor-social development 12 to 36 months	Mental development 12 to 36 months
1.000 (68)						
0.394** (45)	1.000 (58)					
0.146 (49)	0.471*** (39)	1.000 (62)				
0.471*** (58)	0.547*** (48)	0.566*** (56)	1.000 (76)			
0.325** (68)	0.434*** (58)	0.473*** (62)	0.439*** (76)	1.000 (89)		
0.429*** (65)	0.609*** (56)	0.623*** (59)	0.675*** (73)	0.550*** (86)	1.000 (86)	
0.391*** (66)	0.420*** (57)	0.455*** (60)	0.414*** (74)	0.459*** (86)	0.769*** (85)	1.000 (86)

* p <.05
** p <.01
*** p <.001

TABLE IX

SUMMARY OF CLINICAL DATA OF DOWN SYNDROME CHILDREN WITH SEIZURES

	Sex	Study Group	Cardiac Status	Age of onset (months)	Seizure type	Initial electro-encephalogram	Anticonvulsant therapy	Seizure outcome	Onset of independent walking (months)	Mental age (months) (Bayley Scales) at chronological age of 30 months	IQ (Stanford-Binet) at 48 months
1	Male	5-hydroxy-tryptophan	no congenital heart disease	5½	myoclonic	hypsarrhythmic burst-suppression	ACTH and phenobarbitol	complete control	18	15	42
2	Female	5-hydroxy-tryptophan	atrial septa-defect	9	myoclonic	hypsarrhythmic burst-suppression	ACTH and phenobarbitol	complete control	27	14	37
3	Female	placebo	no congenital heart disease	6	myoclonic	hypsarrhythmic burst-suppression	ACTH	complete control	32	16	52
4	Male	placebo	atrio-ventri-cular canal	8	grand mal	pre-hypsarrhythmic	phenobarbitol	complete control	40	11	52
5	Female	5-hydroxy-tryptophan	ventricular septal defect	12	akinetic	right parietal discharge	phenobarbitol	complete control	21	20	55

Developmental Outcome

limpness, followed by unresponsiveness and sleep. Her electroencephalogram showed a rare spike discharge originating from the right parietal area. Table IX presents a summary statement of clinical data, results of electroencephalograms, treatment approach, and developmental outcome of the five children with seizures.

The four children who had an initial hypsarrhythmic electroencephalographic tracing with burst-suppression patterns were of special interest to us; but also caused great concern, since it had been reported that 5-hydroxytryptophan administration to children with Down syndrome was seizurogenic (21) and since the prognosis in patients with infantile spasms in general is not favorable. While the first two children in our cohort indeed had received 5-hydroxytryptophan, patients three and four, however, had been given the placebo. The evaluation of our data, in addition to our recent experience (we have seen four more patients with Down syndrome with infantile spasms who did not receive any tryptophan compounds), and the review of the literature on this subject, suggest that the administration of 5-hydroxytryptophan most likely was not responsible for the development of infantile spasms in the two children in our program.

After the first two children had developed infantile spasms, it was decided that every child in the Down syndrome program should be scheduled for routine electroencephalographic and evoked potential studies at ages 3 , 6, and 12 months.* When infant number three had her first electroencephalogram at the age of 2 months, right occipital discharges were noted. At that time she was asymptomatic and a neurological evaluation did not uncover any pathological findings. Her six months' electroencephalogram, however, showed a hypsarrhythmic pattern without evidence of concommitant clinical seizure acitivity. Again, the neurological examination was normal. Two days later, however, she started to exhibit myoclonic activity compatible with infantile spasm. Like the other two patients, she was given a course of ACTH.

It is of note that all five children, in particular those with infantile spasms, showed marked improvement after initiation of anticonvulsant therapy. These children have remained seizure-free and their

*See chapters on Electroencephalographic Investigations and on Visual and Auditory Evoked Potential Studies.

electroencephalograms are normal. Most importantly, these children have continued to develop well.

SUMMARY

Selected analyses of periodic neurological evaluations of children in the Down Syndrome Program are presented. We observed the cry pattern of ⅔ of these infants to be abnormal. The initially reduced muscle tone was noted to improve over time. While there was no significant difference in muscle tone between boys and girls (except at the 36 months level) children with moderate and severe congenital heart disease were more hypotonic than those children without or with only mild congenital heart disease during the first year of life. Traction response, Landau maneuver, Moro reflex, tonic-neck reflex, deep tendon reflexes, parachute response, and ambulation skills were investigated.

The study of relationships of selected biomedical and behavioral variables found high correlations among muscle tone at 12 and 24 months, sitting at 12 months, walking at 24 months, and psychomotor development. Finally, the five children who developed seizures are discussed with emphasis on infantile spasms.

REFERENCES

1. Cowie, V. A. *A Study of the Early Development of Mongols.* London: Pergamon Press, 1970.
2. Swaiman, K. F. and Wright, F. S. *The Practice of Pediatric Neurology,* Vol. 1. St. Louis: C. V. Mosby Co., 1975.
3. Hall, B. Mongolism in newborns: a clinical and cytogenetic study. *Acta Pediatrica,* Supplement, 1-95, 1964.
4. Penrose, L. S. and Smith, G. F. *Down's Anomaly.* Edinburgh, London and New York: Churchill Livingston, 1966.
5. McIntire, M. S. and Dutch, S. J. Mongolism and generalized hypotonia. *American Journal of Mental Deficiency,* 68:669-670, 1964.
6. Benda, C. E. The central nervous system in mongolism. *American Journal of Mental Deficiency,* 45:42-47, 1940.
7. Diamond, E. F. and Moon, M. S. Neuromuscular development in mongoloid children. *American Journal of Mental Deficiency,* 66:218, 1961.

8.   Loesch-Mdzewska, D. Some aspects of the neurology of Down's syndrome. *Journal of Mental Deficiency Research,* 12:237-246, 1968.

9.   Levinson, A., Friedman, A. and Stamps, R. Variability of mongolism. *Pediatrics,* 16:43-54, 1955.

10. Prechtl, H. and Beintema, D. The neurological examination of the full term newborn infant. *Little Club Clinics in Developmental Medicine,* 12, 1964.

11. Paulson, G. W., Son, Ch.D. and Nance, W.E.W. Neurologic aspects of typical and atypical Down's syndrome. *Diseases of the Nervous System,* 30:632-636, 1969.

12. Parmalee, A. H. Jr. A critical evaluation of the Moro reflex. *Pediatrics,* 33:773, 1964.

13. Paine, R. S., Brazelton, T. B., Donovan, D. E., Drorbough, J. E. Hubbell, J. P., and Sears, E. M. Evolution of postural reflexes in normal infants and in the presence of chronic brain syndromes. *Neurology,* 14:1036-1048, 1964.

14. Penrose, L. S. *Biology of Mental Defect.* New York: Grune and Stratton, 1949.

15. Walter, R. D., Yeager, C. L. and Rubin, H. K. Mongolism and convulsive seizures. *Archives of Neurology and Psychiatry,* 74:559, 1955.

16. Pueschel, S. M. and Rynders, J. R. *Down Syndrome: Advances in Biomedicine and the Behavioral Sciences.* Cambridge, The Ware Press, 1982.

17. MacGillivray, R. C. Epilepsy in Down's anomaly. *Journal of Mental Deficiency Research,* 11:43-48, 1967.

18. Veall, R. M. The prevalence of epilepsy among mongols related to age. *Journal of Mental Deficiency Research,* 18:99-106, 1974.

19. Tangye, Sh. R. The EEG and incidence of epilepsy in Down's syndrome. *Journal of Mental Deficiency Research,* 23:17-24, 1979.

20. Coriat, L. F. and Fejerman, N. Infantile spasms in children with trisomy 21. *La Semana Medica et Pediatrica 76,* 15:493-500, 1963.

21   Coleman, M. Infantile spasms associated with 5-hydroxytryptophan administration in patients with Down's syndrome. *Neurology,* 21:911-919, 1971.

22. Wolcott, G. J. and Chun, R. W. Myoclonic seizures in Down's syndrome. *Developmental Medicine and Child Neurology,* 15:805-808, 1973.

23. Pollack, M. A., Golden G. S., Schmidt, R., Davis, J. A. and Leeds, N. Infantile spasms in Down syndrome: a report of five cases and review of the literature. *Annals of Neurology,* 3:406-408, 1978.

Chapter 11

INTERRELATIONSHIPS OF BIOLOGICAL, ENVIRONMENTAL AND COMPETENCY VARIABLES

Robert B. Reed
Siegfried M. Pueschel
Richard R. Schnell
Christine E. Cronk

INTRODUCTION

In the past many investigations on Down syndrome have focused on single biological structures and functions. There have been numerous discussions of medical issues, epidemiological concerns, as well as psychoeducational matters, without emphasis on interrelationships of such factors.

This chapter highlights correlations of selected study components and interrelationships of biological, environmental, and outcome variables. Such analysis will lead to a better understanding of developmental processes in the young child with Down syndrome.

METHODS

In order to study interrelationships and major factors influencing specified developmental functions in young children with Down syndrome, four behavioral variables were identified by principal component analysis (1). These variables accounted for 80% of the overall variance. Varimax rotation was used to separate the variables into subsets, which in turn provided the basis for creating new summary variables by averaging the actual test scores of the associated variables.

The following summary variables were determined:

General Development At 6 Months is an average of the 6-month scores of Mental and Motor Scales of the Bayley Scales of Infant Development and the 6-month assessments on the Vineland Social Maturity Scale. Because of the limited repertoire of the child with Down syndrome at 6 months of age, the items on all three scales are very similar, and would be expected to be highly correlated. At 6 months of age the behavior of many children with Down syndrome is more like that of normal children of 3 to 5 months of age. This early developmental period is primarily characterized by reflexive behavior and the emergence of various early motor activities.

Motor-Social Development Between 12 and 36 Months is the composite average of scores from assessments at 12, 18, 24, 30 and 36 months on the Motor Scale of the Bayley Scales of Infant Development and the Vineland Social Maturity Scale. The majority of behaviors on both scales reflects to a large extent the development of motor skills. The Motor Scale of the Bayley Scales of Infant Development measures the attainment of ambulatory and manual skills, while the Vineland Social Maturity Scale rates the accomplishment of activities which require a variety of gross and fine motor functions.

*Mental Development Between 12 and 36 Months** is an average of scores from assessments at 12, 18, 24, 30, and 36 months on the

*See also chapter on Psychomotor Development.

Mental Scale of the Bayley Scales of Infant Development, and is an initial estimate of cognitive functioning. Over this measured developmental range the behaviors sampled are largely those involving visual-motor manipulation and simple problem-solving.

*Language Development At 36 Months*** is composed of scores obtained on the Receptive-Expressive Emergent Language Scale at 36 months of age. This instrument evaluates specific receptive and expressive language skills. The emergence of this factor as separate from mental development is in large part due to the fact that the Bayley Mental Scales have only a few language-related items over the 6 to 19 months range, in which children with Down syndrome generally perform at the chronological age of 12 to 36 months. As mentioned above, the Mental Scale of the Bayley Scales of Infant Development mainly stresses manipulation and simple problem-solving skills at these age levels. As children progress, language skills on the Bayley Scales of Infant Development are given more weight, and a stronger relationship between the Receptive-Expressive Emergent Language Scale and the Bayley Mental Scale would be expected.

Each of the aforementioned behavioral variables was studied by regression analysis to determine its relationship to the following variables: congenital heart disease, initial muscle tone scores, muscle tone ratings between 3 and 36 months, parental follow-through, and the parents' coping ability.

*Congenital Heart Disease**** signifies the presence of moderate to severe cardiac problems in children with Down syndrome. These children had serious cardiac defects such as tetralogy of Fallot, atrioventricular canal, and other complex cardiac conditions often accompanied by heart failure necessitating the administration of digitalis and diuretics. In addition, pulmonary hypertension and recurrent bronchopneumonia were frequently observed. The children's growth rate and weight gain were less than those of children without congenital heart disease.

**See also chapter on Speech and Language Evaluations.

***See also Part I of this monograph for a more detailed definition of mild, moderate and severe congenital heart disease.

The muscle tone* observed in children with Down syndrome was given particular attention because hypotonia is one of the well-described manifestations in many children with this chromosomal disorder. Independent ratings of the degree of hypotonia were obtained by the physical therapist, the neurologist and the pediatrician in the course of their periodic examinations. The multiple ratings obtained by the individual observers were summarized in composite scores for the initial examination, for the first year (except the initial muscle tone rating), for the second, and for the third year respectively. Thus we derived four composite scores for each of the three examiners. These twelve individual ratings and their intercorrelations were studied. Subsequently, two muscle tone variables were indentified through regression analysis:

Initial Muscle Tone refers to an average of the first muscle tone examinations by the three professionals.

Muscle Tone Between 3 and 36 Months encompassed all muscle tone ratings after the initial examination averaging nine composite scores over the time period from 3 to 36 months.

Follow-Through Between 6 and 36 Months ** was a rating given to parents on their ability to follow through with furnished guidance. Support to parents and instructions regarding various aspects of care and stimulation had been provided throughout the study. The extent to which parents complied with such guidance was rated semi-annually. The individual ratings were summed up in the final analysis of the data, and converted into dichotomous ratings of the parents' ability and quality of follow-through.

Parental Coping Ability classified parents on a 3-point scale rating the quality of their adaptation to the stressful situation after the birth of their child.

A number of other variables including socioeconomic status, maternal age, gestational age, birth weight, motor activity, and frequency of illnesses were studied. These variables were not found to be significantly related to any of the four behavioral outcome measures, and thus are not included in the results of the analysis.

*See also Part II and chapters on Motor Development and Neurological Investigations.
**See also Part II and chapter on Social Development and Feeding Milestones.

quency of illnesses were studied. These variables were not found to be significantly related to any of the four behavioral outcome measures, and thus are not included in the results of the analysis.

RESULTS

The first part of the analysis describes and interprets the data set for all behavioral variables, while the second part presents a path analysis of factors affecting the behavioral variables.

The means and standard deviations of children with Down syndrome for each of the 21 behavioral measures are provided in Table I. The data of the upper part of this table indicate that children

TABLE I

MEANS AND STANDARD DEVIATIONS OF DEVELOPMENTAL ASSESSMENTS

OBTAINED FROM YOUNG CHILDREN WITH DOWN SYNDROME

AT SIX MONTH INTERVALS[*]

Age in months	Vineland Social Maturity Scale			Bayley Scales of Infant Development					
				Motor Scale			Mental Scale		
	N	mean	S.D.	N	mean	S.D.	N	mean	S.D.
6	85	4.6	.8	81	4.0	1.2	81	3.3	1.1
12	81	9.2	1.6	83	7.2	1.6	88	6.7	1.7
18	67	13.0	2.5	75	10.4	2.6	75	10.5	2.3
24	77	16.3	2.9	80	13.1	3.4	80	13.6	2.6
30	71	19.6	3.1	80	16.6	4.4	80	16.7	3.0
36	74	22.7	3.6	75	19.0	5.2	75	20.6	4.6

Receptive - Expressive Emergent Language Scale

	Receptive			Expressive			Combine		
	N	mean	S.D.	N	mean	S.D.	N	mean	S.D.
36	81	18.8	5.2	81	16.6	5.0	81	17.6	4.8

*Some of these data have been presented in different form in the chapter on Psychomotor Development.

with Down syndrome perform at slightly better than half of what would be expected for their respective chronological age. On the Receptive-Expressive Emergent Language Scale, however, the children's performance on the expressive and combined scores is just below half of the expected age norms.

On the Bayley Mental Scale the rate of performance varies between 55 and 58% of the expected rate (e.g. at 6 months of age the mean of the Bayley Mental Scale score is at 3.3 months). The performance on the Bayley Mental Scale at ages 6 to 36 months appears relatively stable from age level to age level, while there is more variability on the Bayley Motor Scale and on the Vineland Social Maturity Scale. On both latter scales the percentage decreases slightly with increase in chronological age, from 67 to 53% on the Bayley Motor Scale and from 77 to 63% on the Vineland Social Maturity Scale.

Table II presents the correlation coefficients for the same scales applied at different ages. As would be expected, the correlations increase with age and are highest at 30 and 36 months of age. From 18 months of age on, strong correlations (i.e. where at least half of the variance is shared in common) are apparent.

The correlations between different tests administered at different ages are noted in Table III. It can be seen that the correlations between the Bayley Motor Scale and the Vineland Social Maturity Scale rise to about .81 at 24 months of age and then drop off slightly. Similarly the correlations between the Bayley Mental Scale and the Bayley Motor Scale increase up to 18 months, falling off at 24 months, but gradually increasing again to 36 months of age. The Vineland Social Maturity Scale scores at 36 months show a slightly better correlation with Receptive-Expressive Emergent Language Scale scores than do the Bayley Mental Scores, while the Bayley Motor Scores reveal lower correlations with the Receptive-Expressive Emergent Language scores. Part of the reason for the strong correlation between the Vineland Social Maturity Scale and the Receptive-Expressive Emergent Language Scale may be the fact that the information for each of the tests is obtained from the same parents, while the Bayley Scales of Infant Development are administered to the children.

TABLE II

CORRELATION COEFFICIENTS FOR THE SAME TEST

ADMINISTERED AT SIX MONTH INTERVALS

VINELAND SOCIAL MATURITY SCALE

BAYLEY MOTOR SCALE

BAYLEY MENTAL SCALE

	Age in months	6	12	18	24	30	36
				Vineland Social Maturity Scale			
	6	1.000					
Vineland	12	.472	1.000				
Social	18	.462	.712	1.000			
Maturity	24	.425	.587	.790	1.000		
Scale	30	.310	.631	.867	.851	1.000	
	36	.311	.690	.798	.788	.882	1.000
				Bayley Motor Scale			
	6	1.000					
Bayley	12	.574	1.000				
Motor	18	.534	.725	1.000			
Scale	24	.576	.712	.810	1.000		
	30	.510	.594	.698	.825	1.000	
	36	.512	.677	.722	.794	.817	1.000
				Bayley Mental Scale			
	6	1.000					
Bayley	12	.427	1.000				
Mental	18	.438	.722	1.000			
Scale	24	.339	.575	.852	1.000		
	30	.478	.635	.778	.840	1.000	
	36	.531	.603	.716	.738	.827	1.000

*Some of these data have been presented in the chapter of Psychomotor Development.

TABLE III

CORRELATION COEFFICIENTS AMONG DIFFERENT TESTS
ADMINISTERED AT SIX MONTH INTERVALS
VINELAND SOCIAL MATURITY SCALE
BAYLEY MOTOR SCALE AND BAYLEY MENTAL SCALE
RECEPTIVE-EXPRESSIVE EMERGENT LANGUAGE SCALE (REEL)

Scales	Age in months	REEL			Bayley Mental Scale						Bayley Motor Scale					
		R 36	E 36	C* 36	6	12	18	24	30	36	6	12	18	24	30	36
Vineland Social Maturity Scale	6	.367	.305	.360	.367	.221	.266	.104	.190	.266	.374	.405	.280	.306	.247	.440
	12	.520	.524	.546	.424	.591	.645	.480	.531	.626	.539	.622	.570	.598	.520	.517
	18	.624	.626	.646	.391	.624	.730	.687	.711	.656	.556	.738	.750	.785	.797	.746
	24	.622	.673	.681	.312	.570	.62?	.576	.581	.640	.460	.664	.688	.807	.711	.75?
	30	.718	.752	.768	.301	.587	.659	.673	.662	.694	.435	.676	.693	.796	.679	.724
	36	.724	.675	.729	.308	.641	.691	.593	.645	.709	.464	.678	.721	.733	.661	.643
Bayley Motor Scale	6	.352	.319	.349	.526	.402	.402	.347	.444	.393						
	12	.429	.425	.430	.380	.571	.652	.548	.568	.535						
	18	.422	.451	.443	.352	.556	.678	.553	.619	.650						
	24	.591	.548	.585	.398	.542	.602	.607	.606	.652						
	30	.599	.503	.575	.424	.517	.636	.526	.603	.629						
	36	.503	.517	.518	.417	.441	.542	.498	.552	.588						
Bayley Mental Scale	6	.355	.264	.334												
	12	.476	.468	.485												
	18	.571	.551	.576												
	24	.630	.536	.598												
	30	.637	.509	.590												
	36	.721	.638	.699												

*R - Receptive, E - Expressive, C - Combined

Figure 1 presents a summary statement of the underlying pattern of our analysis. Variables are shown here from left to right in approximate time-order sequence: the cardiac condition which exists prior to birth appears at the extreme left, and the behavioral outcome variables are shown at the extreme right of the figure. Arrows represent the potential path of causation indicating that the variable at the base of the arrow may be thought of as having an effect upon the variable at the point of the arrow. It is important to note that the path-analysis procedure does not test a particular assumption of causality.

The path coefficients that reflect the importance of the elemental causal paths were computed by fitting a regression equation for each variable in a box as the dependent variable, and the source of all arrows leading to that box as independent variables. The standardized regression coefficients of these equations constitute the elemental path coefficients. When an independent variable did not contribute significantly to a regression, it was dropped from the equation. Path coefficients for the reduced model are shown in Figure 1. Where a

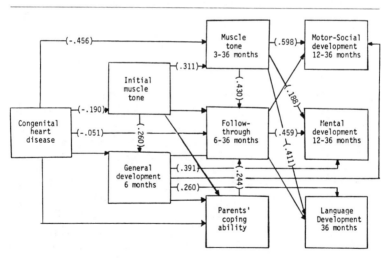

Figure 1:   Overall path diagram relating potential causal

factors to behavioral outcomes.

Numerals in parentheses represent the path coefficients.

path is shown without a coefficient, it represents a potential causal effect that did not turn out to be statistically significant.

In order to present the complex interrelationships noted in Figure 1 in a simplified way, we dissected Figure 1 into three sub-schemes as shown in Figures 2, 3 and 4.

The first section taken out of Figure 1 relates to the influence of moderate and severe congenital heart disease upon other variables. Thus Figure 2 indicates that significant cardiac problems adversely affect the initial muscle tone, the muscle tone observed during the time period from 3 to 36 months, and the ability of parents to follow through with recommended instructions. Cardiac involvement did not have an independent effect on the outcome variables including language, motor, social, and mental developments.

Figure 3 shows relationships of initial muscle tone and early development to later muscle tone as well as language and mental development. Development at 6 months, which itself is influenced by the initial muscle tone, is a predictor for language acquisition and mental development during 12 to 36 months. The initial muscle tone affects future muscle tone (3 to 36 months), which in turn influences mental and language functioning.

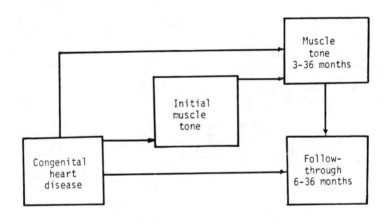

Figure 2: Path diagram: factors affecting muscle tone and follow-through.

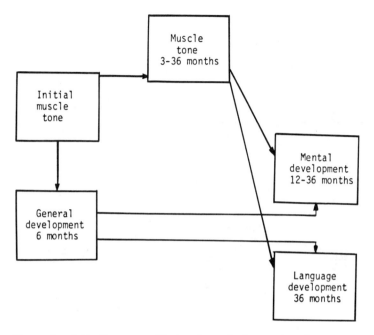

Figure 3:   Path diagram: effects of muscle tone and early

general development on mental development between

12 to 36 months and language acquisition at 36 months.

Figure 4 demonstrates again that muscle tone observed during the 3-to-36-month period is a good predictor of all three outcome variables: language acquisition, motor and social development, and, to a lesser degree, mental functioning between 12 and 36 months. It is of note that muscle tone during the first few years had more explanatory power for these outcome variables than does the measurement of general development at 6 months (Figures 3 and 4). Parental follow-through is positively influenced by the parents' coping ability and by muscle tone observed between 3 and 36 months. Follow-through on the other hand affects all three outcome variables, yet the only significant correlation is with mental development between 12 and 36 months.

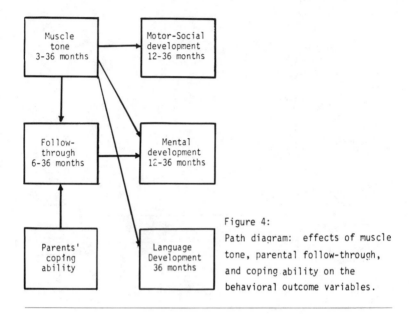

Figure 4:
Path diagram: effects of muscle tone, parental follow-through, and coping ability on the behavioral outcome variables.

DISCUSSION

The above presented data raise a number of questions, such as: why is significant heart disease in these children associated with diminished muscle tone? Why do cardiac problems have a negative effect upon the parental follow-through variable? How does muscle tone influence a variety of developmental parameters?

Clinical experience teaches us that children with Down syndrome who have congenital heart disease, particularly children in cardiac failure, are known to be less active, often display muscle weakness and lethargy, and generally thrive poorly. It is hypothesized that much of the energy ordinarily utilized in normal activity is shunted into the increased cardiac workload in children with congenital heart disease. The frequently observed increased muscle weakness and lethargy was reflected in the muscle tone assessments. Moreover, many of these children who were in cardiac failure received medications (digitalis and a variety of diuretics) which affected their appetite and food intake. This resulted in decreased protein synthesis and in reduced weight gain and growth.

Concerning the parental follow-through variable, many parents were fearful of disturbing children with cardiac problems, and engaged less in early intervention activities. These parents had indicated that they wanted to let the child rest since he/she often appeared exhausted after normal activities such as feeding, dressing, or after crying. Such prolonged rest periods precluded the parents' proceeding with the recommended activities of early stimulation. It is of note that only 3 out of 17 parents whose children had severe cardiac conditions followed through appropriately with furnished guidance.

Another element to be considered is that the child who is lethargic and inactive will ordinarily not elicit favorable responses from parents. In addition, children with significant heart problems often were hospitalized because of respiratory infections, cardiac failure, cardiac catheterization, or cardiac surgery. During these periods there was little interaction with the child even if the parents visited frequently. A number of parents feared that the child might die because of the severity of the cardiac condition, and indeed 12 children with significant congenital heart disease expired during the study period. All these factors undoubtedly interfered with the normal bonding process and parent/child reciprocity.

In an attempt to interpret the interrelationships of selected variables in Figures 3 and 4, it becomes apparent that muscle tone occupies a central role as an intermediate variable. Adequate muscle tone in a child with Down syndrome during the initial examination may be an expression of the intactness of neuronal units which control muscle tone. It can be assumed that other central nervous system functions may display a similar maturational level due to a general inborn integrity of neural tissue which could explain the correlation between the initial muscle tone and early development.

The initial muscle tone also predicts future muscle tone. Generally it is expected that the child with adequate muscle tone will have similar muscle-tone ratings during subsequent examinations. Empirically, muscle tone in children with Down syndrome improves over time (see Part II).

The child with adequate muscle tone usually will be more active than other children with significant hypotonia, and will engage in a variety of motor functions and social skills. The increased sensory input due to greater mobility might reflect in part some children's advanced intellectual development and language acquisition. Parents also might find it more rewarding to handle and care for children with adequate muscle tone and increased motor activity, which could explain the positive influence of muscle tone on the parental follow-through variable.

With regard to the relationship of parental follow-through with the outcome variables, it may be hypothesized that relatively good early developmental progress encourages parents to increase early intervention activities, which in turn affects positively the child's future development.

As presented in Figure 4, the parents' ability to cope with presenting circumstances influences their capacity to follow through with furnished instructions. The parent who has adjusted to the realities of life will more likely relate better to the child and will be able to provide appropriate stimulation.

SUMMARY

The longitudinal study of 89 children with Down syndrome by an interdisciplinary team of professionals permitted these analyses focusing on developmental interrelationships, major influencing factors of specified functions, and predictable outcome competencies. Certain behavioral variables were identified by principal component analysis using varimax rotation. Through subsequent path analysis it was found that the presence of significant congenital heart disease influences adversely the muscle tone, and the parents' ability to follow through with the provided guidance. Muscle tone, however, is a powerful predictor of all the outcome variables including language acquisition, motor and social development, and mental functioning. The general development at 6 months was also noted to influence future language acquisition as well as mental development in subsequent years. The ability to follow through is affected by muscle tone and by the parent's ability to cope. In turn, follow-through had a significant influence on mental development between 12 and 36 months.

The foregoing analysis signifies the importance of the study of variable interrelationships, since it provides information on predicability of specific biological conditions and environmental circumstances. Such assessment will lead to a better understanding of developmental and maturational processes in the child with Down syndrome.

REFERENCES

1. Nie, N., Hull, C., Jenkins, J., Steinbrenner, K., and Bent, B. *Statistical Package for the Social Sciences*. New York: McGraw-Hill Book Company, 1971.

Part IV

Chapter 12

ELECTROENCEPHALOGRAPHIC INVESTIGATIONS

Daune L. MacGregor
Liza Yessayan
Siegfried M. Pueschel

INTRODUCTION

Electroencephalographic findings in Down syndrome have been discussed in several recent publications (1-6). In a review on this subject Seppalainen and Kivalo reported slower alpha rhythm, low frequency waves, frequent discharges of beta waves, increased intermediate fast activity, high percentage of paroxysmal activity with use of activation procedures, and a convulsive threshold higher in persons with Down syndrome than in other mentally retarded individuals (6). Only a few investigators studied the frequency of electroencephalographic abnormalities in Down syndrome, and there is virtually no detailed information available on the effects of 5-hydroxytryptophan and pyridoxine as well as the presence of congenital heart disease on electroencephalographic patterns in Down syndrome.

This chapter will describe the electroencephalographic findings of children followed in the Down syndrome program. In addition, the influence of 5-hydroxytryptophan and pyridoxine and the children's cardiac status on electroencephalographic patterns will be analyzed.

METHODS

Electroencephalographic investigations were not part of the original study design. However, when two children developed infantile spasms during the second project year, it was decided that every child enrolled in our program be scheduled for routine sequential electroencephalographic studies during the first year of life. Although all children were supposed to have electroencephalograms at ages 2, 6, and 12 months, not all were studied at the specified time periods because of intercurrent illnesses, parental concerns, and other factors that interfered with scheduling.

All electroencephalograms were performed in the Seizure Unit, Department of Neurology, at the Children's Hospital Medical Center. Standard procedures were employed using Grass Model 6 eight-channel electroencephalographic machines. Electrodes were placed according to the International 10–20 system. Grass E5GH gold-plated cup electrodes were used with collodium application. Photic stimulation was carried out on all patients with a Grass Photic stimulator PS3B. When necessary, chloral hydrate was administered as a sedative. The records were then read by qualified staff electroencephalographers without knowledge of the child's clinical status or study-group assignment. At the completion of the study the reports were re-evaluated, and the results were tabulated and subjected to routine statistical analysis.

RESULTS

There were a total of 131 electroencephalograms obtained from 85 children enrolled in the Down syndrome program. Table 1 provides a summary statement of the numbers and percentages of normal and abnormal electroencephalograms at 2, 6, and 12 months. The overall percentage of abnormal tracings was 45%. Abnormal records were observed more often in the 2 month group (51.7%) and less often in the 6 month group (36.4%). These differences are not statistically significant.

Table II presents a description of the abnormalities of the electroencephalographic records at ages 2, 6, and 12 months. In 59 abnormal tracings, 88 abnormalities were reported.

Table III details the results of electroencephalographic recordings according to study group and cardiac status. In order to identify possible "treatment" effects, the abnormal records from the respective study groups (Table IV) and selected combinations (Table V) were analyzed statistically. As seen in Table IV, at two months the pattern is one of pyridoxine effect with pyridoxine reducing the risk of having an abnormal electroencephalogram. At 6 months the pattern is an interactive one with the combination of pyridoxine and 5-hydroxytryptophan increasing the risk, while 5-hydroxytryptophan or pyridoxine each administered alone decreases it. At 12 months the pattern is one of 5-hydroxytryptophan effect, with the latter compound reducing slightly the risk of an abnormal electroencephalogram. None of these effects are statistically significant.

As noted in Table V, a possible "treatment" effect upon electroencephalographic patterns was studied by combining certain

TABLE I

NUMBERS AND PERCENTAGES OF NORMAL AND ABNORMAL ELECTROENCEPHALOGRAMS

AT TWO, SIX AND TWELVE MONTHS

Electroencephalograms	Two Months		Six Months		Twelve Months		Total	
	#	%	#	%	#	%	#	%
Normal	14	48.3	21	63.6	37	53.6	72	55
Abnormal	15	51.7	12	36.4	32	46.4	59	45
Total	29		33		69		131	

TABLE II

ABNORMAL ELECTROENCEPHALOGRAPHIC PATTERNS AT TWO, SIX AND TWELVE MONTHS

| | Numbers of Electroencephalograms | | | |
| | Two | Six | Twelve | |
Abnormal Electroencephalograms*	Months	Months	Months	Total
Sleep disturbances:				
absent sleep spindles	5	2	8	15
poorly developed sleep spindles	2	2	10	14
poor differentiation between				
awake and sleep	1	1	1	3
poor organization between				
sleep states	2	2	3	7
abnormalities of K complexes	1	4	4	9
Paroxysmal activity:				
spike-wave discharges		1	1	2
hypsarrhythmia patterns		2	2	4
sharp wave activity	5	1	1	7
Background disturbances:				
slow wave activity	3	5	10	18
excessive beta activity			3	3
poor organization	1		2	3
immature pattern	1		2	3
Total	21	20	47	88

*many records have more than one type of abnormality.

TABLE III

ELECTROENCEPHALOGRAPHIC PATTERNS ACCORDING TO STUDY GROUP AND CARDIAC STATUS
AT TWO, SIX AND TWELVE MONTHS

Numbers of Electroencephalograms

Electroencephalographic Patterns	Two Months		Six Months		Twelve Months	
	Study Group*	Cardiac Status**	Study Group*	Cardiac Status**	Study Group*	Cardiac Status**
	1 2 3 4	1 2 3 4	1 2 3 4	1 2 3 4	1 2 3 4	1 2 3 4
NORMAL	2 4 3 5	8 2 1 3	6 4 6 5	15 3 3 -	9 10 9 10	24 - 8 5
ABNORMAL						
Sleep disturbances:						
absent sleep spindles	2 1 1 1	5 - - -	1 - - 1	1 1 - -	3 2 3 -	4 3 1 -
poorly developed sleep spindles	1 - 1 -	1 - - 1	- 2 - -	2 - - -	5 2 1 2	6 1 2 1
poor differentiation between awake & asleep	- - - 1	1 - - -	- 1 - -	1 - - -	1 - - -	- - 1 -
poor organization between sleep states	1 - 1 -	2 - - -	1 - - 1	1 1 - -	1 - - 2	- - - 3
abnormalities of K complexes	- - - 1	1 - - -	1 2 - 1	3 - 1 -	2 2 - -	2 - 2 -
Paroxysmal activity:						
spike-wave discharges	1 - - -	1 - - -	1 - - -	- - - 1	- - 1 -	- - - 1
hypsarrhythmia patterns	- - - -	- - - -	1 - 1 -	2 - - -	1 - 1 -	1 - 1 -
sharp wave activity	1 1 3 -	4 1 - -	- - 1 -	1 - - -	- - - -	- - - -
Background disturbances:						
slow wave activity	1 - 1 1	2 - 1 -	- - 1 4	4 - - 1	2 4 1 3	7 1 1 1
excessive beta activity	- - - -	- - - -	- - - -	- - - -	1 - 1 1	- - 1 2
poor organization	- 1 - -	1 - - -	- - - -	- - - -	1 1 - -	2 - - -
immature pattern	1 - - -	1 - - -	- - - -	- - - -	1 - - 1	1 - 1 -

*Study group: 1 – Placebo
2 – Pyridoxine
3 – 5-hydroxytryptophan
4 – 5-hydroxytryptophan/pyridoxine

**Cardiac Status: 1 – No congenital heart disease
2 – Mild congenital heart disease
3 – Moderate congenital heart disease
4 – Severe congenital heart disease

TABLE IV

NUMBERS AND PERCENTAGES OF NORMAL AND ABNORMAL ELECTROENCEPHALOGRAMS ACCORDING TO STUDY GROUP

AT TWO, SIX AND TWELVE MONTHS

		Two Months Study Groups*				Six Months Study Groups*				Twelve Months Study Groups*				Total Study Groups*			
		1	2	3	4	1	2	3	4	1	2	3	4	1	2	3	4
Normal	#	2	4	3	5	6	4	6	5	9	10	8	10	17	18	17	20
	%	28.6	57.1	37.5	71.4	54.5	80.0	75.0	55.6	47.4	50.0	61.5	58.8	45.9	56.3	58.6	60.6
Abnormal	#	5	3	5	2	5	1	2	4	10	10	5	7	20	14	12	13
	%	71.4	42.9	62.5	28.6	45.5	20.0	25.0	44.4	52.6	50.0	38.5	41.2	54.1	43.7	41.4	39.4
Total		7	7	8	7	11	5	8	9	19	20	13	17	37	32	29	33

* Study Groups: 1 – Placebo
2 – Pyridoxine
3 – 5-hydroxytryptophan
4 – 5-hydroxytryptophan/pyridoxine

TABLE V

NUMBERS AND PERCENTAGES OF NORMAL AND ABNORMAL ELECTROENCEPHALOGRAMS ACCORDING TO ADMINISTRATION

OF 5-HYDROXYTRYPTOPHAN OR PYRIDOXINE AT TWO, SIX AND TWELVE MONTHS

		Two Months Study Groups*				Six Months Study Groups*				Twelve Months Study Groups*				Total Study Groups*			
		1+2	3+4	1+3	2+4**	1+2	3+4	1+3	2+4**	1+2	3+4	1+3	2+4**	1+2	3+4	1+3	2+4
Normal	#	6	8	5	9	10	11	12	9	19	18	17	20	35	37	34	38
	%	42.9	53.3	33.3	64.3	62.5	64.7	63.2	64.3	48.7	60.0	53.1	54.1	50.7	59.7	51.5	58.5
Abnormal	#	8	7	10	5	6	6	7	5	20	12	15	17	34	25	32	27
	%	57.1	46.7	66.7	35.7	37.5	35.3	36.8	35.7	51.3	40.0	46.9	45.9	49.3	40.3	48.5	41.5
Total	#	14	15	15	14	16	17	19	14	39	30	32	37	69	62	66	65

*Study Groups

1 - Placebo
2 - Pyridoxine
3 - 5-hydroxytryptophan
4 - 5-hydroxytryptophan/pyridoxine

**Combinations of Study Groups

1+2   received no 5-hydroxytryptophan
3+4   received 5-hydroxytryptophan
1+3   received no pyridoxine
2+4   received pyridoxine

study groups. For both 5-hydroxytryptophan and pyridoxine the direction of the effect was toward reducing electroencephalographic abnormalities among those "treated" with the respective compounds. This relationship appears in each of the age groups, although in half of the specific comparisons, the effect was very small (1-2% difference). Again, none of the results are statistically significant. These data do not suggest that 5-hydroxytryptophan and/or pyridoxine enhanced the risk of an abnormal electroencephalogram.

Table VI presents an analysis of the electroencephalographic data according to the children's cardiac status. At all ages, there was no significant variation in the percentage of abnormal electroencephalograms. The lowest observed percentage was 33% among the 18 records of children with moderate congenital heart disease. The findings in the specific age groups were similar. All results were again nonsignificant. Of the 13 children from whom serial tracings were obtained (Table VII) no consistent pattern was noted.

The overall analysis of the results does not reveal any statistically significant differences. It should be noted, however, that there is difficulty in translating these negative findings into a "no difference" conclusion because of the small numbers of children in the various groups (particularly at 2 and 6 months) for whom electroencephalograms were available.

DISCUSSION

In the recent literature, several papers have reviewed electroencephalographic findings in Down syndrome. Particular attention has been paid to the presence of sleep disturbances and hypsarrhythmic patterns.

Smith and Berg noted that although various electroencephalographic abnormalities have been reported in Down syndrome, no specific patterns have been identified (7). In a study of 92 subjects with Down syndrome, Seppalainen and Kivalo found only 12% of electroencephalographic recordings to be completely normal. The most common abnormality was a diffuse cortical disturbance in 82%.

TABLE VI

NUMBERS AND PERCENTAGES OF NORMAL AND ABNORMAL ELECTROENCEPHALOGRAMS

ACCORDING TO CARDIAC STATUS AT TWO, SIX AND TWELVE MONTHS

		Two Months				Six Months				Twelve Months				Total			
		Cardiac Status*				Cardiac Status*				Cardiac Status*				Cardiac Status*			
		1	2	3	4	1	2	3	4	1	2	3	4	1	2	3	4
Normal	#	8	2	1	3	15	3	3	0	24	0	8	5	47	5	12	8
	%	40.0	66.7	50.0	75.0	65.2	75.0	75.0	0	54.5	0	66.7	55.6	54.0	45.4	66.7	53.3
Combined 1+2/3+4	%	43.5		66.7		66.7		50.0		50.0		61.9		46.9		60.6	
Abnormal	#	12	1	1	1	8	1	1	2	20	4	4	4	40	6	6	7
	%	60.0	33.3	50.0	25.0	34.8	25.0	25.0	100.0	45.5	100.0	33.3	44.4	46.0	54.6	33.3	46.7
Combined 1+2/3+4	%	56.5		33.3		33.3		50.0		50.0		38.1		53.1		39.4	
Total	#	20	3	2	4	23	4	4	2	44	4	12	9	87	11	18	15

*Cardiac Status

   1 - No congenital heart disease

   2 - Mild congenital heart disease

   3 - Moderate congenital heart disease

   4 - Severe congenital heart disease

TABLE VII

RESULTS OF ELECTROENCEPHALOGRAMS OF CHILDREN WITH SEQUENTIAL TRACINGS

#	Study Group*	Cardiac Status**	Two Months	Six Months	Twelve Months
1	2	1	Normal	Normal	Normal
2	2	3	Normal	Normal	No spindles poor K complexes
3	3	1	frontal slowing left temporal sharp waves	Normal	Normal
4	4	1	Normal	Generally slow, poor organization sleep patterns; poor K complexes	Borderline slow
5	1	1	Normal	Normal	Normal
6	4	4	Normal	Borderline slow, monotonous	Borderline slow, poor sleep spindles
7	2	1	Normal	Poor spindles and K complexes; poor differentiation sleep-drowsiness	Borderline slow
8	1	1	Abnormal transition sleep states	Borderline slow	Poor background poor spindles
9	3	1	Abnormal transition	Normal	Normal
10	4	1	Normal	Normal	Normal
11	2	1	Borderline poor organization	Normal	Borderline; poor Developed spindles
12	1	1	Biparietal spikes Absent spindles	Hypsarrhythmia	Borderline; poor developed spindles
13	3	2	Multifocal sharp waves	Normal	Asymmetry of spindles

* Study Group: 1 - Placebo
              2 - Pyridoxine
              3 - 5-hydroxytryptophan
              4 - 5-hydroxytryptophan/pyridoxine

**Cardiac Status: 1 - No congenital heart disease
                  2 - Mild congenital heart disease
                  3 - Moderate congenital heart disease
                  4 - Severe congenital heart disease

Paroxysmal activity included spike-wave discharges in 4.3%, and sharp wave forms in 1.7%. Abnormalities of rhythm were seen in 14%, high frequency beta activity in 12%, and immature patterns for age in 10% (6).

Loesch-Mdzewska reported on the electroencephalographic findings in 31 children with Down syndrome, ages 3–18 years (4). Sixteen percent were considered normal; the abnormalities included disturbances of background activity with dominant delta and theta activity of medium voltage (16%), moderate diffuse dysrhythmias (48%) and spike-wave complexes (13%). In 10% of the records sharp wave activity was observed, but considered normal for age (4).

Ellingson and coworkers in examining the electroencephalograms of 94 patients with Down syndrome age 1 month to 41 years noted that 23% of the subjects had one or more abnormal records. In the age group under 36 months, only 19% were abnormal (2). The disturbances recorded included spike as well as polyspike and wave complexes, diffuse slow activity and asynchrony and/or asymetry. The authors concluded that the rates of electroencephalographic abnormalities are higher and age-related in persons with Down syndrome, but that these abnormalities are not well correlated with specific behavioral or neurological symptoms.

In another paper, Ellingson and co-investigators reported the results of 279 electroencephalographic recordings obtained on 202 subjects with Down syndrome aged 1 month to 36 years (1). The overall rate of abnormalities was 21%; 2% showed asymmetry and/or asynchrony without distinctly abnormal wave forms, 10% had excessive diffuse slow activity for age, and 9% had paroxysmal discharges. The overall rate of electroencephalographic abnormalities was felt to be significantly not greatly elevated (20–25%). The rate was again age-related, with the majority of abnormalities seen during the childhood years. Paroxysmal activity was confined to young children and usually not associated with a history of seizures. No pathognomonic or specific electroencephalographic patterns were identified, nor was there any evidence that the karyotype (trisomy 21, translocation, mosaicism) influences rates or types of observed abnormalities.

The overall rate of electroencephalographic abnormalities in our series is almost double (45%) that of Ellingson and coworkers; it probably reflects the younger age range of our group of children (2 months to 1 year). This confirms other investigators' observations that the greatest number of electroencephalographic abnormalities in a Down syndrome population are seen in the younger age groups.

A hypsarrhythmia pattern has also been reported in association with Down syndrome. In our series, four children were found to have this abnormality.* Coleman reported 9 infants of a group of 60 children with Down syndrome who developed infantile spasms after administration of 5-hydroxytryptophan; four of whom had a hypsarrhythmia pattern recorded (8). Treatment with L-tryptophan was also studied by Airaksinen (9). Seven infants with Down syndrome who were given L-tryptophan and 14 untreated controls with Down syndrome were followed for one year. A hypsarrhythmia tracing was found on routine recording in one of the treated children; his electroencephalogram remained abnormal even after L-tryptophan was discontinued.

The association of infantile spasms and Down syndrome was reviewed by Pollack and coworkers (10). They noted that 24 patients with Down syndrome and infantile spasms have been described so far; of these 12 were reported to have a hypsarrhythmic electroencephalogram. Administration of 5-hydroxytryptophan was not felt responsible for the development of infantile spasms. These investigators felt that a hypsarrhythmia pattern appears to be more closely related to a patient's age rather than to a specific metabolic or neuropathological abnormality.

Early reports on sleep disturbances in Down syndrome noted changes in total sleep time and rapid-eye-movement sleep. Petre-Quadens and DeLee studied nocturnal recordings of 45 mentally retarded patients, 10 of whom had Down syndrome (11). There was a significant increase in the total length of sleep, particularly stage 4, and a decrease of stages 1, 2 and 3.

Fukuma and his associates studied ten children with Down syndrome ages 7 to 17 years with all-night polygraphy (electroencephalogram, electromyogram and eye movement records) matched with ten children with mental retardation of unknown origin and eight normal children. The Down syndrome group showed a prolongation of total sleep time, increased percentages of stages 1-2, diminished

*For detailed discussion of the children with hypsarrythmia see chapter on Neurological Investigations.

percentages of stages 3–4, rapid-eye-movement sleep in the total sleep time, prolonged intervals between successive rapid-eye-movement periods, and decreased rapid-eye-movement period frequency (12). The numbers of sleep stage shifts and of awakenings before rising were lower and there was a slight increase of indeterminate sleep. This was felt to indicate a poor quality of sleep and immaturity of cerebral function especially in the formation of sleep stages.

Sleep spindles are more conspicuous in children than in adults, and are thought to facilitate the development of cortical functions of the brain (12). Abnormal development of spindles has been shown to be incompatible with learning (11). Fukuma and co-investigators also noted that the records generally reflected a decreased number of spindles and when spindling was present it appeared irregular in frequency and amplitude (12). Our series also showed abnormalities of spindling, including complete lack of spindle formation or poorly developed spindles (Table II).

Clausen summarized the sleep characteristics of children with Down syndrome to comprise lack of waking alpha activity, fewer sleep spindles, atypical K complexes, increased total sleep time, longer rapid-eye-movement latency, less rapid-eye-movement sleep, fewer eye movements and increased indeterminate sleep (13).

Petre-Quadens and DeGreef studied the effects of 5-hydroxytryptophan on sleep in infants with Down syndrome. These investigators were to determine to what extent the amount, density and periodicity of eye movements during sleep in normal newborns differed from those of infants with trisomy 21, and to correlate the effects of 5-hydroxytryptophan with changes in these patterns (15). The number of eye movements during rapid-eye-movement sleep was decreased in subjects with Down syndrome and the distribution of high density eye movement patterns within consecutive rapid-eye-movement periods differed considerably from those seen in normal newborn infants. After 5-hydroxytryptophan administration, the density of eye movements increased in children with Down syndrome older than one year, and their distribution showed a periodic alteration similar to the rapid-eye-movement rhythm seen in normal children (11). The effect, however, was limited with return to baseline levels after two months of treatment. Further study of six infants with Down syndrome after the age of 2 months who received oral 5-hydroxytryptophan for periods of 12 to

36 months failed to induce any long-term effect in eye movement frequency. A discussion of the possible relationship between number of sleep spindles and higher eye movement frequency was given suggesting regulation by the same system as demonstrated by alteration in both following 5-hydroxytryptophan administration.

SUMMARY

Eighty-five children with Down syndrome underwent electroencephalographic studies during their first year of life. The electroencephalograms were reviewed to determine the type and frequency of abnormal tracings in this population. The results were subjected to statistical analysis to examine the effect of 5-hydroxytryptophan and/or pyridoxine administration and the presence and severity of congenital heart disease.

In total, 45% of records were found to be abnormal at all ages. These abnormalities included sleep disturbances, paroxysmal activity and nonspecific background disturbances as detailed in Table II. The analyses of the data do not suggest that 5-hydroxytryptophan and/or pyridoxine increase the risk of having an abnormal electroencephalogram. No statistically significant differences were found in the proportion of abnormal electroencephalograms, or the frequencies of various electroencephalographic disturbances with respect to age, administration of 5-hydroxytryptophan and/or pyridoxine, or severity of congenital heart disease. The relationship between the electroencephalographic abnormalities and Down syndrome is discussed in particular reference to infantile spasms, sleep disturbances and 5-hydroxytryptophan administration.

REFERENCES

1. Ellingson, R.J., Eisen, J.D. and Ottersberg, G. Clinical electroencephalographic observations on institutionalized mongoloids confirmed by karyotype. *Electroencephalography and Clinical Neurophysiology*. 34:193–196, 1973.
2. Ellingson, R.J., Menolascino, F.J. and Eisen, J.D. Clinical EEG relationships in mongoloids confirmed by karyotype. *American Journal of Mental Deficiency*, 74:645–650, 1970.

3. Elul, R., Hanley, J. and Simmons, J.Q. Non-Gaussian behavior on the EEG in Down's syndrome suggests decreased neuronal connections. *Acta Neurologica Scandinavia*, 51:21–28, 1975.

4. Loesch-Mdzewska, D. Some aspects of neurology of Down's syndrome. *Journal of Mental Deficiency Research*, 12:237–246, 1968.

5. Schlack, H.G. and Schmidt-Schuh, H. Neurophysiological and behavioral changes during mental work in children with Down's syndrome. *Neuropadiatrie*, 8:374–386, 1977.

6. Seppalainen, A.M. and Kivalo, E. EEG findings and epilepsy in Down syndrome. *Journal of Mental Deficiency Research*, 11:116–125, 1967.

7. Smith, G.F. and Berg, J.M. *Down's Anomaly*. Edinburgh, London and New York: Churchill Livingstone, 1976.

8. Coleman, M. Infantile spasms associated with 5-hydroxytryptophan administration in patients with Down's syndrome. *Neurology*, 21:911–919, 1971.

9. Airaksinen, E.M. Tryptophan treatment of infants with Down's syndrome. *Annals of Clinical Research* (Helsinki), 6:33–39, 1974.

10. Pollack, M.A., Golden, G.S., Schmidt, R., Davis, J.A. and Leeds, N. Infantile spasms in Down syndrome: A report of 5 cases and review of the literature. *Annals of Neurology*, 3:406–408, 1978.

11. Petre-Quadens, O. and DeLee, C. 5-hydroxytryptophan and sleep in Down's syndrome. *Journal of Neurological Sciences*, 26:443–453, 1976.

12. Fukuma, E., Umezawa, Y., Kobayashi, K. and Motoike, M. Polygraphic study on the nocturnal sleep of children with Down's syndrome and endogenous mental retardation. *Folia Psychiatrica et Neurologica Japonica*, 28:333–345, 1974.

13. Clausen, J., Sersen, E.A. and Lidsky, A. Sleep patterns in mental retardation: Down's syndrome. *Electroencephalography and Clinical Neurophysiology*, 43:183–191, 1977.

14. Castaldo, V. Down's syndrome: A study of sleep patterns related to level of mental retardation. *American Journal of Mental Deficiency*, 74:187–190, 1969.

15. Petre-Quadens, O. and DeGreef, A. Effects of 5-HTP on sleep in mongol children. *Journal of the Neurological Sciences*, 13:115–119, 1971.

16. Lee, J.C.M., Ornitz, E.M., Tanguay, P.E., and Ritro, E.R. Sleep EEG patterns in a case of Down's syndrome—before and after 5-HTP. *Electroencephalography and Clinical Neurophysiology*, 27:686, 1969.

Chapter 13

VISUAL AND AUDITORY EVOKED POTENTIAL STUDIES

Siegfried M. Pueschel
Kazuie Iinuma
Joan Katz
Yoichi Matsumiya

Introduction

Since central nervous dysfunction is one of the manifestations most often observed in persons with Down syndrome, many investigators have studied both structural and functional elements of the brain in children with this chromosomal disorder (1-6).

Aside from histopathological and biochemical examinations of neural tissues and cognitive assessments of children with Down syndrome (7-14), researchers have in recent years also employed electroencephalograms* and evoked potential studies in an attempt to elucidate neurophysiological aberrations (15–26). Investigating visual, auditory and somatosensory evoked potentials, Callner and coworkers observed that the amplitude of late components was markedly larger, and that there was only little change of amplitude with increasing age in persons with Down syndrome when compared with normal controls (15). Yellin and co-investigators also found the amplitude of visual and auditory evoked potentials in persons with Down syndrome to be increased and their peak latencies to be longer, than equivalent responses in normal subjects (16,17). Moreover, Bigum and coworkers reported that there was no significant interhemispheric difference in visual evoked responses obtained from children with Down syndrome, while the amplitude of visual evoked responses recorded from the occipital scalp and somatosensory responses from the central scalp were more homogenous in children with Down syndrome than in the control subjects. In addition there were greater amplitudes and later occurring peak latencies of the components (18). Other reports from the literature on evoked potentials in Down syndrome also discussed abnormal responses to various sensory stimuli in this population (19–25).

The selected neurophysiological investigations reported in this chapter were prompted by the unexpected occurrence of seizures in several infants enrolled in the Down Syndrome Program. Since two of the infants with infantile spasms had been administered 5-hydroxytryptophan, and since Coleman had suggested 5-hydroxytryptophan to be seizurogenic (26), we attempted to gain insight into the neurophysiological functions in these children, using visual evoked potentials and auditory evoked potentials.

METHODS

Evoked potential studies began after the majority of children had been admitted to the Down Syndrome Program. Since the patients were to have serial examinations during the first year of life, only a limited number of infants were available for these investigations.

*See also chapter on Electroencephalographic Investigations.

A total of 30 visual evoked potential and 31 auditory evoked potential recordings were obtained from 18 infants with Down syndrome. Eleven visual evoked potentials and auditory evoked potentials were recorded between 0 and 2 weeks of age; ten visual evoked potentials and eleven auditory evoked potentials were recorded between 2 weeks and 5 months of age, and nine visual evoked potentials and auditory evoked potentials were obtained between 6 and 12 months of age. The personnel involved with recording and analysis of the auditory evoked potentials and visual evoked potentials were unaware of the "type of medication" the children had been administered.

The examinations of evoked potentials were performed while the infant was sleeping in a dimly illuminated room. Gold cup electrodes were secured by collodion at the vertex (Cz), left and right occipital areas (0_1 and 0_2), and the left and right central locations (C_3 and C_4). All electrodes were referred to the linked ear lobes. The strobe flash was presented binocularly by a Grass PS-1 photostimulator with intensity setting at 4. The auditory stimuli consisted of 95 db SPL clicks presented binaurally through earphones. The strobe flashes and auditory click stimuli were randomly mixed and presented with an interstimulus interval of 4 seconds.

The potentials were amplified by a Grass Model 7 polygraph with a band-pass filter set at 1 and 500 cycles. The records were stored on a 7 channel Mnemotron FM tape recorder for later averaging by a PDP-12 computer. The PDP-12 averaged 100 responses during 1024 msec following the stimulus off-line. The visual evoked potentials and auditory evoked potentials were plotted by an MFE 815 plotamatic X-Y transcriber. The positivity obtained at the active electrode with respect to the earlobes was recorded as an up-going deflection. The potentials from the right and left occiputs, as well as from the vertex, were examined for visual evoked potentials; and those recorded over both central regions and at the vertex were evaluated for auditory evoked potentials. The waveforms, amplitude, and latency of each evoked potential wave were also analyzed.

According to Goff and coworkers (27), the most prominent positive wave in visual evoked potentials which appears near 100 msec in the older age group in this study, was named P_{100}; the negative wave in visual evoked potentials with a peak latency about 70 msec followed by P_{100} was identified as N_{70}. In auditory evoked potentials, the most prominent positive wave with a peak latency about 200 msec was called P_{200}, and the preceding and following negative waves were named N_{100} and N_{300} respectively. Finally, the second positive wave after N_{300} was called P_{400}. Examples of the nomenclature of each evoked potential component are shown in Figures 1 and 2.

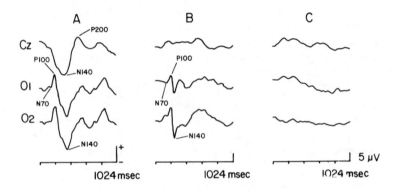

Figure 1:   Three representative visual evoked potential waveforms obtained from the vertex (Cz) and left and right occipital areas (O_1 and O_2).

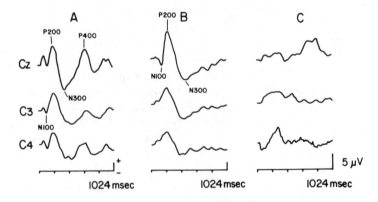

Figure 2:   Three representative auditory evoked potential waveforms obtained from the vertex (Cz) and specified left and right scalp locations (O_1 and O_2).

Results

During the analysis of the data the "medication" code of the 18 participating children was broken: there were 11 children who had been given a placebo (Group I), three children to whom pyridoxine (Group II) had been administered, and four children who had been on 5-hydroxytryptophan (Group III). There were no children from the 5-hydroxytryptophan/pyridoxine group in the evoked potential study.

The visual evoked potentials of infants with Down syndrome displayed various waveforms which were classified as follows:

- *Type A* show visual evoked potentials with a well-organized early negative wave (N_{70}), an early positive wave (P_{100}) and a late negative wave (N_{140}) over both occipital areas. There is also a biphasic potential at the vertex which appears to be equivalent to the commonly called vertex potential (N_{140}–P_{200}) of older children.
- *Type B* are well-organized visual evoked potentials over both occipital areas as in Type A, but with poorly organized visual evoked potentials at the vertex.
- *Type C* represent poorly organized visual evoked potentials with only one or two prominent components over both occiputs or very distorted and/or attenuated visual evoked potentials.

Examples of the various types of visual evoked potentials are seen in Figure 1, and the visual evoked potential waveshape classification and its relation to study group and age are presented in Table I. As noted, a definite trend of waveshape among the three study subgroups is not apparent. However, well-organized visual evoked potentials (Type A) were more often found in the older age groups than in the 0-to-2-week age group.

The waveshapes of the auditory evoked potentials were also quite variable; they were similarly classified into the following three types:

- *Type A* have well-organized early negative (N_{100}), late positive (P_{200}), negative (N_{300}), and positive (P_{400}) components.

TABLE I

VISUAL EVOKED POTENTIAL

WAVESHAPES ACCORDING TO AGE AND STUDY SUB-GROUP IN INFANTS WITH DOWN SYNDROME

	Type A Well organized at occiputs and the vertex			Type B Well organized at occiputs, poorly organized at vertex			Type C Poorly organized distorted and/or attenuated			
	Group*			Group*			Group*			
	I	II	III	I	II	III	I	II	III	Total
Age										
0 - 2 wks	4	0	0	4	0	1	2	0	0	11
3 wks - 5 mos	4	2	2	0	0	1	0	0	0	9
6 - 12 mos	5	2	1	2	0	0	0	0	0	10
Total	13	4	3	6	0	2	2	0	0	30

*Group I - Placebo

Group II - Pyridoxin

Group III - 5-hydroxytryptophan

— *Type B* show auditory evoked potentials with only a few prominent components such as the early negative (N_{100}), late positive (P_{200}) and negative (N_{300}) components.

— *Type C* demonstrate distorted or attenuated auditory evoked potentials.

Typical examples of each of the three types of auditory evoked potential waveforms are seen in Figure 2. There was no appreciable difference in the waveforms among the three study subgroups (Table II). As had been noted in the visual evoked potentials, the well-organized auditory evoked potentials also appeared more often in the older groups than in the younger age group.

In further analysis of the data, visual evoked potentials obtained from O_1 were used. Latencies of the wave N_{70}, the major early negative wave in evoked potentials, and the wave P_{100}, the most prominent positive peaks, were measured. The peak latencies of these

TABLE II

AUDITORY EVOKED POTENTIAL

WAVESHAPE ACCORDING TO AGE AND STUDY SUB-GROUP IN INFANTS WITH DOWN SYNDROME

	Type A Well organized Group*			Type B Poorly organized Group*			Type C Distorted and/or attenuated Group*			
	I	II	III	I	II	III	I	II	III	Total
Age										
0 - 2 wks	2	0	0	7	0	1	1	0	0	11
3 wks - 5 mos	3	1	2	1	1	2	0	0	0	10
6 - 12 mos	5	2	1	0	1	0	1	0	0	10
Total	10	3	3	8	2	3	2	0	0	31

*Group I - Placebo

Group II - Pyridoxin

Group III - 5-hydroxytryptophan

two waves, N_{70} and P_{100}, are shown in Figure 3. The latency values of the three study subgroups are fairly equally distributed, yet there was a tendency of progressive decrement with increasing age in all three groups.

When the auditory evoked potentials recorded from the vertex (C 2) were examined, the peak latencies of the P_{200} and N_{300} waves did not reveal any noticeable differences among the three study subgroups (Figure 4). The same tendency as observed for the latencies of the visual evoked potential to decrease with advancing age, was also noted in the analysis of the auditory evoked potentials.

In addition, the amplitude of the P_{100}-N_{140} component of the visual evoked potentials recorded at 0_1 was measured. As noted in Figure 5, the amplitude distribution for the age at the time of recording suggests no real difference among the three study subgroups. Although the amplitude of the visual evoked potentials is more variable than their latency, the data of Figure 5 indicate a tendency toward increasing amplitude with increasing age.

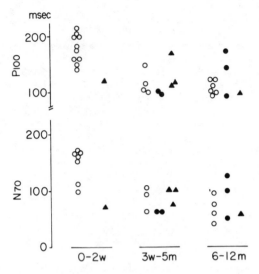

Figure 3: Visual evoked potential latencies of waves N_{70} and P_{100} according to age and study subgroup (placebo o, pyridoxine ●, 5-hydroxytryptophan ▲).

The amplitude of the P_{200}-N_{300} component of the auditory evoked potentials as shown in Figure 6 is more variable than that of the visual evoked potentials and there was no appreciable difference among the study subgroups.

Discussion

Although numerous reports have been published on evoked potentials in Down syndrome (15-25), only one article dealt with evoked potential studies after 5-hydroxytryptophan administration (21). In their investigations Barnet and coworkers studied auditory evoked potentials in 42 Down syndrome and 56 normal infants. To some of their infants with Down syndrome 5-hydroxytryptophan had been administered, and one subject had been given 5-hydroxytryptophan and pyridoxine (21). These authors, however, did not provide detailed information on those infants, and in their analysis they did not differentiate between children with Down syndrome who received these compounds or who did not.

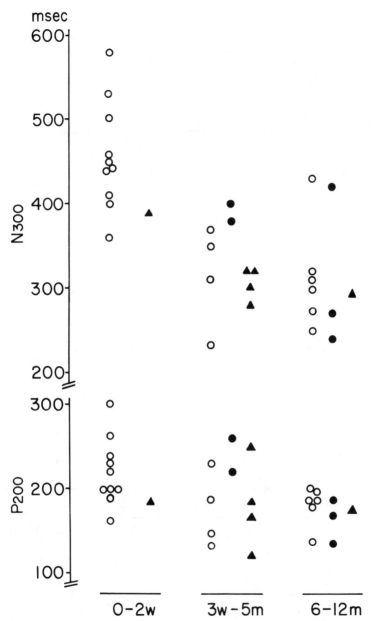

Figure 4:   Auditory evoked potential latencies of waves P200 and N300 according to
age and study subgroup (placebo o, pyridoxine ●, 5-hydroxytryptophan ▲).

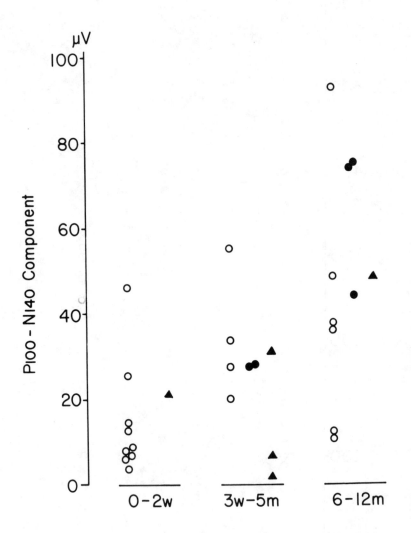

Figure 5: Visual evoked potential amplitude of P_{160} and N_{140} component according to age and study subgroup (placebo ○, pyridoxine ●, 5-hydroxytryptophan ▲)

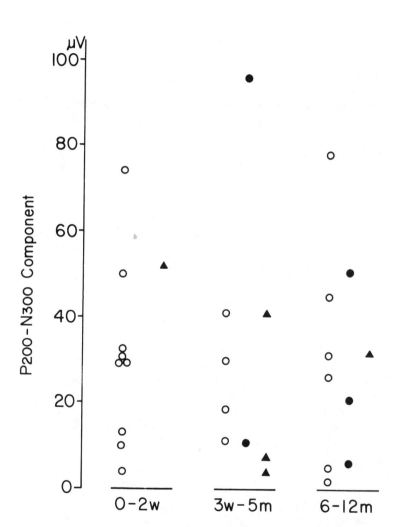

Figure 6:   Auditory evoked potential amplitude of P_{200} and N_{300} component according to age and study subgroup (placebo o, pyridoxine ●, 5-hydroxytryptophan ▲).

Because of our Down Syndrome Study's double-blind design, the children's random assignment to the various study subgroups was not known to the investigators. Moreover, the evoked potential study was started rather late in the program. Therefore we had only a small number of children available for evoked-potential studies, with an uneven distribution among the study subgroups. While the placebo group was well represented, the pyridoxine and the 5-hydroxytryptophan groups only numbered a few children each; and no child who had received the combination of both "medications" was enrolled in the evoked potential study. Thus a proper statistical analysis of a possible "treatment" effect could not be carried out. It appears, however, that there is no appreciable difference among the various groups with respect to waveform, latency, or amplitude of the evoked potentials.

Unfortunately, no equivalent data obtained from normal children are available for comparison in this study. However, other investigators who contrasted evoked potentials of children with Down syndrome with those of normal children felt that a reduced inhibitory control of afferent stimulation in the reticular and basal ganglionic structures produces the abnormal evoked responses in Down syndrome (15). It was also suggested that the reduced neural inhibition was related to the diminished tonic effect on the cortex from brain stem structures (18,20). The impaired response habituation to repetitive stimuli in Down syndrome was thought to be due to brain stem factors which may affect arousal level and selective attention (16), while the longer latencies of the late components, according to Straumanis and coworkers, may be caused by differences in neural organization of sensory association and nonspecific cortical areas (24).

SUMMARY

A total of 30 visual evoked potentials and 31 auditory evoked potentials were recorded for 18 children with Down syndrome during their first year of life. There was no appreciable difference in visual evoked potential and auditory evoked-potential waveforms among children from various study subgroups. Well-organized visual evoked potentials and auditory evoked potentials were noted at a higher frequency in infants beyond the newborn period. Latency values of visual evoked potentials and auditory evoked potentials were fairly randomly distributed among the study subgroups; yet there was a tendency toward progressive decrement with increasing age. The assessment of specific components of visual evoked-potential and auditory evoked-potential amplitudes also revealed no marked difference among the study subgroups.

REFERENCES

1. Benda, C.E. The central nervous system in mongolism. *American Journal of Mental Deficiency*, 45:42-47, 1940.
2. Colon, E.J. The structure of the cerebral cortex in Down's syndrome. *Neuropaediatrie*, 3:362-376, 1972.
3. Schochet, S.S., Jr., Lampert, P.W. and McCormick, W.F. Neurofibrillary tangles in patients with Down's syndrome: A light and electron microscopic study. *Acta Neuropathologica* (Berlin) 23(4):342-346, 1973.
4. Brink, M. and Grundlingh, E.M. Performance of persons with Down's syndrome on two projective techniques. *American Journal of Mental Deficiency*, 81(3):265-270, 1976.
5. Carr, J. Mental and motor development in young mongol children. *Journal of Mental Deficiency Research*, 14(3):205-220, 1970.
6. Connolly, J.A. Intelligence levels of Down's syndrome children. *American Journal of Mental Deficiency*, 83(2):193-196, 1978.
7. Rees, S. The incidence of ultrastructural abnormalities in the cortex of two retarded human brains. (Down's syndrome). *Acta Neuropathologica* (Berlin), 37(1):65-68, 1977.
8. Meyer, A. and Jones, T.B. Histological changes in the brain in mongolism. *Journal of Mental Science*, 85:206, 1939.
9. Banik, N.L., Davison, A.N., Palo, J. and Savolainen, H. Biochemical studies on myelin isolated from the brains of patients with Down's syndrome. *Brain*, 98(2):213-218, 1975.
10. Giza, T., Szafran, A., Kobielowa, Z., Ostrowski, A., and St. Epiniewski, M. Amino acids in cerebrospinal fluid of children with Down's syndrome. *Polski Tygodnik Lekarski* (Warsaw) 27(4):128-130, 1972.

11. Schlack, H.G. and Schmidt-Schuh, H. Neurophysiological and behavioral changes during mental work in children with Down's syndrome. *Neuropaediatrie*, 8(4):374–386, 1977.

12. Cicchetti, D. and Stroufe, L.A. The relationship between affective and cognitive development in Down's syndrome infants. *Child Development*, 47:920–929, 1976.

13. Dameron, L.E. Developmental intelligence of infants with mongolism. *Child Development*, 34:733–738, 1963.

14. Dicks-Mireaux, M.J. Mental development of infants with Down's syndrome. *American Journal of Mental Deficiency*, 77(1):26–32, 1972.

15. Callner, D.A., Dustman, R.E., Madsen, J.A., Schenkenberg, T., and Beck, E.C. Life span changes in the averaged evoked responses of Down's syndrome and nonretarded persons. *American Journal of Mental Deficiency*, 82(4):398–405, 1978.

16. Yellin, A.M., Lodwig, A.K. and Jerison, H.J. Effects of rate and repetitive stimulus presentation on the visual evoked brain potentials of young adults with Down's syndrome. *Biological Psychiatry*, 14(6):913–923, 1979.

17. Yellin, A.M., Lodwig, A.K. and Jerison, H.J. Auditory evoked brain potentials as a function of interstimulus interval in adults with Down's syndrome. *Audiology*, 19:255–262, 1980.

18. Bigum, H.B., Dustman, R.E. and Beck, E.C. Visual and somatosensory evoked responses from mongoloid and normal children. *Electroencephalography and Clinical Neurophysiology* 28:576–585, 1970.

19. Dustman, R.E. and Callner, D.A. Cortical evoked responses and response decrement in nonretarded and Down's syndrome individuals. *American Journal of Mental Deficiency*, 83(4):391–397, 1979.

20. Barnet, A.B., Lodge, A. Click evoked EEG responses in normal and developmentally retarded infants. *Nature*, 214:252–255, 1969.

21. Barnet, A.B., Ohlrich, E.S. and Shanks, B.L. EEG evoked responses to repetitive auditory stimulation in normal and Down's syndrome infants. *Developmental Medicine and Child Neurology*, 13(3):321–329, 1971.

22. Gliddon, J.B., Busk, J. and Galbraith, G.C. Visual evoked responses as a function of light intensity in Down's syndrome and nonretarded subjects. *Psychophysiology*, 12(4):416–422, 1975.

23. Gliddon, J.B., Galbraith, G.C. and Busk, J. Effect of preconditioning visual stimulus duration on visual-evoked responses to a subsequent test flash in Down syndrome and nonretarded individuals. *American Journal of Mental Deficiency*, 80(2):186–190, 1975.

24. Straumanis, J.J., Jr., Shagass, C., and Overton, D.A. Evoked response in Down's syndrome of young adults. *Electroencephalography and Clinical Neurophysiology*, 29(3):324, 1970.

25. Straumanis, J.J., Jr., Shagass, C., and Overton, D.A. Somatosensory evoked responses in Down syndrome. *Archives of General Psychiatry*, 29(4):544–549, 1973.

26. Coleman, M. Infantile spasms associated with 5-hydroxytryptophan administration in patients with Down's syndrome. *Neurology*, 21:911–919, 1971.

27. Goff, G.D., Matsumiya, Y., Allison, T. and Goff, W.R. The scalp topography of human somatosensory and auditory evoked potentials. *Electroencephalography and Clinical Neurophysiology*, 42:57–76, 1977.

Chapter 14

AUDIOLOGICAL ASSESSMENTS

Martin C. Schultz
Siegfried M. Pueschel

INTRODUCTION

Several reports in the literature discuss audiological impairments in persons with Down syndrome. Rigrodsky and coworkers observed that 26 of 43 patients with Down syndrome had hearing deficits when the criterion of 20 decibels or greater Hearing Levels for any two frequencies in one ear was used (1). In contrast, McIntire and co-investigators found only 8.3% of children with Down syndrome to have a hearing impairment. Glovsky reported in 1966 that 20 of 38 children with Down syndrome were classified as having a perceptive hearing loss, 7 had a mixed loss, 1 a conductive loss, and 2 normal hearing, while 8 of his subjects could not be successfully tested (3). Fulton and Lloyd found that of 79 children and young adults with Down syndrome ranging in age from 7 to 27 years, 46 children had essentially normal hearing, 17 showed conductive loss, 7 had a mixed loss, and another 7 had a sensorineural hearing loss; 2 children could not be reliably tested (4).

In the last decade, newly developed assessment techniques have permitted investigators to evaluate children's hearing abilities in more varied ways. Brooks and his group, dissatisfied with pure tone audiometry, employed electroacoustic impedance testing and observed that only 23% of patients with Down syndrome had normal hearing (5). Schwartz and Schwartz examined 39 noninstitution-alized children with Down syndrome ranging in age from 2 weeks to 10 years, 11 months, with a mean age of 3 years and 1 month. Pneumo-otoscopy and acoustic impedance measurements revealed middle-ear effusion in more than 60% of their children (6). Similarly, Balkany and co-investigators noted that when otoscopy, audiometry and impedance tympanometry were performed, 78% of patients with Down syndrome showed a significant hearing loss. The vast majority had a conductive hearing impairment, and the degree of hearing loss was mild to moderate, ranging from 15 to 40 dB (7). In another paper, the same authors reported that some children with Down syndrome had significant middle-ear abnormalities, including fixa-tion and superstructure deformity of the stapes and dehiscence of the Fallopian canal (8).

Since the significance of hearing loss in young children lies in its effect on all phases of psychological and emotional development (9-12), the assessment of audiological function in children with Down syndrome seems to be of paramount importance.

METHODS AND RESULTS

Each child from our study population of 89 children with Down syndrome was scheduled to undergo a series of audiological tests at 15 months, and again at 36 months of age. Attempts were made to obtain a variety of response measures to several acoustical signals.

The procedures and results are covered in four sections dealing with techniques for evaluation, classification of hearing status, information on the utility of solicited parental reports about hearing, and observations on testing at 15 and 36 months.

Techniques for Evaluation

Seven different categories of signals were used in the evaluation of the children: voice detection level, Speech Hearing Level or Speech Reception Threshold, speech discrimination, environmental sounds (e.g., telephone, vacuum cleaner, doorbell), broad-band noise, narrow-band noise, and pure tones. For the 73 children successfully tested at 15 months of age, only three signal classes yielded high response rates: 66 children responded to environmental sounds, 65 to a broad-band noise and 64 to voice detection, but all three classes were required to test the 73 children successfully.

Five different classes of responses to stimulation were evaluated for efficacy at 15 months: startle, auropalpebral, cessation of activity, initiation of activity, and localization. The localization response occurred so seldom that it is omitted from present consideration. In Table I, the number of children who gave weak, strong or paroxysmal responses is displayed as the negative-diagonal for each type of response.*

The behaviors giving clearest indication of signal reception were startle and cessation of activity, and the combination served as the criterion in successful testing of better than three-quarters of the 15 month old children.

Classification of Hearing Status

The children were classified by hearing status, for each ear independently where possible, by whichever procedures would allow classification. Pure-tone results were obtained for 24 children at 15

---

*Cross-tabulation was done to determine how many additional children could be successfully tested if some type of response was evaluated in addition to the negative-diagonal class. A second group of positively responding children is found in this table by combining any first group with the number shown, on the same row, under the response mode appearing as the column heading. For example, 59 children gave good startle response to stimulation and 10 additional children showed cessation of activity; thus 69 children were tested successfully by examining these two types of responses. Because only two-dimensional cross-tabulations were done, no conclusions can be drawn about the additional number of children who could be successfully tested using yet a third or fourth type of response signal.

TABLE I

SINGLE AND DUPLEX RESPONSE MODES SERVING FOR SUCCESSFUL TESTING OF CHILDREN

WITH DOWN SYNDROME AT 15 MONTHS OF AGE

	Startle response	Auro-palpebral	Cessation of activity	Initiation of activity
Startle response	59	6	10	2
Auropalpebral	36	28	34	5
Cessation of activity	8	2	61	0
Initiation of activity	49	21	50	12

TABLE II

CLASSIFICATION OF HEARING STATUS BY NON-PURE TONE RESULTS AT 15 MONTHS

Hearing Status	Right ear %	Left ear %
Normal hearing	45.8	47.8
Mild hearing loss	40.3	38.3
Moderate hearing loss	9.7	9.7
Moderately severe hearing loss	2.8	2.8
Severe hearing loss	1.4	1.4

months, but 51 children were not tested by pure tones at that age. Using procedures other than pure tones or speech, results were obtained on 72 children for the right ear, 73 for the left; one child was not tested and 16 were listed as questionable (see Table II).

When contrasted with the pure tone results for the 24 children on whom both classes of results were obtained, there was agreement of results in 62.5% for the right ear, and 58.3% for the left ear; that is, they were identically classified by both kinds of procedures. For the remaining nine children (37.5%) whose results would lead to some difference in categorization, the child would be labelled as having more acute hearing or less hearing loss by the nonpure tone result.

The 15-month data summary was a hearing level successfully obtained for 73 children, a questionable result for another 15 children, and only one child on whom all procedures were considered inapplicable. The pure-tone results at 15 months offered no help to resolving these labelling difficulties.

The 36-month data are quite different. Hearing levels were obtained on 54 children by techniques other than pure tones or speech signals: a questionable result was found on another 28 children, and for seven children these procedures were considered inapplicable. Of these seven children a pure-tone result was obtained on six, but the pure-tone results did not assist in resolving the questionable data for any of the 28 children.

The Utility of Solicited Parental Reports on Hearing Status

Parents were asked to indicate how loud a signal was required for a response if the signal were voice, music, a noisy toy or other environmental sound (e.g. ringing of telephone or door bell). The parents graded loudness for each on the following scale: extremely loud, loud, average, soft, and extremely soft.

The results were examined for any relationship of parent's perception of the loudness of a home-generated signal, and auditory classification by formal testing. No apparent relationship was found.

Parental reports were also examined for relationships with the child's general responsiveness under formal testing; i.e., whether children requiring a louder home-generated signal were less or more likely to startle or to cease activity as a clear response to sound.

Again, no apparent relationship was obtained. The combination suggests that a solicited parental report of the child's home responsiveness was of little value in predicting a hearing loss, or in predicting whether a child would be testable in the clinical situation.

Observations on Testing at 15 and 36 Months

Multiple additional questions were of interest in the design of the study, focusing in part on the results of early testing and later profiles of results (tonal thresholds, speech-detection levels, recognition scores), the influence of a child's general behavior and physiological state on the results at 15 months and 36 months, the relations among 15 months' results, and the type and magnitude of a hearing loss at 36 months.

It is of note that approximately half of the study population (52%) was found to have some hearing impairment at 15 months, whereas results from the recent literature give a 65-75% prevalence of hearing loss (5-8). The explanation for this discrepancy may reside in the young age and in the special composition of our study population. Their parents' involvement in an ongoing interdisciplinary program allowed for more sensitive monitoring of the health of the children. Prompt treatment of upper respiratory infections and/or otitis media may have contributed to the lower frequency of hearing loss.

SUMMARY

The audiological status of 89 children with Down syndrome was evaluated when they were 15 and 36 months of age. Using a variety of signals and response indicators, 73 children were successfully tested at 15 months, and 54 children at 36 months. There was agreement as to classification of the child's hearing status for 62.5% of the children by pure-tone or other-than-pure-tone results. Approximately 48% of the children were noted to have normal hearing at 15 months, and another 40% to have only a mild hearing loss. Solicited parental reports were not found to be useful for predicting a child's responsiveness under formal testing conditions, or for predicting the results from such testing.

References

1. Rigrodsky, S., Prunty, F. and Glovsky, L. A study of the incidence, types and associated etiologies of hearing loss in an institutionalized mentally retarded population. *Training School Bulletin,* 58:30-44, 1961.

2. McIntire, M.S., Menolascino, F.J. and Wiley, J.H. Mongolism—some clinical aspects. *American Journal of Mental Deficiency,* 69:794-800, 1965.

3. Glovsky, L. Audiological assessment of a mongoloid population. *Training School Bulletin,* 63:27-36, 1966.

4. Fulton, R.T. and Lloyd, L.L. Hearing impairment in a population of children with Down syndrome. *American Journal of Mental Deficiency,* 73:298-302, 1968.

5. Brooks, D.N., Wooley, H., and Kanjilal, G.C. Hearing loss and middle ear disorders in patients with Down syndrome (mongolism). *Journal of Mental Deficiency Research,* 16:21-29, 1972.

6. Schwartz, D.M. and Schwartz, R.H. Acoustic impedance and otoscopic findings in young children with Down syndrome. *Archives of Otolaryngology,* 104:652-656, 1978.

7. Balkany, T.J., Downs, M.P., Jafek, B.W., and Krajicek, M.J. Hearing loss in Down syndrome: A treatable handicap more common than generally recognized. *Clinical Pediatrics,* 18(2):116-118, 1979.

8. Balkany, T.J., Mischke, R.E. and Downs, M.P. Ossicular abnormalities in Down syndrome. *Otolaryngology and Head and Neck Surgery,* 87:372-384, 1979.

9. Smith, D.W. and Wilson, A.A. The child with Down syndrome (mongolism). Philadelphia: W.B. Saunders Company, 1973.

10. Needleman, H. Effects of hearing loss from early recurrent otitis media on speech and language development. In *Hearing Loss in Children.* B.F. Jaffe (Ed.). Baltimore: University Park Press, 1977, pp. 640-649.

11. Menyuk, P. Effects of hearing loss on language acquisition in the babbling stage. In *Hearing Loss in Children* B. Jaffe, (Ed.). Baltimore: University Park Press, 1977, pp. 621-629.

12. Howie, V.N. *Comparison between impedance audiometry and pneumatic otoscopy in the diagnosis of middle ear effusion in the infant.* Fourth Annual Meeting SENTAC, New Orleans, 1976.

ACKNOWLEDGEMENTS

Several persons made significant contributions to the design and conduct of the audiological components of this study. Most of the planning and initial data-gathering was done by Richard S. Schweitzer. Sylvia Topp and later Raymond Hurley continued his early work and the latter two were succeeded in turn by Susan Norton. We are grateful for their able service.

Chapter 15

OPHTHALMOLOGICAL MANIFESTATIONS

Robert A. Petersen

INTRODUCTION

The ocular manifestations in children with Down syndrome are important characteristics frequently helpful in making the clinical diagnosis of this chromosomal disorder (1). In addition, children with Down syndrome have more eye problems than normal children, which may contribute to their disability. Many of these eye abnormalities can be corrected so that these patients can achieve their optimal ocular function.

This chapter describes the eye findings in the group of children followed in the Down Syndrome Program and also reviews the pertinent literature on this subject.

METHODS

Of the 89 children in the final study sample, 54 had examinations by an opthalmologist. The pediatrician in the study had not observed obvious eye pathology in the other children. The parents of these 35 patients were queried by mail about the presence of eye disorders; 23 of the 35 patients responded stating that they had not noted any eye problems in their children. The ocular status of the remaining 12 patients is unknown. Of the 54 patients who were examined by opthalmologists, 39 were seen at the Department of Opthalmology of Children's Hospital Medical Center. Reports were obtained on another 11 children who had been examined by local opthalmologists. Hence, this report will deal with the 50 patients who underwent detailed opthalmological examinations.

RESULTS AND DISCUSSION

Eyelids

The commonest and most characteristic abnormalities in patients with Down syndrome concern the eyelids.* The incidence of anomalies of the palpebral fissures varies in the literature from 43% to 100% (1-4). Of our 50 patients, 29 had almond-shaped palpebral fissures and 31 had an oblique slant of the palpebral fissures. One patient was reported to have normal eyelids, and the palpebral fissures were not described in 16 patients. There was unilateral ptosis in two patients.

One anomaly which had been reported in the literature in at least three infants with Down syndrome is congenital eversion of the upper eyelids which was treated either by tarsorrhaphy (5) or by conservative management with spontaneous resolution (6). We did not see this complication in any of our patients.

---

*Phenotypic eye findings of all children with Down syndrome in this program are described in the first chapter of this monograph.

Blepharitis has been mentioned in most previous reports, with the incidence between 2% and 41% (1-4). Of our 50 patients, 18 had blepharitis and 26 had no episodes of eyelid inflammation. No mention was made of such problems in 6 children.

Keratoconus

Most publications report that 5% of patients with Down syndrome have keratoconus (1,3,4,7,8). Of our 50 patients none had keratoconus. We have seen keratoconus in several adult patients with Down syndrome, but not in young children.

Brushfield Spots

Brushfield spots are frequently seen in children with Down syndrome. The incidence is reportedly between 38% and 85% (9). Of our 50 patients, 25 had Brushfield spots, 8 did not and in 17 instances no mention was made as to whether or not Brushfield spots were present.

Cataracts

Cataracts are said to be present during late adolescence in almost 100% of patients with Down syndrome if the patients are examined carefully by means of a slit lamp with the pupils dilated (1). These cataracts are usually arcuate opacities around the fetal nucleus, or polychromatic crystalline opacities more peripherally located in the lens. The incidence of minor congenital opacities (3-11%) is probably not different from that observed in the general population (1). Falls states that although the cataractous changes may be progressive, they rarely become dense enough to require surgery (1). Other authors (2,3) estimate that about 12 to 15% of patients have visually significant cataracts. Of our 50 patients, only two had congenital cataracts.

Strabismus

There was a high prevalence of strabismus in the patients enrolled in this study. Twenty-one children had esotropia, one patient had constant exotropia, and another two had intermittent exotropia. In 25 patients strabismus was not present. Other studies have given somewhat lower prevalence figures for strabimus within the range of 12 to 23% (1) and 34% (10). One of our patients had accomodative esotropia which was successfully treated with glasses, and four children required operations. Amblyopia was present in one eye of eight patients. This was treated by the usual occlusion therapy.

Nystagmus

Nystagmus of unspecified type has been reported in several papers to be about 15% (2-4,10). Of our 50 patients, 11 had nystagmus, three had spasmus nutans, and three others had latent (occlusional) nystagmus. In one child the nystagmus was due to poor vision. The other patients could not be classified as to the etiology or type of nystagmus.

Refractive Errors

An increased occurence of refractive errors has been reported by several authors. High myopia has been present in between 5% (3,4) and 30-35% (1) of patients in previous reports. Four of our patients had high myopia (4 diopters or greater) in both eyes, and two other patients had this refractive error in only one eye. An additional five patients had lower degrees of myopia in both eyes. Hyperopia of two diopters or greater was noted in three patients bilaterally, and in two patients in only one eye each. Twenty-four of our patients were emmetropic.

Visual Acuity

Not much information is available on visual acuity of children with Down syndrome. The best estimate of visual acuity we could obtain in 29 of our patients was the ability to fix and follow with each eye. One child had optokinetic nystagmus. In 18 patients some subjective visual acuity testing was possible. In 12 patients who were tested with Allen cards, 19 eyes had visual acuity of 10/30 or better and five eyes had vision that was worse than 10/30. Six patients were capable of reading a letter chart. In this group four eyes had visual acuity of 20/40 or better and eight eyes had visual acuity between 20/50 and 20/200. In one other study, 18 of 44 patients were capable of being tested with a letter chart, and of these, 12 had visual acuity of 20/40 or better and six children had visual acuity of between 20/50 and 20/100 (4).

Other Ocular Findings

A number of other abnormalities were noted only rarely in the examination of the children referred for ophthalmological evaluation. These included myopic-appearing discs in four patients and myopic degeneration of the retina in two patients, both of which would be expected in a group of patients with high myopia. These findings have also been noted in previous studies (1). Two of our patients had congenital obstruction of the nasolacrimal ducts, a common abnormality in normal infants (13), but which has rarely been reported in Down syndrome (14). Other abnormalities, each occuring in only one individual, include large optic cups, tortuous retinal vessels, dystichiasis, posterior embryotoxon, granularity in the corneal stroma anterior to Descement's membrane, oculodigital reflex, and pseudopapilledema. Since all of these anomalies may occur in otherwise normal individuals, there is no reason to believe that they are related specifically to Down syndrome.

Another rare anomaly reported in a patient with Down syndrome is bilateral congenital dacryocutaneous fistulae (15). We have seen this anomaly unilaterally in three otherwise normal infants but never in a child with Down syndrome.

SUMMARY

Fifty patients with Down syndrome underwent detailed eye examinations. There were several findings which were important either from the standpoint of bringing to mind the diagnosis of this chromosomal disorder, or from a functional point of view. The anomalies which help define the phenotype of Down syndrome include almond-shaped and slanted palpebral fissures, epicanthus and telecanthus, and Brushfield spots of the iris.

Abnormalities which were common in our group of patients and which required ophthalmological evaluation and treatment included blepharitis, strabismus, nystagmus, and refractive errors. While we

saw only two patients with congenital cataracts and none with keratoconus, these are vision-threatening abnormalities which require
prompt attention by an ophthalmologist.

REFERENCES

1. Falls, H. F. Ocular changes in mongolism. *Annals of the New York Academy of Sciences*, 171:627-636, 1970.

2. Eissler, R. and Longenecker, L. P. The common eye findings in mongolism. *American Journal of Ophthalmology*, 54:398-406, 1962.

3. Cullen, J. F. and Butler, H. G. Mongolism (Down's syndrome) and keratoconus. *British Journal of Ophthalmology*, 47:321-330, 1963.

4. Lyle, W. M., Woodruff, M. E. and Zuccaro, V. S. A review of the literature on Down's syndrome and an optometrical survey of 44 patients with the syndrome. *American Journal of Optometry*, 49:715-727, 1972.

5. Gilbert, H. D., Smith, R. E., Barlow, M. H., and Mohr, D. Congenital upper eyelid eversion and Down's syndrome. *American Journal of Ophthalmology*, 75:469-472, 1973.

6. Stern, N., Campbell, C. H. and Faulkner, H. W. Conservative management of congenital eversion of the eyelids. *American Journal of Ophthalmology*, 75:319-320, 1973.

7. Pierse, D. and Eustace, P. Acute keratoconus in mongols. *British Journal of Ophthalmology*, 55:50-54. 1971.

8. Kenyon, K. R. and Kidwell, E. J. Corneal hydrops and keratoconus associated with mongolism. *Archives of Ophthalmology*, 94:494, 1976.

9. Donaldson, D. D. The significance of spotting of the iris in mongoloids, Brushfield spots. *Archives of Ophthalmology*, 65:26-31, 1960.

10. Hiles, D. A., Hoyme, S. H. and McFarlane, F. Down's syndrome and strabismus. *American Orthoptic Journal*, 24:63-68, 1974.

11. Williams, E. J., McCormick, A. Q. and Tischler, B. Retinal vessels in Down's syndrome. *Archives of Ophthalmology*, 89:269-271, 1973.

12. Ahmad, A. and Pruett, R. C. The fundus in mongolism. *Archives of Ophthalmology,* 94:772-776, 1976.

13. Petersen, R. A. and Robb, R. M. The natural course of congenital obstruction of the nasolacrimal duct. *Journal of Pediatric Ophthalmology,* 15:246-250, 1978.

14. Awan, K. J. Uncommon ocular changes in Down's syndrome (mongolism). *Journal of Pediatric Ophthalmology,* 14:215-216, 1977.

15. Klein, K. H. Über eine seltene Anomalie an den Tränenwegen bei Mongolismus. *Kinderärztliche Praxis.* 29:189-190, 1961.

Chapter 16

CARDIAC ASSESSMENTS

Lucy Parisi-Buckley

INTRODUCTION

The association of congenital heart disease with Down syndrome has been recognized for some time. Although Down had mentioned in his original description (1) that "the circulation is feeble," it was not until 1894 that Garrod first suggested the special connection between congenital cardiac lesions and Down syndrome (2). Since then, numerous investigators have described this association.

The frequency of congenital heart disease and the type of cardiac malformations reported in the literature have been noted to vary greatly with the age of patients, the accuracy of diagnoses, the mode of ascertainment, and the composition of the study population. Among 3532 children with Down syndrome collected from several studies between 1950 and 1976 (3-12), 16 to 63% were found to have congenital heart disease, with the highest prevalence in the pediatric hospital and necropsy series (Table I).

The major cardiac anomalies in Down syndrome comprise the endocardial cushion defects (complete atrioventricular canal and partial endocardial cushion defect) and ventricular septal defect. Tetralogy of Fallot, patent ductus arteriosus and secundum type atrial septal defects occur less frequently, and other cardiac lesions are very rare.

TABLE I

CONGENITAL HEART DISEASE AMONG CHILDREN WITH DOWN SYNDROME

A COMPOSITE OF NINE STUDIES

Reference	Author(s) and Year of Publication	Total Number of Children with Down Syndrome	Children with Congenital Heart Disease		Mode of Ascertainment
			Number	Percent	
(3)	Evans (1950)	63	28	44	Autopsy cases
(4)	Granata et al (1952)	56	24	43	Clinical study
(5)	Liu & Corlett (1959)	166	27	16	Clinical study
(6)	Berg et al (1960)	141	79	56	Autopsy cases
(7)	Rowe & Uchida (1961)	174	70	40	Clinical study
(8)	Cumming (1962)	80	40	50	Clinical study
(9)	Ito (1965)	62	26	42	Hospital review
(10)	Fabia & Drolette (1970)	2421	691	29	Clinical study
(11)	Greenwood & Nadas (1976)	369	230	62	Hospital review
	Composite Total	3532	1215	34	

This chapter reviews the clinical course of infants with Down syndrome and congenital heart disease who participated in the Down Syndrome Program.

METHODS

Study was made of clinical data extracted from the hospital records, electrocardiograms, radiological and catheterization reports, operative notes and postmortem findings for all infants with Down syndrome and congenital heart disease enrolled in this program. Furthermore, the diagnostic files of the New England Regional Infant Cardiac Program were searched for data on these infants, and a computerized summary of each infant was obtained and tabulated.

RESULTS

Of the 114 infants admitted to the Down Syndrome Program, 43 (39%) had congenital heart disease.* A detailed analysis of the cardiac anomalies and of the outcome of these patients are summarized in Tables II and III. No patient assigned to a major diagnostic category had significant additional cardiac anomalies.

Thirty-three patients were managed medically with an overall mortality of 30 percent. There were no deaths in the group of ten children who underwent surgery. The most common malformations (52%) were endocardial cushion defects, and 40% of these patients died: 4 of the 11 with complete atrioventricular canal and 5 of the 11 with partial endocardial cushion defect. The next most common lesion (28%) was ventricular septal defect, and two of 12 with this cardiac lesion expired. One of three patients with tetralogy of Fallot, and the patient with patent ductus arteriosus also died. However, all five patients (11%) with small secundum type atrial septal defect, or with no significant heart disease survived.

*It is of note that in this chapter all 114 children who originally entered the study are analyzed with respect to their cardiac status, while in the previous chapters, of this monograph only the 89 children in the final study sample are considered. Of the total of 114 children with Down syndrome, 43 had congenital heart disease; and of the 89 children in the final study sample, 26 had congenital heart disease.

TABLE II

CARDIAC DIAGNOSES IN CHILDREN

ENROLLED IN THE DOWN SYNDROME PROGRAM

Cardiac Lesion	Number	Percent
Complete atrioventricular canal	11	26
Partial endocardial cushion defect	11	26
Ventricular septal defect	12	28
Tetralogy of Fallot	3	7
Patent ductus arteriosus	1	2
Atrial septal defect or non-significant heart disease	5	11
Total	43	100

The age and mode of death according to diagnosis is shown in Table IV. The majority of patients (10 of 13) succumbed to complications of heart disease including chronic congestive heart failure, recurrent respiratory infections, pulmonary artery hypertension, and pulmonary vascular obstructive disease.

Complete Atrioventricular Canal

Among the 11 patients with complete atrioventricular canal, the combination of primum atrial septal defect, large ventricular septal defect, and common atrioventricular valve was confirmed at autopsy in 4 patients, and by cardiac catheterization in the remaining 7 children (including two with surgical repair). The catheter data of children between 1 to 15 months of age revealed an expected rise in the right atrial and ventricular oxygen saturations, systemic right ventricular pressure and single common atrioventricular valve or "smiling crocodile" appearance on left ventricular angiography with absent to mild mitral incompetence.

TABLE III

MANAGEMENT AND OUTCOME OF CHILDREN WITH

DOWN SYNDROME AND CONGENITAL HEART DISEASE

Cardiac Lesion	Total Number	Mortality Number	Mortality Percent	Medical Management Number	Surgical Intervention Palliative Number	Surgical Intervention Total Correction Number
Complete atrioventricular canal	11	4	36	6	4	2*
Partial endocardial cushion defect	11	5	45	11	0	0
Ventricular septal defect	12	2	17	9	0	3
Tetralogy of Fallot	3	1		1	2	2*
Patent ductus arteriosus	1	1		1	0	0
Atrial septal defect or non-significant heart disease	5	0		5	0	0
Total	43	13	30	33(77)**	6(7)**	7*(16)**

*Includes patients with previous palliation.
**Numbers in parentheses give the percentages

TABLE IV

MODE OF DEATH IN CHILDREN WITH DOWN SYNDROME AND CONGENITAL HEART DISEASE

Cardiac Lesion	Total Number	Died Number	Mean age of death (months)	Cause of Death			
				Congestive heart failure and respiratory infection Number	Respiratory Infection Number	Other Number	
Complete atrioventricular canal	11	4	13.5	4			
Partial endocardial cushion defect	11	5	24.0	2	2	1 (apnea)	
Ventricular septal defect	12	2	23.0	2			
Tetralogy of Fallot	3	1	1.8			1 (Duod. Atresia)	
Patent ductus arteriosus	1	1	3.5			1 (sudden infant death)	
Atrial septal defect or non-significant heart disease	5	0					
Total	43	13	17.2	8	2	3	

All patients had a loud systolic murmur noted by 6 weeks of age and required treatment for congestive failure and respiratory infection by 5 months of age. These 11 children had significant cardiomegaly and increased pulmonary blood flow on x-ray. One child developed calcific aneurysmal dilatation of the main pulmonary artery segment after banding. Ten patients had a superior counter clockwise frontal vector with right or combined ventricular hypertrophy on electrocardiogram, while one child had a QRS axis of + 100 degrees. Catheterization confirmed elevated pulmonary vascular resistance, large left to right shunt (>3 to 1); and mild systemic arterial desaturation (80-90%) was noted. In addition to the complete atrioventricular canal, three patients had a patent ductus arteriosus with equivocal mitral regurgitation and one muscular ventricular septal defect.

Of six patients treated medically, four died between 6 to 21 months of age (mean 13.5 months) of chronic congestive failure and pneumonia.

Partial Endocardial Cushion Defect

Since none of the patients with partial endocardial cushion defect underwent surgical treatment or came to autopsy, the diagnosis of primary atrial septal defect, isolated or associated with mitral disease and/or a small ventricular septal defect, was made clinically in seven patients, and confirmed by catheterization in four patients. The catherization data of children between 10 to 19 months of age revealed expected large left-to-right atrial shunts, less than systemic right ventricular pressure, and abnormal mitral valve attachment or "gooseneck deformity" on left ventricular angiography with absent to moderate mitral incompetence.

All patients had a loud systolic murmur noted by 3 months of age: two infants succumbed by 8 weeks, seven required therapy for congestive heart failure and respiratory infection by 10 months, and two others have never been treated. The 11 children with partial endocardial cushion defect had significant cardiomegaly with increased pulmonary vascularity on x-ray. Two patients developed marked dilatation of the main pulmonary artery segment along with severe pulmonary artery hypertension. All patients had a superior counter-clockwise frontal loop on electrocardiogram, with right or combined ventricular hypertrophy and atrial enlargement. In addition to the partial endocardial cushion defect, one patient had a pulmonary sequestration, and one patient had an aberrant right subclavian artery. Five of the eleven patients died: three in the neonatal period and two with complications of pulmonary vascular disease. Only one of six survivors has not developed significant pulmonary artery hypertension.

Ventricular Septal Defect

Among the 12 patients with ventricular septal defect, the diagnosis was confirmed at autopsy in two patients, and documented by cardiac catheterization with a left-to-right ventricular shunt in four patients (including three surgical repair). The diagnosis was made clinically in the others - four patients with significant defects and two patients with small defects and severe extracardiac anomalies. Ten patients had membraneous defects: six closed spontaneously, two children were surgically repaired successfully, and two others developed pulmonary vascular obstructive disease. Two patients had endocardial cushion type defects: one survived surgical repair and the other died from pulmonary vascular obstructive disease. In addition to the ventricular septal defect, two patients had an aberrant right subclavian artery, one with abnormal tricuspid valve attachment.

Ten patients had a loud systolic murmur noted by three months of age, and required digitalization for congestive heart failure. They had growth failure and recurrent respiratory infections by 6 months of age. Classic clinical signs of a moderate to large sized shunt were supported by x-ray findings of cardiomegaly with pulmonary hypervascularity and electrocardiogram evidence of combined or right ventricular hypertrophy. In none of these children, except the two with endocardial cushion defects, was the mean QRS electrical axis less than 0 degrees. Nine patients were managed medically and seven are alive. The three surgical patients who had pulmonary artery hypertension documented by cardiac catheterization four to nine months prior to patch closure are asymptomatic, but one has developed aortic regurgitation.

Tetralogy of Fallot

There were three patients with well documented cyanotic lesions due to diminished pulmonary blood flow and right-to-left ventricular shunts. While all three had cyanosis and murmurs at birth with severe infundibular and valvular pulmonary stenosis, the two patients with tetralogy of Fallot had malalignment ventricular septal defects with aortic override, and the patient with double outlet right ventricle had endocardial cushion type ventricular septal defect, with both great vessels arising from the right ventricle. The diagnosis of severe tetralogy of Fallot was confirmed at autopsy in a seven week old infant with duodenal atresia who developed the "dumping syndrome" with glucose intolerance and intractable diarrhea and acidosis following gastrointestinal surgery. The diagnosis was established at open-heart surgery in the two other patients who had required palliative shunts.

One patient with tetralogy of Fallot had congenital stridor, and catheterization at 12.5 months of age revealed pulmonary venous (81%) and systemic arterial (65%) desaturation. Although stridor and carbon dioxide retention improved following arytenoidectomy at 16 months of age, the baby developed a cerebrovascular accident and required an emergency Blalock shunt. Definitive surgical repair was successful and there are no neurologic sequelae and the patient is very active with mild cardiomegaly on x-ray and complete right bundle branch block on electrocardiogram.

The patient with double outlet right ventricle had required Waterston shunt after unsuccessful Blalock shunt at 6 months of age. Intracardiac repair at 2.9 years of age, which included patch closure of the ventricular septal defect (redirecting aorta to left ventricle), was complicated by acute tubular necrosis, respiratory failure, and bacteremia. Repeat catheterization revealed significant residual pulmonary stenosis.

Isolated Patent Ductus Arteriosus

The autopsy of a 3½ month-old infant who died suddenly after a short course of diarrhea revealed a wide patent ductus arteriosus, a

TABLE V

CARDIAC DIAGNOSES IN INFANTS WITH DOWN SYNDROME
FROM THE NEW ENGLAND REGIONAL INFANT CARDIAC PROGRAM
DURING THE TIME PERIOD JULY 1968 TO JUNE 1979

Cardiac Lesion	Number	Percent
Complete atrioventricular canal	67	45
alone	58	
complex	9	
Partial endocardial cushion defect	13	9
Ventricular septal defect	34	23
alone/with atrial septal defect	24	
with patent ductus arteriosus	10	
Tetralogy of Fallot	14	10
alone	10	
with double outlet right ventricle & pulmonary stenosis	4	
Patent ductus arteriosus	6	4
Atrial septal defect	3	2
Primary lung disease/persistent fetal circulation	5	3
Other	6	4
TOTAL	148	100

TABLE VI

MANAGEMENT AND OUTCOME OF INFANTS WITH DOWN SYNDROME AND CONGENITAL HEART DISEASE

IN THE NEW ENGLAND REGIONAL INFANT CARDIAC PROGRAM

Cardiac Lesion	Total Number	Mortality Number	Mortality Percent	Medical Management Total Number	Medical Management Died Number	Surgical Intervention Palliate Total Number	Palliate Died Number	Total Repair Total Number	Total Repair Died Number
Complete atrioventricular canal	67	40	60	39	23	21	13	9	5
Partial endocardial cushion defect	13	6	46	13	6				
Ventricular septal defect	34	10	29	19	7	2	1	13	2
Tetralogy of Fallot	14	9	64	6	4	8	5	2	0
Patent ductus arteriosus	6	2		2	2	4	0		
Atrial septal defect	3	1		3	1				
Primary lung disease/ persistent fetal circulation	5	2		5	2				
Others	6	6		3	3	3	3		
TOTAL	148	76	51	90	48	38	22	24	7

fenestrated patent foramen ovale, and bilateral pulmonary edema. A loud continuous murmur with bounding pulses but without clinical evidence of congestive failure had been present during life.

Atrial Septal Defect or No Significant Heart Disease

All five patients in this subgroup demonstrated a systolic murmur in infancy with confusing clinical and laboratory findings. Three had significant extra cardiac anomalies and two had severe neonatal problems. None of the children have required cardiac medication or surgery, and all are asymptomatic at the time of this writing.

A tentative diagnosis of a small left-to-right shunt or mild pulmonary stenosis had been made in all five patients by 7 weeks of age. There was no evidence of cyanosis, and neither the murmur nor pulmonary second heart sound were impressive. Initial electrocardiograms revealed indeterminant or right-axis deviation with clockwise frontal vector and right ventricular predominance, but within normal limits for age. Serial chest films indicated equivocal heart size and pulmonary vascularity.

DISCUSSION

While the true occurence rate and diagnostic distribution of cardiac defects in patients with Down syndrome remains uncertain, the overall incidence reported in the literature is approximately 34% (3-12). Cardiovascular abnormalities were present in 43 of 114 (39%) infants enrolled in the Down Syndrome Program. Anatomic diagnosis was confirmed by autopsy, surgical intervention and cardiac catheterization in 60% of the cases, and in 40% the diagnosis was made clinically. The leading malformations, complete atrioventricular canal, partial endocardial cushion defect and ventricular septal defect contributed 4/5 of the patients, while tetralogy of Fallot, patent ductus arteriosus and secundum atrial septal defect were less common. There were no surgical deaths among this group, but 13 patients (30%) died from complications of pulmonary artery hypertension, congestive heart failure and respiratory failure.

In the context of this discussion, it is of interest to contrast the results of our investigations with data from the New England Regional Cardiac program where a total of 3626 critically ill infants with congenital heart disease were admitted between 1968 and 1979, and of these, 148 (4.1 %) had Down syndrome. The distribution and outcome of the various heart lesions of the patients with Down syndrome are summarized in Tables V and VI. Also in this series, the most common lesions are complete atrioventricular canal (45 %), partial endocardial cushion defect (9 %), ventricular septal defect (23 %), tetralogy of Fallot (10 %), and isolated patent ductus arteriosus (4 %). The remaining patients are divided among secundum artial septal defects (2 %), primary lung disease, persistent fetal circulation (3 %), and miscellaneous category (4 %).

SUMMARY

Of the originally admitted 114 children with Down syndrome, 43 (39 %) had congenital heart disease. The most common cardiac lesions were atrioventricular canal, partial endocardial cushion defect, and ventricular septal defect. These and other less frequent cardiac defects have been described. Thirteen children died.

It is clear that infants with Down syndrome and significant congenital heart disease carry a grave prognosis. Because of the higher frequency and earlier development of pulmonary artery hypertension and pulmonary vascular obstructive disease, prognosis depends on early recognition and treatment. Fortunately, recent technologic advancements have revolutionized infant cardiac care (13), and significantly improved the outlook for these patients.

REFERENCES

1. Down J. L. H. *Observations on an ethnic classification of idiots.* London Hospital Report, 3:259, 1866.
2. Garrod, A. E. On the association of cardiac malformations with other congenital defects. *St. Bartholomew Hospital Report,* 30:53, 1894.

3. Evans, R. P. Cardiac anomalies in mongolism. *British Heart Journal,* 12:258, 1950.

4. Granata, G., Bencini, A., and Parenzan, L. Contributo alla conoscenza delle malformazioni cardiache congenite nei soggetti mongoloidi. *Pediatria* (Napoli), 60:281, 1952.

5. Liu, M. C. and Corlett, K. A study of congenital heart defects in mongolism. *Archives of Diseases in Childhood,* 34:410, 1959.

6. Berg, J. M., Crome, L. and France, N. E. Congenital cardiac malformations in mongolism. *British Heart Journal,* 22:331, 1960.

7. Rowe, R. D. and Uchida, I. A. Cardiac malformation in mongolism: A prospective study of 184 mongoloid children. *American Journal Medicine,* 31:726, 1961.

8. Cumming, G. R. *Cardiopatia en pacients con anomalias cromosomales.* Memorias del IV Congreso Mundial De Cardiologia. Mexico: L-A Congenitos Hemodinamica, 1962.

9. Ito, T. Personal communication to Engle, M. A. and Ehlers, K. H.: Cardiovascular malformations in association with chromosmal aberrations. In: *Pediatric Cardiology.* Hammish Watson (Ed.) St. Louis: D. V. Mosby Co., 668, 1968.

10. Fabia, J. and Drolette, T. Life tables up to age 10 for mongols with and without congenital heart defects. *Journal of Mental Deficiency Research,* 14:235, 1970.

11. Greenwood, R. D. and Nadas, A. S. The clinical course of cardiac disease in Down's syndrome. *Pediatrics,* 58:893, 1976.

12. Cullum, L. and Liebman, J. The association of congenital heart disease with Down's syndrome (Mongolism). *American Journal of Cardiology,* 24:354, 1969.

13. Fyler, D. C. and Buckley, L.P. Extracardiac anomalies associated with congenital heart disease. In: *Associated Congenital Anomalies.* ElShafie,M. and Klippel,C. H.(Eds.)Baltimore: Williams and Wilkins, 125, 1981.

EPILOGUE

Claire D. Canning*

The conclusion of the Down Syndrome Program closed a very special chapter for my family. In all our lives there are particular moments that are memorable, a rainbow of colors, both happy and sad, that intermingle to become that stained-glass window of human life. If we are lucky, there are a handful of people who have profoundly touched our lives and made it better.

I look back upon the Down Syndrome Program at Children's Hospital Medical Center in Boston as one of the most helpful of my life's experiences. I think of the guidance of the professionals, their dedication for special people, and their outstanding warmth. I think of all the staff involved in the program and appreciate their gentle counseling that was coupled with honesty. All of them taught us to hope that life would be good and happy once again, and that our children with Down syndrome were feeling, promising persons whose potential we had to try a little harder to unfold.

I think of the social services that meant so much, the gentle questions and guidance, the parent meetings where we learned we were not alone, and shared our experiences and feelings with one another. I think of the physical therapy sessions that taught us to develop our children's weak muscles so that we could continue these exercises at home, to enable our babies to better explore and lead fuller lives. I think of the nutritional sessions that guided us through swallowing problems, introducing new foods, and eventual self-feeding skills. I think of the occupational therapists who taught us

*Mrs. C.D. Canning is a parent whose child was enrolled in the Down Syndrome Program.

how to make or choose learning toys that also have exceptional play value. I think of the encouraging pediatric guidance through our children's more frequent respiratory infections, and of the invaluable feeling of knowing someone who cared and understood was always accessible through those early years. When difficult problems arose, we were reassured by most competent neurologists, cardiologists, and capable specialists in each field. Genetic counseling for ourselves and our families added another valuable dimension to the program.

Through every session, I never ceased to be amazed that all the staff of such intellectual capability had such respect for life and optimal development of each child with Down syndrome in the study.

It is good that the mind tends more to remember happy events, but I also still remember, though more dimly, the frustrations involved in being part of the Down Syndrome Program. I remember how my husband juggled his own office schedule to be part of every session, and how often we altered our own plans. I am grateful that at least one of our other children usually took a day off from school to share with us all the things we would learn so we could carry them on at home.

I remember traveling to Boston in a blizzard, in all kinds of weather, when sometimes our child with Down syndrome was just too tired or off-schedule to perform for the psychologist things she routinely did at home. I remember the frustration of those times, but I also realize that, as all our other children reserved performance for home, our special child was exhibiting "normal" behavior!

Thanks, in large measure, to the privilege of being part of the Down Syndrome Program, the aching, all-permeating sadness of our early days as parents of an exceptional child is over, replaced by hope and only fleeting moments of chronic sorrow. Now we are filled with optimism for the future. We are grateful to our special child, too, for having taught us some of life's most beautiful lessons in loving.

We have learned also that now we are ready to help others. I feel certain that many parents who had participated in the Down Syndrome Program are now community leaders in mental retardation, active on many advisory boards that oversee better services for the developmentally disabled. I have come to think of myself as a "peaceful activist" who would not hesitate in the least to march to the State House to help assure that all handicapped persons achieve their inalienable rights.

The past ten years have seen remarkable progress for persons with Down syndrome. Our family was privileged to have been part of the first intensive study of children with Down syndrome who are being reared at home, as opposed to institutional studies. With others in the program, we feel a commitment to see that programs offering guidance to new parents are continued in many of our communities. In our gratitude, we can band together and attest to the value of "people power" to assure a full and happy life for our children. Then perhaps they, too, can feel the words of the poster which first greeted us on the wall at Children's Hospital: "I am so glad that you are here. It helps me to realize how beautiful my world is" (Rilke).

INDEX

American Sign Language, 256
Aneuploidy, 27
Ankle
    clonus, 273
    motor activity, 155, 157, 165, 170

Bayley Scales of Infant Development
    in anthropometric studies, 133
    according to cardiac status, 218,
        219, 222–223
    and correlation of variables, 286,
        287, 289, 290–292
    and language skills, 257
    and psychomotor development,
        207–208, 210–216, 217–223
    and study evaluations, 34, 62, 70,
        71–75, 81
Blepharitis, 345, 347
Bone age; see Physical features
Brushfield spots of the iris, 345, 347

Cataracts, 345, 348
Children's Hospital Medical Center,
    Boston, 28, 31, 35,
    Department of Ophthalmology, 344
    Developmental Education Clinic,
        17, 36
Cognitive development, 207–209
Communication, 256, 258
Congenital anomalies, 42–47
    see also Heart disease, congenital
Cry, 264, 265, 282

Demographic data, 39–40
Diseases, intercurrent, 50–54
Down syndrome, mosaic, 40–41, 209

Electroencephalographic studies, 33,
    277, 280, 281, 303–316, 320
    according to cardiac status, 311
Environment, 47–50
Epicanthus, 347
Epilepsy; see Seizures
Eyelids, 344

Feeding, 228, 229, 234–243, 249, 251
    milestones
        according to age, 242
        according to cardiac status, 237
        according to sex, 236
Feet, 191–193
5-Hydroxyindole
    levels, 33, 61, 63, 65–66, 69–75,
        77, 79
    pathway, 80
5-Hydroxyindoleacetic acid, 79, 80
5-Hydroxytryptamine (5-HTP)
    levels, 60, 61, 73, 78, 79
    transport across blood-brain
    barrier, 79
    see also Serotonin
5-Hydroxytryptophan (5-HT)
    benefits of, 28, 29, 30
    and electroencephalographic
        patterns, 304, 305, 308–310, 312
    and evoked potentials, 323–330
    and Food and Drug
        Administration, 28, 32
    and motor development, 144
    and seizures, 320
    and sleep, 315–316
    study group evaluation, 30, 32, 42,
        60–81
    as therapy, 60, 280, 282

368